HAMSTUDY
BASIC
2017/2018

Frank VanderZande VE7AV

Published by Radio Amateurs of Canada

HAMSTUDY Basic 2017/2018

ISBN 978-0-9780869-3-0

Radio Amateurs of Canada
720 Belfast Road, Suite/Bureau 217
Ottawa, Ontario K1G OZ5
613-244-4367   877-273-8304

Welcome to the world of Amateur Radio

This is the third edition of Hamstudy published by Radio Amateurs of Canada. This manual is based on self-study courses which have been offered at www.hamstudy.com for more that 16 years.

The study guide has been designed to get you started in the hobby with 20 to 35 hours of study. You will need to become familiar with 100 topics on which the examination is based. Your multiple choice examination will consist of one question from each of the 100 topics. The complete August 2016 question bank is included in this edition.

The pass mark is 70%. Aim for a mark of 80% or higher because that will give you access to all of the Amateur Radio bands.

The focus of this manual is on the topics that are addressed in the examination. There is much more that one could and should learn about the hobby, but that can start after you write and pass the exam to obtain your own call-sign.

In Canada, www.rac.ca is the best source for information about Amateur Radio on the web. This is also where you can be directed to a list of accredited examiners for your area.

You are also encouraged to join and support Radio Amateurs of Canada and receive the very informative bi-monthly magazine "TCA - The Canadian Amateur".

Joining a local Amateur Radio Club in or near your own community is also recommended. Meeting and talking to people who have a common interest in the hobby is an excellent way to learn more about our hobby.

Good luck with your studies.

73 – Frank VanderZande VE7AV

Cover photo: VE7NNN - Greg VanderZande
View from "Binks Knoll"
Overlooking Grand Forks BC
949 Meters above sea level

HAMSTUDY Basic 2017/2018

TABLE OF CONTENTS

TABLE OF CONTENTS continued

REGULATIONS

INTRODUCTION

The definition of the amateur radio service is found in the Radiocommunication Regulations. It is:

> "amateur radio service" means a radiocommunication service in which radio apparatus are used for the purpose of self-training, intercommunication or technical investigation by individuals who are interested in radio technique solely with a personal aim and without pecuniary interest."

Regulations pertaining to the amateur radio service are contained in the Radiocommunication Regulations and the Standards for the Operation of Radio Stations in the Amateur Radio Service (RBR-4).

The authority to make regulations and standards is derived from the Radiocommunication Act.

Innovation, Science and Economic Development Canada (formerly Industry Canada) is the federal government department responsible for the administration of the Radiocommunication Act. There still remain many references to Industry Canada in the question bank.

Authority to make regulations and standards is also derived from the Radiocommunication Act.

SUPPLEMENT

Download the "Standard for the Operation of Radio Stations in the Amateur Radio Service" RBR-4 from the internet. You need to become familiar with this document.

The Amateur Radio Service Center is responsible nationally for all amateur radio matters. Correspondence and enquiries should be directed to:

> Amateur Radio Service Centre
> 2 Queen Street East
> Sault Ste Marie, ON
> Toll free: 888-780-3333
> Fax: 613-991-5575
> E-mail: spectrum.amateur@ic.gc.ca

B-001-1-1.... Authority to make regulations governing radiocommunications is derived from:

1. *the Radiocommunication Act*
2. the Radiocommunication Regulations
3 the Standards for the Operation of Radio Stations in the Amateur Radio Service
4. the ITU Radio Regulations

B-001-1-2.... Authority to make "Standards for the Operation of Radio Stations in the Amateur Radio Service" is derived from:

1. the Radiocommunication Regulations
2. *the Radiocommunication Act*
3. the Standards for the Operation of Radio Stations in the Amateur Radio Service
4. the ITU Radio Regulations

B-001-1-3.... The Department that is responsible for the administration of the Radiocommunication Act is:

1. Transport Canada
2. *Industry Canada*
3. Communications Canada
4. National Defence

B-001-1-4.... The "amateur radio service" is defined in:

1. the Radiocommunication Act
2. the Standards for the Operation of Radio Stations in the Amateur Radio Service
3. the FCC's Part 97 rules
4. *the Radiocommunication Regulations*

RADIO AUTHORIZATION

INTRODUCTION

The radio authorization required to operate an amateur radio station is the Amateur Radio Operator Certificate. This certificate is issued after passing the Basic qualification examination. The pass mark is 70%. There are two other qualification examinations. These are Advanced (pass mark 70%) and 5 w.p.m. Morse code.

Download "RIC-3 Information on the Amateur Radio Service" from the web for complete details.

The Amateur Radio Service Center does not charge a fee for issuing Amateur Radio Operator Certificates.

If asked by an federal government spectrum management representative, amateur radio operators must show their radio authorization, or a copy thereof, to the official, within 48 hours of the request.

Whenever a change of address is made, the Amateur Radio Service Center is to be notified of the change of address.

SUPPLEMENT

Your callsign appears on the "Amateur Radio Operator Certificate" and is valid for life.

Additional or specially requested callsigns are available subject to administrative rules and fees.

Canada eliminated the 12 wpm morse code qualification in 2001. The 5 wpm morse code qualification is still available.

Obtaining the Basic qualification with honours (mark of 80% or above) or obtaining the 5 wpm morse code qualification, will give you access to all amateur bands, including those below 30 MHz. Obtaining the Advanced qualification will also give you access to these same amateur bands.

When a callsign is issued, Radio Amateurs of Canada's website will display this information. It is always a good idea to check the listing for accuracy soon after a certificate has been applied for.

QUESTIONS

B-001-2-1.... What must you do to notify your mailing address changes?

1. telephone your local club, and give them your new address
2. contact an accredited examiner and provide details of your address change
3. contact Industry Canada and provide details of your address change
4. write amateur organizations advising them of your new address, enclosing your certificate

B-001-2-2.... An Amateur Radio Operator Certificate is valid for:

1. five years
2. three years
3. one year
4. life

B-001-2-3.... Whenever a change of address is made:

1. Industry Canada must be notified within 14 days of operation at the new address
2. the station shall not be operated until a change of address card is forwarded to Industry Canada
3. Industry Canada must be advised of any change in postal address
4. within the same province there is no need to notify Industry Canada

B-001-2-4.... The Amateur Radio Operator Certificate:

1. must be put on file
2. must be kept in a safe place
3. must be retained at the station
4. must be kept on the person to whom it is issued.

B-001-2-5.... The holder of an Amateur Radio Operator Certificate shall, at the request of a duly appointed radio inspector, produce the certificate, or copy thereof, to the inspector, within ____48____ hours after the request:

1. 48
2. 12
3. 24
4. 72

B-001-2-6.... The fee for an Amateur Radio Operator Certificate is:

1. free
2. $32
3. $10
4. $24

B-001-2-7.... The Amateur Radio Operator Certificate should be:

1. retained in a safety deposit box
2. retained on the radio amateur's person
3. retained in the radio amateur's vehicle
4. retained at the address provided to Industry Canada

ENFORCEMENT

INTRODUCTION

Misrepresentation or contraventions of the Radiocommunication Act, Radiocommunication Regulations and terms or conditions of radio authorizations may be cause for the Minister to revoke a person's Amateur Radio Operator Certificate. A reasonable opportunity to make representation to the Minister would be afforded before such action would be taken.

No advance written notice is required for the Minister to revoke a radio authorization for situations involving failure to comply with requests to pay fees.

Spectrum Management officials may at any reasonable time, for the purpose of enforcing the Radiocommunication Act, enter any place in which the official believes, on reasonable grounds, there is any radio apparatus, interference-causing equipment or radio-sensitive equipment. In the case of a dwelling-house, a Radio Inspector normally requires the consent of the occupant unless acting under the authority of a warrant.

Transmitting a false or fraudulent distress signal, message or call, may result, upon conviction, in fines of up to $5,000 and/or imprisonment for up to one year. Out of amateur band transmissions and the retransmission of decoded encrypted subscription programs are prohibited.

SUPPLEMENT

The Radiocommunication Act is the document which states the offences and penalties for non compliance of rules governing radiocommunications.

For the most part, the amateur radio service is self regulating. Amateurs have a long established record of resolving most problems themselves or with assistance of other amateurs.

Radio Amateurs of Canada has established an "Official Observer" program. Designated "Official Observers" actively look for and report on stations that have unusually good signals or operating procedures, and which set an example by displaying the best that Amateur Radio has to offer. At least 70% of notices sent are "Good Operator Notices". Troubling operating practices or technical difficulties are also noted. In these situations an "Official Observer" may issue an "Advisory Notice".

QUESTIONS

B-001-3-1.... Out of amateur band transmissions:

1. must be identified with your call sign
2. are permitted
3. are prohibited - penalties could be assessed to the control operator
4. are permitted for short tests only

B-001-3-2.... If an amateur pretends there is an emergency and transmits the word "MAYDAY", what is this called?

1. a traditional greeting in May
2. an emergency test transmission
3. nothing special: "MAYDAY" has no meaning in an emergency
4. false or deceptive signals

B-001-3-3.... A person found guilty of transmitting a false or fraudulent distress signal, or interfering with, or obstructing any radio communication, without lawful cause, may be liable, on summary conviction, to a penalty of:

1. a fine, not exceeding $5 000, or a prison term of one year, or both
2. a fine of $10,000
3. a prison term of two years
4. a fine of $1,000

B-001-3-4.... What government document states the offences and penalties for non compliance of the rules governing radiocommunications?

1. the Radiocommunications Law Reform Act of 2002
2. the Official Radio Rules of Canada
3. the Radiocommunication Act
4. the Radiocommunications Regulations

B-001-3-5.... Which of the following is NOT correct? The Minister may suspend an Amateur Radio Operator Certificate:

1. where the holder has contravened the Radiocommunication Act, its Regulations, or the terms and conditions of the certificate
2. where the certificate was obtained through misrepresentation
3. with no notice, or opportunity to make representation thereto
4. where the holder has failed to comply with a request to pay fees or interest due

B-001-3-6.... Which of the following statements is NOT correct?

1. where entry is refused, and is necessary to perform his duties under the Act, a radio inspector may obtain a warrant
2. a radio inspector may enter a dwelling without the consent of the occupant and without a warrant
3. in executing a warrant, a radio inspector shall not use force, unless accompanied by a peace officer, and force is authorized
4. the person in charge of a place entered by a radio inspector shall give the inspector information that the inspector requests

CERTIFICATES

INTRODUCTION

The Amateur Radio Operator Certificate has the following qualifications:

- Basic
- Basic with Honours (80% or higher mark on the exam)
- Advanced
- Morse Code 5 w.p.m

A Basic qualification examination must be passed successfully before taking examinations for additional qualifications. Examinations for additional qualifications may be taken in any order.

There is no age limit or citizenship requirements but you must have a valid address in Canada. Amateur Radio Operator Certificates are valid for life.

Amateur Radio Operator Certificate holders are permitted to operate stations in the amateur radio service. Amateur Digital Radio Operator's Certificates can be exchanged for certificates with Basic & Advanced Qualifications. The Canadian Radiocommunication Operator General Certificate Maritime (RGMC) can also be exchanged for a Amateur Radio Operator Certificate with Basic Qualifications.

SUPPLEMENT

Holders of the following professional and previously issued Amateur certificates may obtain an Amateur Radio Operator Certificate without requiring further examination:

Radiocommunication Operator General Certificate (Maritime)
Radio Operator's First Class Certificate
Radio Operator's Second Class Certificate
Radiotelephone Operator's General Certificate (Aeronautical)
Radiotelephone Operator's General Certificate (Maritime)
Radiotelephone Operator's General Certificate (Land)
First-Class Radioelectronic Certificate
Amateur Radio Operator's Certificate (equivalent to - Basic, Advanced & Morse Code 12 wpm)
Amateur Radio Operator's Advanced Certificate (equivalent to - Basic, Advanced & Morse Code 12 wpm)
Amateur Digital Radio Operator's Certificate (equivalent to - Basic & Advanced)
Amateur Operator's Certificate (equivalent)

QUESTIONS

B-001-4-1.... What age must you be to hold an Amateur Radio Certificate with Basic Qualification?

1. 70 years or younger
2. 18 years or older
3. *there are no age limits*
4. 14 years or older

B-001-4-2.... Which examination must be passed before an Amateur Radio Operator Certificate is issued?

1. *Basic*
2. Advanced
3. personality test
4. morse code

B-001-4-3.... Holders of which one of the following certificates may be issued an Amateur Radio Operator Certificate?

1. Canadian Restricted Operator Certificate - Maritime (ROC-M)
2. *Canadian Radiocommunication Operator General Certificate Maritime (RGMC)*
3. Canadian Restricted Operator's Certificate - Maritime Commercial (ROC-MC)
4. Canadian Restricted Operator Certificate - Aeronautical (ROC-A)

B-001-4-4.... After an Amateur Radio Operator Certificate with Basic qualifications is issued, the holder may be examined for additional qualifications in the following order:

1. Morse code after passing the Basic with Honours
2. Advanced after passing Morse code
3. Morse code after passing the Advanced
4. *any order*

B-001-4-5.... One Morse code qualification is available for the Amateur Radio Operator Certificate. It is:

1. *5 wpm*
2. 7 wpm
3. 15 wpm
4. 12 wpm

B-001-4-6.... The holder of an Amateur Radio Operator Certificate with the Basic Qualification is authorized to operate the following stations:

1. a station authorized in the aeronautical service
2. a station authorized in the maritime service
3. any authorized station except stations authorized in the amateur, aeronautical or maritime services
4. *a station authorized in the amateur service*

B-001-4-7.... What conditions must candidates to amateur radio certification meet?

1. be at least 14 years of age and a Canadian citizen or permanent resident.
2. be a Canadian citizen
3. be a Canadian citizen or permanent resident
4. *have a valid address in Canada*

8

PRIVILEGES

INTRODUCTION

The Radiocommunication Act states that no person shall, except and in accordance with a radio authorization, install, operate or possess radio apparatus that would comprise an amateur radio station. In the amateur radio service, the Amateur Radio Operator Certificate is the authorization. Privileges are dependent on qualifications. Pass marks are 70% except 100% for morse code.

Basic Qualification
- access to all amateur bands above 30 MHz.
- passing the examination with a mark of 80% or higher will be recorded as "Basic with Honours" and comes with the privilege of access to all amateur bands including bands below 30 MHz.

Advanced Qualification
- access to all amateur bands
- use the maximum allowable transmitter powers
- build transmitting equipment, establish repeaters and club stations
- operate remotely controlled fixed stations, including the use of radio links

Morse Code (5 w.p.m.) Qualification
- access to all amateur radio bands twwice

SUPPLEMENT

HF bands are those amateur radio frequency bands below 30 MHz.

Amateur radio operators may install an amateur radio station for another person if that other person is the holder of a valid Amateur Radio Operator Certificate.

The Advanced qualification is required to build transmitting equipment.

Amateur Radio Operators certified prior to April 2, 2002 are allowed to operate on all amateur bands including those bands below 30 MHz.

There is an international trend of eliminating morse code as a requirement for licensing or certification. Morse code still has a large following amongst Amateur Operators. We highly recommend that new operators consider learning morse code. This is still one of the most thrilling modes of communications between Amateurs.

QUESTIONS

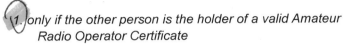

B-001-5-1.... Radio apparatus may be installed, placed in operation, repaired or maintained by the holder of an Amateur Radio Operator Certificate with Advanced qualification on behalf of another person:

1. if the other person is the holder of an Amateur Radio Operator Certificate to operate in the amateur radio service
2. pending the granting of a radio authorization, if the apparatus covers the amateur and commercial frequency bands
3. pending the granting of an Amateur Radio Operator Certificate, if the apparatus covers the amateur frequency bands only
4. if the transmitter of a station, for which a radio authorization is to be applied for, is type approved and crystal controlled

B-001-5-2.... The holder of an Amateur Radio Operator Certificate may design and build from scratch transmitting equipment for use in the amateur radio service provided that person has the:

1. Advanced qualification
2. Basic and Morse Code qualification
3. Morse Code with Honours qualification
4. Basic qualification

B-001-5-3.... Where a friend is not the holder of any type of radio operator certificate, you, as a holder of an Amateur Radio Operator Certificate with Basic qualification, may, on behalf of your friend:

1. install an amateur station but not operate or permit the operation of the apparatus
2. install and operate the radio apparatus, using your own call sign
3. modify and repair the radio apparatus but not install it
4. not install, place in operation, modify, repair, maintain, or permit the operation of the radio apparatus

B-001-5-4.... A radio amateur with Basic and Morse Code qualifications may install an amateur station for another person:

1. only if the other person is the holder of a valid Amateur Radio Operator Certificate
2. only if the final power input does not exceed 100 watts
3. only if the station is for use on one of the VHF bands
4. only if the DC power input to the final stage does not exceed 200 watts

HAMSTUDY Basic 2017/2018

STANDARDS

INTRODUCTION

The Standards for the Operation of Radio Stations in the Amateur Radio Service (RBR-4) and the Radiocommunication Regulations, spell out terms and conditions for operating an amateur radio station in Canada.

There is no minimum power limit within amateur frequency bands.

All amateur radio stations must be operated in accordance with a radio authorization.

Operation of amateur radio equipment is not permitted on frequencies outside of amateur radio bands. Radio equipment approved for use and licenced for frequencies in the land mobile service may also be used on amateur radio band frequencies if the owner holds an Amateur Radio Operator Certificate.

Amateur radio stations may only communicate with other similarly authorized amateur radio stations.

It is not permissible to use amateur radio apparatus to amplify the output of licence-exempt transmitters.

Transmissions that are superfluous (in excess of what is needed or not essential) are not permitted.

SUPPLEMENT

Download RBR-4 "Standards for the Operation of Radio Stations in the Amateur Radio Service" from the internet. Every Amateur Radio Operator needs to be aware of the contents of this document, namely:

- Frequency Bands
- Operator Qualifications
- Bandwidths
- Frequencies for Radio Control of Models
- Communications on behalf of Third Parties
- Operation Outside Canada
- Interference
- Station Identification
- Restrictions on Capacity and Power Output
- Unmodulated Carriers and Retransmission
- Amplitude Modulation and Frequency Stability

- Environmental Process
- Change of Address
- Measurements

QUESTIONS

B-001-6-1.... An amateur radio station with a maximum input power to the final stage of 2 watts:

1. *must be operated by a person with an Amateur Certificate and call sign*
2. must be licensed by Industry Canada
3. need not be licensed in isolated areas only
4. is exempt from regulatory control by Industry Canada

B-001-6-2.... An Amateur station may be used to communicate with:

1. any stations which are identified for special contests
2. armed forces stations during special contests and training exercises
3. *stations operated under similar authorizations*
4. any station transmitting in the amateur bands

B-001-6-3.... Which of the following statements is NOT correct?

1. a considerate operator does not transmit unnecessary signals
2. a courteous operator refrains from using offensive language
3. a radio amateur may not operate, or permit to be operated, a radio apparatus which he knows is not performing to the Radiocommunication Regulations
4. *a radio amateur may use a linear amplifier to amplify the output of a licence-exempt transmitter outside any amateur radio allocations*

B-001-6-4.... Which of the following statements is NOT correct?

1. except for a certified radio amateur operating within authorized amateur radio allocations, no person shall possess or operate any device for the purpose of amplifying the output power of a licence-exempt radio apparatus
2. a person may operate or permit the operation of radio apparatus only where the apparatus is maintained to the Radiocommunication Regulations tolerances
3. *an amateur radio operator transmitting unnecessary or offensive signals does not violate accepted practice*
4. a person may operate an amateur radio station when the person complies with the Standards for the Operation of Radio Stations in the Amateur Radio Service

B-001-6-5.... Which of the following statements is NOT correct? A person may operate radio apparatus authorized in the amateur service:

1. *on aeronautical, marine or land mobile frequencies*
2. only where the person complies with the Standards for the Operation of Radio Stations in the Amateur Radio Service
3. only where the apparatus is maintained within the performance standards set by Industry Canada regulations and policies
4. except for the amplification of the output power of licence-exempt radio apparatus operating outside authorized amateur radio service allocations

B-001.6.6.... Some VHF and UHF FM radios purchased for use in the amateur service can also be programmed to communicate on frequencies used for the land mobile service. Under what conditions is this permissible?

1. *the radio is certified under the proper Radio Standard Specification for use in Canada and licensed by Industry Canada on the specified frequencies*
2. the radio operator has a Restricted Operator's Certificate
3. the equipment has a RF power output of 2 watts or less
4. the equipment is used in remote areas north of 60 degrees latitude

RESTRICTIONS

INTRODUCTION

Amateur radio stations may only communicate with other amateur radio stations. The radio communications must not use or involve:

- radiocommunications in support of industrial, business or professional activities
- programming originated from a broadcast station
- commercially recorded material
- music
- code or cipher that is secret (internationally recognized Q codes are permitted)
- false or deceptive signals or communications
- profane or indecent language
- broadcasting to the general public

New digital encoding techniques to transmit data over amateur radio spectrum is permitted, provided the encoding or cipher is not secret.

SUPPLEMENT

Amateur operators discuss all kinds of topics on amateur bands. The tradition has been to avoid conversations which are risque and also those that deal with religion or politics.

It should always be kept in mind that conversations conducted using amateur radio are not private and could be received by anyone.

If the message has the potential to harm or offend others, it is probably not appropriate for the amateur service.

Turn down the volume of background broadcasting or other non-amateur signals so they are not re-transmitted by your station.

QUESTIONS

B-001-7-1.... Which of the following CANNOT be discussed on an amateur club net?

1. recreation planning
2. code practice planning
3. emergency planning
4. business planning

B-001-7-2.... When is a radio amateur allowed to broadcast information to the general public?

1. never
2. only when the operator is being paid
3. only when broadcasts last less than 1 hour
4. only when broadcasts last longer than 15 minutes

B-001-7-3.... When may false or deceptive amateur signals or communications be transmitted?

1. never
2. when operating a beacon transmitter in a "fox hunt" exercise
3. when playing a harmless "practical joke"
4. when you need to hide the meaning of a message for secrecy

B-001-7-4.... Which of the following one-way communications may not be transmitted in the amateur service?

1. broadcasts intended for the general public
2. radio control commands to model craft
3. brief transmissions to make adjustments to the station
4. morse code practice

B-001-7-5.... You wish to develop and use a new digital encoding technique to transmit data over amateur radio spectrum. Under what conditions is this permissible?

1. when the encoding technique is published in the public domain
2. when it is used for commercial traffic
3. when it includes sending the amateur station's call sign
4. when it is used for music streaming content

B-001-7-6.... When may an amateur station in two-way communication transmit an encoded message?

1. during a declared communications emergency
2. during contests
3. only when the encoding or cipher is not secret
4. when transmitting above 450 MHz

B-001-7-7.... What are the restrictions on the use of abbreviations or procedural signals in the amateur service?

1. there are no restrictions
2. they are not permitted because they obscure the meaning of a message to government monitoring stations
3. only "10-codes" are permitted
4. they may be used if the signals or codes are not secret

B-001-7-8.... What should you do to keep your station from re-transmitting music or signals from a non-amateur station?

1. turn up the volume of your transmitter
2. speak closer to the microphone to increase your signal strength
3. adjust your transceiver noise blanker
4. turn down the volume of background audio

B-001-7-9.... The transmission of a secret code by the operator of an amateur station:

1. is permitted for contests
2. must be approved by Industry Canada
3. is not permitted
4. is permitted for third-party traffic

B-001-7-11.... In the amateur radio service, business communications:

1. are only permitted if they are for the safety of life or immediate protection of property
2. are not prohibited by regulation
3. are permitted on some bands
4. are not permitted under any circumstance

Finish question section on page 225

INSTALLATION & QUALIFICATIONS

INTRODUCTION

Amateur radio operators may establish their amateur radio stations anywhere in Canada. Installations may be subject to environmental and aeronautical assessments.

There are no limitations as to the number of stations that may be established.

Amateur radio operators who are holders of the Basic and Advanced qualifications may also install and operate:

- club stations
- automatic repeater stations (in band)
- transmitters or RF amplifiers that are not commercially manufactured for use in the amateur service
- remotely controlled fixed stations, including the use of radio links

SUPPLEMENT

The 6 meter band has unique propagation characteristics that suit the operation of beacon stations. This band has the largest number of beacon stations operated by amateurs. Beacon stations transmit signals intended for one way communication. Six meter band enthusiasts monitor for these transmissions to help them determine whether or not sky wave propagation is possible to specific regions.

The Northern California DX Foundation and the International Amateur Radio Union operate an International Beacon Network in certain HF bands. Search for NCDXF/IARU Beacon Network on the internet.

QUESTIONS

B-001-8-1.... Where may the holder of an Amateur Radio Operator Certificate operate an amateur radio station in Canada?

1. *anywhere in Canada*
2. anywhere in Canada during times of emergency
3. only at the address shown on Industry Canada records
4. anywhere in your callsign prefix area

B-001-8-2.... Which type of station may transmit one-way communications?

1. *beacon station*
2. repeater station
3. HF station
4. VHF station

B-001-8-3.... Amateur radio operators may install or operate radio apparatus:

1. *at any location in Canada*
2. only at the address which is on record at Industry Canada
3. at the address which is on record at Industry Canada and at one other location
4. at the address which is on record at Industry Canada and in two mobiles

B-001-8-4.... In order to install any radio apparatus, to be used specifically for receiving and automatically retransmitting radiotelephone communications within the same frequency band, a radio amateur must hold an Amateur Radio Operator Certificate, with a minimum of:

1. basic and Morse code qualifications
2. *basic and advanced qualifications*
3. basic qualification
4. basic with Honours qualification

B-001-8-5.... In order to install any radio apparatus, to be used specifically for an amateur radio club station, the radio amateur must hold an Amateur Radio Operator Certificate , with a minimum of the following qualifications:

1. *basic and advanced*
2. basic with Honours
3. basic
4. basic, advanced and Morse code

B-001-8-6.... In order to install or operate a transmitter or RF amplifier that is neither professionally designed nor commercially manufactured for use in the amateur service, a radio amateur must hold an Amateur Radio Operator Certificate, with a minimum of which qualifications:

1. basic, advanced and Morse code
2. basic and Morse code
3. basic with Honours
4. *basic and advanced*

USING AMATEUR RADIO STATIONS

INTRODUCTION

To install and operate an amateur radio station, individuals must be holders of an Amateur Radio Operator Certificate with appropriate qualifications.

The owner and operator share the responsibility for the proper operation of an amateur radio station.

Where the owner is unable to be in control of the operation of an amateur radio station, the owner may choose any qualified amateur radio operator to be the control operator. The control operator must be able to control the operation of transmitting equipment at the station's control point.

Unqualified persons may operate amateur radio stations only under the supervision and in the presence of the holder of an Amateur Radio Operator Certificate with appropriate qualifications.

SUPPLEMENT

Before making your "first contact", spend some time listening and becoming acquainted with the methods of communications being used on the ham band of interest.

The first contact will no doubt be very exciting and memorable. Most amateurs are friendly and are more than willing to respond to any questions you may have. But, like in any walk of life, there may be an occasion when you encounter an operator whose operating procedures and mannerisms turns you off. Don't let a negative encounter prevent you from investigating the various possibilities of this exciting hobby.

QUESTIONS

B-001-9-1.... Who is responsible for the proper operation of an amateur station?

1. only the station owner who is the holder of an Amateur Radio Operator Certificate
2. *both the control operator and the station owner*
3. the person who owns the station equipment
4. only the control operator

B-001-9-2.... If you transmit from another amateur's station, who is responsible for its proper operation?

1. you
2. *both of you*
3. the station owner, unless the station records show that you were the control operator at the time
4. the station owner

B-001-9-3.... What is your responsibility as a station owner?

1. you must allow another amateur to operate your station upon request
2. you must be present whenever the station is operated
3. you must notify Industry Canada if another amateur acts as the control operator
4. *you are responsible for the proper operation of the station in accordance with the regulations*

B-001-9-4.... Who may be the control operator of an amateur station?

1. any person over 21 years of age with a Basic qualification
2. *any qualified amateur chosen by the station owner*
3. any person over 21 years of age with Basic and Morse code qualifications
4. any person over 21 years of age

B-001-9-5.... When must an amateur station have a control operator?

1. a control operator is not needed
2. whenever the station receiver is operated
3. *whenever the station is transmitting*
4. only when training another amateur

B-001-9-6.... When an amateur station is transmitting, where must its control operator be?

1. anywhere in the same building as the transmitter
2. at the station's entrance, to control entry to the room
3. anywhere within 50 Km of the station location
4. *at the station's control point*

B-001-9-7.... Why can't family members without qualifications transmit using your amateur station if they are alone with your equipment?

1. they must not use your equipment without your permission
2. they must first know how to use the right abbreviations and Q signals
3. they must first know the right frequencies and emission modes for transmitting
4. *they must hold suitable amateur radio qualifications before they are allowed to be control operators*

B-001-9-8.... The owner of an amateur station may:

1. permit anyone to take part in communications only if prior written permission is received from Industry Canada
2. permit anyone to use the station without restrictions
3. *permit any person to operate the station under the supervision, and in the presence of the holder of the amateur operator certificate*
4. permit anyone to use the station and take part in communications

B-001-9-9.... Which of the following statements is correct?

1. a person, holding only Basic qualification, may operate another station on 14.2 MHz.
2. radio amateurs may permit any person to operate the station without supervision
3. *any person may operate an amateur station under supervision, and in the presence of, a person holding appropriate qualifications*
4. any person may operate a station in the amateur radio service

18

HARMFUL INTERFERENCE

INTRODUCTION

Interference that seriously degrades, obstructs or repeatedly interrupts a radio communication service is referred to as harmful interference.

It is unlawful to deliberately interfere with another station's communication.

When interference to the reception of radiocommunications is caused by the operation of an amateur station, the Minister may require that the radio amateur takes the necessary steps to prevent the interference. When possible, operators should take immediate steps to resolve such interference situations before it becomes necessary to involve Industry Canada.

If two amateur stations want to use the same frequency, both station operators have an equal right to operate on the frequency. Be considerate.

(This topic continues on page 21)

SUPPLEMENT

Interference can also be broadly defined as any modification to the reception of sound or picture signals that makes them unacceptable.

Interference can originate from a variety of sources. Electrical and electronic appliances in homes, offices and industry, neon signs, motor vehicle ignition systems, medical equipment, power lines and radio transmitters all contribute to background noise that can interfere with radio and television reception.

This problem is compounded by the fact that many radios and televisions were not designed to operate in today's radio frequency environment, in which the number of electrical devices and radio transmissions has greatly increased.

When an electronic device picks up interference, the problem is often assumed to be the fault of the radio transmitting source. But in fact, the affected equipment often lacks the circuitry required to operate properly in the presence of radio signals, or it has a defect that makes it susceptible to interference.

QUESTIONS

B-001-10-1.... What is a transmission called that disturbs other communications?

1. harmful interference
2. interrupted CW
3. transponder signals
4. unidentified transmissions

B-001-10-2.... When may you deliberately interfere with another station's communications?

1. never
2. only if the station is operating illegally
3. only if the station begins transmitting on a frequency you are using
4. you may expect, and cause, deliberate interference because it can't be helped during crowded band conditions

B-001-10-4.... What rule applies if two amateurs want to use the same frequency?

1. both station operators have an equal right to operate on the frequency
2. the station operator with a lesser qualification must yield the frequency to an operator of higher qualification
3. the station operator with a lower power output must yield the frequency to the station with a higher power output
4. station operators in ITU regions 1 and 3 must yield the frequency to stations in ITU region 2

B-001-10-5.... What name is given to a form of interference that seriously degrades, obstructs or repeatedly interrupts a radiocommunication service?

1. intentional interference
2. adjacent interference
3. disruptive interference
4. harmful interference

B-001-10-6.... Where interference to the reception of radiocommunications is caused by the operation of an amateur station:

1. the amateur station operator is not obligated to take any action
2. the amateur station operator may continue to operate without restrictions
3. the Minister may require that the necessary steps for the prevention of the interference be taken by the radio amateur
4. the amateur station operator may continue to operate and the necessary steps can be taken when the amateur operator can afford it

HARMFUL INTERFERENCE - continued

INTRODUCTION

In many bands, the amateur radio service has primary user status. However, in some bands, such as 430-450 MHz. and 902-928 MHz, the amateur radio service has secondary user status.

The 902-928 MHz and 2300 to 2450 MHz bands are heavily used by licence exempt low power devices.

Transmissions from secondary users may not cause interference to primary user stations. Secondary users may not claim interference from primary user transmissions.

Avoid all transmissions, including test transmissions, if there is a possibility of causing interference to primary users.

Identification and resolution of interference may require the assistance of an experienced individual. Seek assistance for difficult situations.

SUPPLEMENT

Audio rectification interference occurs when an electronic circuit (usually an amplifier), which ideally should respond only to audio frequency signals, responds to external radio frequency (RF) signals. Typically, the circuit picks up signals from a nearby radio transmitter in addition to the sound the listener wants to hear. The unwanted signal may be constant or intermittent, faint or uncontrollably loud.

Televisions, radios, stereos, telephones, electronic organs and public address systems are all prone to audio rectification interference. When audio rectification occurs, it indicates that the device lacks sufficient shielding or filtering to function properly when in a strong radio signal environment. The solution is to modify the affected audio device.

Radio transmitters that are defective or of inadequate design, may radiate excessive spurious emissions or harmonic signals which can result in interference to the reception of broadcast stations. In this case, a solution needs to be designed for the transmitting device.

QUESTIONS

B-001-10-3.... If the regulations say that the amateur service is a secondary user of a frequency band, and another service is a primary user, what does this mean?

1. *amateurs are allowed to use the frequency band only if they do not cause interference to primary users*
2. nothing special - all users of a frequency band have equal rights to operate
3. amateurs are only allowed to use the frequency band during emergencies
4. amateurs must increase transmitter power to overcome any interference caused by primary users

B-001-10-7.... Radio amateur operation must not cause interference to other radio services operating in which of the following bands?

1. 7.0 to 7.1 MHz
2. 144.0 to 148.0 MHz
3. *430.0 to 450.0 MHz*
4. 14.0 to 14.2 MHz

B-001-10-8.... Radio amateur operations are not protected from interference caused by another service operating in which of the following frequency bands?

1. 144 to 148 MHz
2. 222 to 225 MHz
3. 50 to 54 MHz
4. *902 to 928 MHz*

B-001-10-9.... Which of the following is NOT correct? The operator of an amateur station:

1. shall not cause harmful interference to a station in another service which has primary use of that band
2. may conduct technical experiments using the station apparatus
3. *may make trials or tests, even though there is a possibility of interfering with other stations*
4. may make trials or tests, except if there is a possibility of interference to other stations.

B-001-10-10.... Which of these amateur bands may be heavily occupied by licence exempt devices?

1. 3.5 to 4.0 MHz
2. 430 to 450 MHz
3. *902 to 928 MHz*
4. 135.7 to 137.8 kHz

B-001-10-11.... The amateur radio service is authorized to share a portion of what Industrial Scientific Medical (ISM) band that is heavily used by licence exempt devices?

1. 430 to 450 MHz
2. 144 to 148 MHz
3. *2300 to 2450 MHz*
4. 1240 to 1300 MHz

22

EMERGENCY COMMUNICATIONS

INTRODUCTION

Distress communications involve the immediate safety of life of individuals or the immediate protection of property. For distress communications, any frequency, mode and power may be used to communicate with any other station. In such situations there are no restrictions on message content.

An amateur station may provide a radiocommunication service on behalf of recognized public service agencies during peace time civil emergencies and exercises.

During disasters, transmissions necessary to meet essential communication needs and transmissions to assist with relief operations are permitted when normal communication systems are overloaded, damaged or disrupted. Most communications are handled by nets using predetermined frequencies in amateur bands. Operators not directly involved with disaster communications are requested to avoid making unnecessary transmissions on or near frequencies being used for disaster communications.

Except when a station is directly involved with a distress situation, it is not permissible to interfere with the working of another station. Under normal circumstances, amateur radio stations only communicate with other amateur stations. An amateur radio station in distress may use any means of radiocommunication and without power limitations.

SUPPLEMENT

Many amateurs have prepared themselves and equipped their stations to be capable of assisting in providing communications in times of disaster or emergencies. If this aspect of amateur radio is of interest, a starting point would be to ask questions of local amateurs or check out the Amateur Radio Emergency Service (ARES) on the web.

Public Safety Canada is responsible for handling national situations. Each of the provinces and territories have their own organizations to handle provincial emergencies. Likewise, most cities and municipalities have organizations to handle locally occurring emergencies within their own jurisdiction.

QUESTIONS

B-001-11-1.... Amateur radio stations may communicate:

1. with anyone who uses international Morse code
2. with non amateur stations
3. with any station involved in a real or simulated emergency
4. *only with other amateur stations*

B-001-11-2....During relief operations in the days following a disaster, when may an amateur use his equipment to communicate on frequencies outside amateur bands?

1. when relaying messages on behalf of government agencies
2. when messages are destined to agencies without amateur radio support
3. *never*
4. when normal communication systems are overloaded, damaged or disrupted

B-001-11-3.... If you hear an unanswered distress signal on an amateur band where you do not have privileges to communicate:

1. you may offer assistance using international Morse code only
2. you may offer assistance after contacting Industry Canada for permission to do so
3. *you should offer assistance*
4. you may not offer assistance

B-001-11-4.... In the amateur radio service, it is permissible to broadcast:

1. music
2. commercially recorded material
3. programming that originates from a broadcast undertaking
4. *radiocommunications required for the immediate safety of life of individuals or the immediate protection of property*

B-001-11-5.... An amateur radio station in distress may:

1. only use radiocommunication bands for which the operator is qualified to use
2. use any means of radiocommunication, but only on internationally recognized emergency channels
3. *use any means of radiocommunication*
4. use only Morse code communications on internationally recognized emergency channels

B-001-11-6.... During a disaster, when may an amateur station make transmissions necessary to meet essential communication needs and assist relief operations?

1. never - only official emergency stations may transmit in a disaster
2. *when normal communication systems are overloaded, damaged or disrupted*
3. when normal communication systems are working but are not convenient
4. only when the local emergency net is activated

B-001-11-7.... During an emergency, what power output limitations must be observed by a station in distress?

1. 1000 watts PEP during daylight hours, reduced to 200 watts PEP during the night
2. 1500 watts PEP
3. *there are no limitations for a station in distress*
4. 200 watts PEP

B-001-11-8.... During a disaster:

1. use only frequencies in the 80 metre band
2. use only frequencies in the 40 metre band
3. use any United Nations approved frequency
4. *most communications are handled by nets using predetermined frequencies in amateur bands. Operators not directly involved with disaster communications are requested to avoid making unnecessary transmissions on or near frequencies being used for disaster communications*

Finish question section on page 225

REMUNERATION & PRIVACY

INTRODUCTION

Amateur radio operators are prohibited from demanding or accepting remuneration in any form for transmitting or receiving radiocommunications.

Radiocommunications transmitted by broadcast and amateur stations are not protected by law for privacy.

Intercepted communications from other than broadcasting or amateur stations may only be divulged:

- for the purpose of preserving or protecting property, or preventing serious harm to any person, including the bringing of emergency assistance to any person

- when giving evidence in any criminal or civil proceeding

- by officials to other officials in the administration of justice

- on behalf of Canada, for the purpose of international affairs, national defence or security

SUPPLEMENT

Communications between amateur stations are generally heard by others, including non-amateurs. Many people own scanning receivers and they often listen to conversations on popular VHF/UHF amateur frequencies.

Amateurs using HF frequencies for long distance communications will sometimes receive a QSL card from a short wave listener (SWL) with details of some previous contact. The SWL's objective is to collect the amateur's confirmation of this reception report. Not many years ago, before a person could obtain a ham licence in some eastern block countries, a certain number of QSL cards verifying reception reports had to be obtained.

HF = high frequency (3 - 30 MHz.)
VHF = very high frequency (30 - 300 MHz.)
UHF = ultra high frequency (300- 3000 MHz.)

QSL cards are postcards indicating at least the callsign, date-time, frequency, signal report and mode.

B-001-12-1.... What kind of payment is allowed for third-party messages sent by an amateur station?

1. donation of amateur equipment
2. donation of equipment repairs
3. *no payment of any kind is allowed*
4. any amount agreed upon in advance

B-001-12-2.... Radiocommunications transmitted by stations other than a broadcasting station may be divulged or used:

1. if transmitted by any station using the international Morse code
2. *if it is transmitted by an amateur station*
3. if transmitted in English or French
4. during peacetime civil emergencies

B-001-12-3.... The operator of an amateur station:

1. shall charge no less than $10 for each message that the person transmits or receives
2. shall charge no more than $10 for each message that the person transmits or receives
3. may accept a gift or gratuity in lieu of remuneration for any message that the person transmits or receives
4. *shall not demand or accept remuneration in any form, in respect of a radiocommunication that the person transmits or receives*

B-001-12-4.... Which of the following is NOT an exception from the penalties under the Act, for divulging, intercepting or using information obtained through radiocommunication, other than broadcasting?

— remember

1. *where it is to provide information for a journalist*
2. where it is for the purpose of preserving or protecting property, or for the prevention of harm to a person
3. where it is for the purpose of giving evidence in a criminal or civil proceeding in which persons are required to give evidence
4. where it is on behalf of Canada, for the purpose of international or national defence or security

IDENTIFICATION

INTRODUCTION

Canadian amateur stations normally use call signs that start with the letters VA, VE, VO or VY. These are from call sign blocks assigned to Canada by the International Telecommunication Union (ITU).

Call signs are assigned by Amateur Radio Service Center and are indicated on Amateur Radio Operator Certificates.

Amateur radio stations must identify their station by transmitting their assigned call sign in English or in French at the beginning and at the end of each period of exchange of communication or test transmission, and at intervals of not more than 30 minutes.

Transmissions made for the control of models (hobby type planes, boats, cars, etc.) need not be identified by a call sign.

SUPPLEMENT

Canadian call sign prefixes:

VE1 or VA1 Nova Scotia	VE8 Northwest Territories
VE2 or VA2 Quebec	VE9 New Brunswick
VE3 or VA3 Ontario	VE0 International Waters
VE4 or VA4 Manitoba	VO1 Newfoundland
VE5 or VA5 Saskatchewan	VO2 Labrador
VE6 or VA6 Alberta	VY1 Yukon Territory
VE7 or VA7 British Columbia	VY2 Prince Edward Island
	VY0 Nunavut Territory

The policy for issuing call signs and special event prefixes are detailed in Radiocommunication Information Circular RIC-9. You may also hear Canadian prefixes starting with CF, CG, CH, CI, CJ, CK, CY, CZ, VB, VC, VD, VF, VG, VX, XJ, XK, XL, XM, XN and XO. These are more likely to be heard on HF bands to celebrate special events. CY0 is used for operations on Sable Island and CY9 for operations on St-Paul Island.

QUESTIONS

B-001-13-1.... Which of the following call signs is a valid Canadian amateur radio call sign?

1. SM2CAN
2. VA3XYZ
3. BY7HY
4. KA9OLS

B-001-13-2.... How often must an amateur station be identified?

1. at least every thirty minutes, and at the beginning and at the end of a contact
2. at the beginning of a contact and at least every thirty minutes after that
3. at least once during each transmission
4. at the beginning and end of each transmission

B-001-13-3.... What do you transmit to identify your amateur station?

1. your "handle"
2. your first name and your location
3. your full name
4. your call sign

B-001-13-4.... What identification, if any, is required when two amateur stations begin communications?

1. no identification is required
2. each station must transmit its own call sign
3. both stations must transmit both call signs
4. one of the stations must give both stations call signs

B-001-13-5.... What identification, if any, is required when two amateur stations end communications?

1. each station must transmit its own call sign
2. no identification is required
3. one of the stations must transmit both stations call signs
4. both stations must transmit both call signs

B-001-13-6.... What is the longest period of time an amateur station can transmit, without identifying by call sign?

1. 20 minutes
2. 15 minutes
3. 30 minutes
4. 10 minutes

B-001-13-7.... When may an amateur transmit unidentified communications?

1. only for brief tests not meant as messages
2. only if it does not interfere with others
3. only for two-way or third-party communications
4. never, except to control a model craft

B-001-13-8.... What language may you use when identifying your station?

1. English or French
2. any language being used for a contact
3. any language being used for a contact, providing Canada has a third-party communications agreement with that country
4. any language of a country which is a member of the International Telecommunication Union

B-001-13-9.... The call sign of an amateur station must be transmitted:

1. at intervals not greater than three minutes when using voice communications
2. at intervals not greater than ten minutes when using Morse code
3. when requested to do so by the station being called
4. at the beginning and at the end of each exchange of communications and at intervals not greater than 30 minutes

Finish question section on page 225.

28

THIRD PARTY COMMUNICATIONS

INTRODUCTION

Canada does not prohibit international communications on behalf of third parties. Other countries may permit their amateur stations to communicate on behalf of third parties without having to enter into special arrangements with Canada.

International third-party communications, in cases of emergency or disaster relief, is expressly permitted unless specifically prohibited by the other country.

Messages originating from, or destined to, persons authorized by any country to operate in the amateur radio service are not communications on behalf of a third party. Canadian Forces Affiliated Radio System (CFARS) and United States Military Affiliated Radio System (MARS) messages are also not considered communications on behalf of a third party.

If a non-amateur is permitted to operate an amateur station, the communication is on behalf of a third party. The control operator is required to continuously monitor and supervise the third party's participation.

SUPPLEMENT

Some questions on this topic are dated and need to be updated by Industry Canada. Third party restrictions that were previously in effect have been eliminated.

MORE ON IDENTIFICATION

USA amateur operators operating their stations in *Canada* identify with their FCC call signs, adding the word "mobile" or "portable" or the oblique character "/" followed by the appropriate Canadian call sign prefix. For example, W1AW operating in British Columbia would identify W1AW/VE7 when using Morse code. Each amateur station is required to indicate their geographical location as nearly as possible by city and state or province at least once during a contact. The operation of amateur stations in the territory of the other country is covered in "Treaty Series 1952 No. 7 - Operation of Certain Radio Equipment or Stations, Convention between Canada and the United States of America".

Announcing the prefix before the call sign is the procedure used by amateur radio operators from other countries while in Canada. Example VE7/VK4GPP.

QUESTIONS

B-001-14-1.... If a non-amateur friend is using your station to talk to someone in Canada, and a foreign station breaks in to talk to your friend, what should you do?

1. *since you can talk to foreign amateurs, your friend may keep talking as long as you are the control operator*
2. have your friend wait until you determine from the foreign station if their administration permits third-party traffic
3. report the incident to the foreign amateur's government
4. stop all discussions and quickly sign-off

B-001-14-2.... If you let an unqualified third party use your amateur station, what must you do at your station's control point?

1. you must key the transmitter and make the station identification
2. you must monitor and supervise the communication only if contacts are made on frequencies below 30 MHz
3. *you must continuously monitor and supervise the third-party's participation*
4. you must monitor and supervise the communication only if contacts are made in countries which have no third-party communications

B-001-14-3.... Radio amateurs may use their stations to transmit international communications on behalf of a third party only if:

1. the amateur station has received written authorization from Industry Canada to pass third party traffic
2. the communication is transmitted by secret code
3. *such communications have been authorized by the other country concerned*
4. prior remuneration has been received

B-001-14-6.... Amateur third party communications is:

1. the transmission of commercial or secret messages
2. a simultaneous communication between three operators
3. none of these answers
4. *the transmission of non commercial or personal messages to or on behalf of a third party*

B-001-14-4.... A person operating a Canadian amateur station is forbidden to communicate with amateur stations of another country:

1. *when that country has notified the International Telecommunications Union that it objects to such communications*
2. without written permission from Industry Canada
3. until he has properly identified his station
4. unless he is passing third party traffic

B-001-14-5.... International communications on behalf of third parties may be transmitted by an amateur station only if:

1. English or French is used to identify the station at the end of each transmission
2. *the countries concerned have authorized such communications*
3. the countries for which the traffic is intended have registered their consent to such communications with the ITU
4. radiotelegraphy is used

B-001-14-8.... One of the following is not considered to be communication on behalf of a third party, even though the message is originated by, or addressed to, a non-amateur:

1. messages that are handled within a local network
2. messages addressed to points within Canada
3. *messages originated from Canadian Forces Affiliated Radio System (CFARS)*
4. all messages received from Canadian stations

Finish question section on page 225 & 226.

QUALIFICATIONS & HF BANDS

INTRODUCTION

The Amateur Radio Operator Certificate has three qualifications. The privileges are:

- Basic - operate on all amateur bands above 30 MHz with commercially built, power limited transmitters. Obtaining 80% or higher marks on your exam (passing with honours) will qualify you to use all amateur bands including HF.
- Advanced - operate on all HF amateur bands, install and operate non-commercially manufactured transmitters at highest power levels, club stations, automatic repeaters, remotely controlled stations including radio links
- 5 WPM Morse code - operate on all amateur bands

In Canada, the HF amateur bands are:

160 metres - 1.8 to 2.0 MHz
80 metres - 3.5 to 4.0 MHz
40 metres - 7.0 to 7.3 MHz
30 metres - 10.100 to 10.150 MHz
20 metres - 14.000 to 14.350 MHz

17 metres - 18.068 to 18.168 MHz
15 metres - 21.000 to 21.450 MHz
12 metres - 24.890 to 24.990 MHz
10 metres - 28.000 to 29.700 MHz

SUPPLEMENT

Amateur radio operators may use all amateur frequency bands above 30 MHz for radio control of models.

The qualifications required to operate an amateur radio station varies from country to country.

The International Telecommunications Union (ITU) Radio Regulations creates the amateur radio service with minimum mandatory requirements. These requirements are incorporated in Canadian regulations.

Countries are free to impose higher standards or requirements than those required by ITU.

QUESTIONS

B-001-15-1.... If you let another amateur with additional qualifications than yours control your station, what operating privileges are allowed?

1. only the privileges allowed by your qualifications
2. any privileges allowed by the additional qualifications
3. all the emission privileges of the additional qualifications, but only the frequency privileges of your qualifications
4. all the frequency privileges of the additional qualifications, but only the emission privileges of your qualifications

B-001-15-2.... If you are the control operator at the station of another amateur who has additional qualifications to yours, what operating privileges are you allowed?

1. any privileges allowed by the additional qualifications
2. all the emission privileges of the additional qualifications, but only the frequency privileges of your qualifications
3. all the frequency privileges of the additional qualifications, but only the emission privileges of your qualifications
4. only the privileges allowed by your qualifications

B-001-15-3.... In addition to passing the Basic written examination, what must you do before you are allowed to use amateur frequencies below 30 MHz?

1. you must notify Industry Canada that you intend to operate on the HF bands
2. you must pass a Morse code test
3. you must attend a class to learn about HF communications
4. you must pass a Morse code or Advanced test or attain a mark of 80% on the Basic exam

B-001-15-5.... In Canada, the 75/80 metre amateur band corresponds in frequency to:

1. 3.0 to 3.5 MHz
2. 4.0 to 4.5 MHz
3. 4.5 to 5.0 MHz
4. 3.5 to 4.0 MHz

B-001-15-4.... The holder of an amateur radio certificate may operate radio controlled models:

1. if the control transmitter does not exceed 15 kHz of occupied bandwidth
2. on all frequencies above 30 MHz
3. if the frequency used is below 30 MHz
4. if only pulse modulation is used

B-001-15-6.... In Canada, the 160 metre amateur band corresponds in frequency to:

1. 1.8 to 2.0 MHz
2. 1.5 to 2.0 MHz
3. 2.0 to 2.25 MHz
4. 2.25 to 2.5 MHz

B-001-15-7.... In Canada, the 40 metre amateur band corresponds in frequency to:

1. 6.5 to 6.8 MHz
2. 6.0 to 6.3 MHz
3. 7.7 to 8.0 MHz
4. 7.0 to 7.3 MHz

B-001-15-8.... In Canada, the 20 metre amateur band corresponds in frequency to:

1. 14.000 to 14.350 MHz
2. 13.500 to 14.000 MHz
3. 15.000 to 15.750 MHz
4. 16.350 to 16.830 MHz

B-001-15-9.... In Canada, the 15 metre amateur band corresponds in frequency to:

1. 18.068 to 18.168 MHz
2. 14.000 to 14.350 MHz
3. 28.000 to 29.700 MHz
4. 21.000 to 21.450 MHz

Finish question section on page 226.

BANDWIDTH

INTRODUCTION

Permitted bandwidths in amateur bands:

1 kHz	- 10.1 to 10.15 MHz
6 kHz	- All other HF bands below 28.0 MHz
20 kHz	- 28.0 to 29.7 MHz
30 kHz	- 50.0 to 148.0 MHz
100 kHz	- 220.0 to 225.0 MHz
12 MHz	- 430.0 to 928.0 MHz

The bandwidth of a transmitted signal is the frequency band occupied by that signal at a level of 26 dB below the maximum amplitude.

Typical necessary bandwidths for selected emissions:

- single-sideband radiotelephony - 3 kHz
- slow-scan television - 2.7 kHz
- fast-scan television - 5.25 MHz
- AMTOR - 300 Hz

SUPPLEMENT

The overall gain of a communications system can be improved by:

- narrowing the received bandwidth which reduces receiver noise.

- narrowing the transmitted bandwidth which results in spreading all the available power over less spectrum.

Bandwidths are affected by the amount of information to be communicated.

- Morse Code transmissions use very little bandwidth since the only information being transmitted are "dots & dashes" at relatively low speeds.

- Television transmissions convey a lot of information (moving pictures, color, sound, and other signals). Therefore, TV requires large bandwidths.

QUESTIONS

B-001-16-1.... What is the maximum authorized bandwidth within the frequency range of 50 to 148 MHz?

1. 20 kHz
2. the total bandwidth shall not exceed that of a single-sideband phone emission
3. the total bandwidth shall not exceed 10 times that of a CW emission
4. *30 kHz*

B-001-16-2.... The maximum bandwidth of an amateur station's transmission allowed in the band 28 to 29.7 MHz is:

1. 6 kHz
2. 15 kHz
3. *20 kHz*
4. 30 kHz

B-001-16-3.... Except for one band, the maximum bandwidth of an amateur station's transmission allowed between 7 and 28 MHz is:

1. *6 kHz*
2. 15 kHz
3. 20 kHz
4. 30 kHz

B-001-16-4.... The maximum bandwidth of an amateur station's transmission allowed in the band 144 to 148 MHz is:

1. 6 kHz
2. 20 kHz
3. *30 kHz*
4. 15 kHz

B-001-16-5.... The maximum bandwidth of an amateur station's transmission allowed in the band 50 to 54 MHz is:

1. 20 kHz
2. *30 kHz*
3. 6 kHz
4. 15 kHz

B-001-16-6.... Which of the following bands of amateur frequencies has a maximum allowed bandwidth of less than 6 kHz. That band is:

1. 18.068 to 18.168 MHz
2. *10.1 to 10.15 MHz*
3. 24.89 to 24.99 MHz
4. 1.8 to 2.0 MHz

B-001-16-7.... Single sideband is not permitted in the band:

1. 18.068 to 18.168 MHz
2. *10.1 to 10.15 MHz*
3. 24.89 to 24.99 MHz
4. 7.0 to 7.3 MHz

B-001-16-8.... What precaution must an amateur radio operator take when transmitting near band edges?

1. watch the standing wave ratio so as not to damage the transmitter
2. restrict operation to telegraphy
3. make sure that the emission mode is compatible with agreed band plans
4. *ensure that the bandwidth required on either side of the carrier frequency does not fall out of band*

B-001-16-9.... Which of the following answers is NOT correct? Based on the bandwidth required, the following modes may be transmitted on these frequencies:

1. AMTOR on 14.08 MHz
2. 300 bps packet on 10.145 MHz
3. *fast-scan television (ATV) on 145 MHz*
4. fast-scan television (ATV) on 440 MHz

Finish question section on page 226

POWER RESTRICTIONS

INTRODUCTION

Amateur Radio Operator Certificate holders with the Basic qualification are limited to maximum transmitting powers of:

- 250 watts DC input to the final transmitter stage
- 560 watts PEP for single sideband emissions expressed as output power measured across an impedance matched load
- 190 watts carrier power for any other emissions expressed as output power measured across an impedance matched load

Amateur Radio Operator Certificate holders with Basic and Advanced qualifications are limited to maximum transmitting powers of:

- 1000 watts DC input to the final transmitter stage
- 2250 watts PEP for single sideband emissions expressed as output power measured across an impedance matched load
- 750 watts carrier power for any other emissions expressed as output power measured across an impedance matched load

SUPPLEMENT

The maximum power levels permitted in Canada are considerably higher than what is permitted in most of Europe, Australia, New Zealand, etc. In the USA, the maximum power amateur operators are allowed is 1500 watts.

It is considered a good operating practice to reduce transmitter power levels to the minimum required for a particular communication.

QUESTIONS

B-001-17-1.... What amount of transmitter power should radio amateurs use at all times?

1. *the minimum legal power necessary to communicate*
2. 25 watts PEP output
3. 250 watts PEP output
4. 2000 watts PEP output

B-001-17-2.... What is the most FM transmitter power a holder of only Basic qualification may use on 147 MHz?

1. 1000 watts DC input
2. 200 watts PEP output
3. *250 watts DC input*
4. 25 watts PEP output

B-001-17-3.... Where in your station can you verify that legal power limits are respected?

1. at the power amplifier RF input terminals inside the transmitter or amplifier
2. *at the antenna connector of the transmitter or amplifier*
3. on the antenna itself, after the transmission line
4. at the power supply terminals inside the transmitter or amplifier

B-001-17-4.... What is the maximum transmitting output power an amateur station may use on 3750 kHz, if the operator has Basic and Morse code qualifications?

1. 1000 watts PEP output for SSB operation
2. 1500 watts PEP output for SSB operation
3. 2000 watts PEP output for SSB operation
4. *560 watts PEP output for SSB operation*

B-001-17-5.... What is the maximum transmitting power an amateur station may use for SSB operation on 7055 kHz, if the operator has Basic with Honours qualification?

1. 1000 watts PEP output
2. *560 watts PEP output*
3. 2000 watts PEP output
4. 200 watts PEP output

B-001-17-6.... The DC power input to the anode or collector circuit of the final RF stage of a transmitter, used by a holder of an Amateur Radio Operator Certificate with Advanced qualifications, shall not exceed:

1. 250 watts
2. 500 watts
3. *1000 watts*
4. 750 watts

B-001-17-7.... The maximum DC input to the final stage of an amateur transmitter, when the operator is the holder of both the Basic and Advanced qualifications, is:

1. 250 watts
2. *1000 watts*
3. 1500 watts
4. 500 watts

B-001-17-8.... The operator of an amateur station, who is the holder of a Basic qualification, shall ensure that the station power, when expressed as RF output power measured across an impedance matched load, does not exceed:

1. 2500 watts peak power
2. 1000 watts carrier power for transmitters producing other emissions
3. *560 watts peak envelope power, for transmitters producing any type of single sideband emission*
4. 150 watts peak power

B-001-17-9.... The holder of an Amateur Radio Operator Certificate with the Basic qualification is limited to a maximum of ___250___ watts when expressed as direct current input power to the anode or collector circuit of the transmitter stage supplying radio frequency energy to the antenna?

1. 1000
2. 750
3. *250*
4. 100

Finish question section on page 226

UNMODULATED CARRIERS & RETRANSMISSIONS

INTRODUCTION

An amateur station which automatically retransmits the signals of other stations is a repeater station.

Radiotelephone signals cannot be automatically retransmitted below 29.50 MHz unless the received signals are from stations operated by persons qualified to transmit on frequencies below 29.50 MHz.

Transmitting a signal without information (unmodulated carrier) is permitted for brief tests below 30 MHz.

SUPPLEMENT

Repeater stations are usually located on the highest locations, in order to obtain a large coverage area for the transmitter. Weak or low level signals are received and retransmitted at a higher power level making wide area communications between handheld, mobiles and base stations possible. Repeater stations are sometimes linked to increase coverage areas even further. Repeater frequencies are coordinated with repeater councils operating in the area of operation. This is necessary to avoid overlapping areas of coverage.

Some FM repeaters can be found at the upper end of the 10 meter band. When the 10 meter band is open to many areas of the world, operating through these repeaters can create interesting situations. For instance, a signal can be repeated by more than one repeater at the same time.

The two meter band is occupied by many Canadian repeater stations.

QUESTIONS

B-001-18-1.... What kind of amateur station automatically retransmits the signals of other stations?

1. *repeater station*
2. space station control and telemetry link
3 .remote-control station
4. beacon station

B-001-18-2.... An unmodulated carrier may be transmitted only:

1. if the output to the final RF amplifier is kept under 5 W
2. *for brief tests on frequencies below 30 MHz*
3. when transmitting SSB
4. in frequency bands below 30 MHz

B-001-18-3.... Radiotelephone signals in a frequency band below _____ MHz cannot be automatically retransmitted, unless these signals are received from a station operated by a person qualified to transmit on frequencies below the above frequency.

1. 29.7 MHz
2. 50 MHz
3. 144 MHz
4. *29.5 MHz*

B-001-18-4.... Which of the following statements is NOT correct? Radiotelephone signals may be retransmitted:

1. in the 29.5 - 29.7 MHz band, when received in a VHF band, from a station operated by a person with only Basic qualification
2. in the 50 - 54 MHz frequency band, when received from a station operated by a person with only Basic qualification
3. in the 144 - 148 MHz frequency band, when received from a station operated by a person with only Basic qualification
4. *in the 21 MHz band, when received in a VHF band, from a station operated by a person with only Basic qualification*

STABILITY, ACCURACY & OVERMODULATION

INTRODUCTION

Amateur stations must be equipped with a means of determining the transmit frequency to the same degree of accuracy as would a crystal calibrator.

If radiotelephone is used, a means of indicating or preventing overmodulation of the transmitter is required.

The stability of amateur transmitters below 148 MHz is required to be equal or better than the stability obtainable using crystal control.

Transmitters using amplitude modulation are limited to 100 percent modulation.

SUPPLEMENT

Today's generation of commercially built radio equipment is very stable with accurate frequency displays.

The crystal calibrator is still standard in most HF equipment. If the calibrator circuitry uses a 100 kHz crystal, harmonics at multiples of the crystal frequency will be present in the receiver when the calibrator is turned on. The operator tunes for a zero beat on these signals and checks that the receiver frequency readout displays a frequency that is a multiple of 100 kHz. If not, receiver adjustments are made.

When an amplitude modulated transmitter is overmodulated (more than 100%), the RF modulated envelope is distorted and the modulation that is transmitted is no longer an exact replica of the original modulating signal. This difference is expressed as distortion and creates undesirable harmonics and splatter.

An oscilloscope is the best test instrument for measuring overmodulation.

QUESTIONS

B-001-19-1.... When operating on frequencies below 148 MHz:

1. the bandwidth for any emission must not exceed 3 kHz
2. the frequency stability of the transmitter must be at least two parts per million over a period of one hour
3. *the frequency stability must be comparable to crystal control*
4. an overmodulation indicator must be used

B-001-19-2.... A reliable means to prevent or indicate overmodulation must be employed at an amateur station if:

1. *radiotelephony is used*
2. DC input power to the anode or collector circuit of the final RF stage is in excess of 250 watts
3. radiotelegraphy is used
4. persons other than the holder of the authorization use the station

B-001-19-3.... An amateur station using radiotelephony must install a device for indicating or preventing:

1. resonance
2. antenna power
3. plate voltage
4. *overmodulation*

B-001-19-4.... The maximum percentage of modulation permitted in the use of radiotelephony by an amateur station is:

1. 75 percent
2. *100 percent*
3. 50 percent
4. 90 percent

B-001-19-5.... All amateur stations, regardless of the mode of transmission used, must be equipped with:

1. a DC power meter
2. an overmodulation indicating device
3. *a reliable means of determining the operating radio frequency*
4. a dummy antenna

INTERNATIONAL TELECOMMUNICATIONS UNION

INTRODUCTION

Canada is a member of the International Telecommunications Union (ITU) and adheres to ITU Radio Regulations.

ITU regulations state that:

- radiocommunications between amateur stations of different countries shall be permitted unless the administration of one of the countries concerned, has notified that it objects to such radiocommunications.

- administrations shall verify the operational and technical qualifications of any person wishing to operate an amateur station. Morse code is no longer a mandatory requirement to gain access to HF bands.

- transmissions between amateur stations of different countries shall be limited to messages of a technical nature or personal remarks of relative unimportance

Curious?

SUPPLEMENT

The amateur service is recognized in the International Telecommunications Union (ITU) "Radio Regulations.

Article 1 of the Radio Regulations defines various radio services. Section 1.56 and 1.57 state:

"amateur service: A radiocommunication service for the purpose of self-training, intercommunication and technical investigations carried out by amateurs, that is, by duly authorized persons interested in radio technique solely with a personal aim and without pecuniary interest."

"amateur-satellite service: A radiocommunication service using space stations on earth satellites for the same purposes as those of the amateur service."

There are three ITU regions. Region 1 is mainly Europe, South AFrica and Northern Asia. Region 2 covers North and South America. Region 3 includes Southeast Asia and Australia.

B-001-20-1.... What type of messages may be transmitted to an amateur station in a foreign country?

1. messages of any type, if the foreign country allows third-party communications with Canada
2. messages that are not religious, political, or patriotic in nature
3. *messages of a technical nature or personal remarks of relative unimportance*
4. messages of any type

B-001-20-2.... The operator of an amateur station shall ensure that:

1. communications are exchanged only with commercial stations
2. all communications are conducted in secret code
3. charges are properly applied to all third party communications
4. *communications are limited to messages of a technical or personal nature*

B-001-20-3.... Which of the following is NOT a provision of the ITU Radio Regulations which apply to Canadian radio amateurs?

1. it is forbidden to transmit international messages on behalf of third parties, unless those countries make special arrangements
2. radiocommunications between countries shall be forbidden, if the administration of one of the countries objects
3. *transmissions between countries shall not include any messages of a technical nature, or remarks of a personal character*
4. administrations shall take such measures as they judge necessary to verify the operational and technical qualifications of amateurs

B-001-20-4.... The ITU Radio Regulations limit those radio amateurs, who have not demonstrated proficiency in Morse code, to frequencies above:

1. 1.8 MHz
2. 3.5 MHz
3. 28 MHz
4. *none of the other answers*

B-001-20-5.... In addition to complying with the Radiocommunication Act and Regulations, Canadian radio amateurs must also comply with the regulations of the:

1. American Radio Relay League
2. *International Telecommunications Union*
3. Radio Amateurs of Canada Inc.
4. International Amateur Radio Union

ITU REGIONS & CEPT

INTRODUCTION

The International Telecommunications Union (ITU) has three regions. These roughly cover:

- Region 1 - Europe and Africa
- Region 2 - North & South America
- Region 3 - Southeast Asia & Australia

Canadian amateurs operating their amateur radio station in other countries must comply with the rules and regulations applicable to amateur radio operators of the visited country. This includes frequency limitations.

When operating your amateur radio station from a marine vessel while in international waters, the frequency band limitations differ by Regions. Refer to RBR-4

SUPPLEMENT

Canada has negotiated reciprocal operating agreements which allow Canadians to operate their amateur radio stations while temporarily visiting certain countries when in possession of a CEPT permit. A translation of CEPT means European Conference of Postal and Telecommunications Administrations.

Class 1 CEPT permits are issued to amateurs with Basic and Morse Code qualifications. This allows use of all amateur frequency bands authorized in the visited country.

Class 2 CEPT permits are issued to amateurs with Basic qualifications . This allows use of all amateur frequency bands above 30 MHz. authorized in the visited country.

Canada is also a signatory to the "Inter-American Convention on an International Amateur Radio Permit" (IARP). The USA and most South American countries participate in this convention.

Canadian-issued CEPT & IARP permits have no legal status in Canada. Applications are processed by Radio Amateurs of Canada (RAC).

QUESTIONS

B-001-21-1.... In which International Telecommunication Union Region is Canada?

1. region 4
2. region 3
3. region 2
4. region 1

B-001-21-2.... A Canadian radio amateur, operating his station in the state of Florida, is subject to which frequency band limits?

1. those applicable to US radio amateurs
2. ITU region 2
3. ITU region 3
4. ITU region 1

B-001-21-3.... A Canadian radio amateur, operating his station 7 kilometres (4 miles) offshore from the coast of Florida, is subject to which frequency band limits?

1. those applicable to Canadian radio amateurs
2. ITU region 1
3. those applicable to US radio amateurs
4. ITU region 2

B-001-21-4.... Australia, Japan and Southeast Asia are in which ITU region?

1. Region 4
2. Region 2
3. Region 3
4. Region 1

B-001-21-5.... Canada is located in ITU region?

1. region 1
2. region 2
3. region 3
4. region 4

EXAMINATIONS

INTRODUCTION

Examinations are normally conducted by accredited examiners. Fees, if required, are negotiated between the examiner and the candidate.

In some rare situations, Spectrum Management and Telecommunications district offices may administer an examination. The fee charged for taking an examination is currently $20 per qualification.

Persons with disabilities may be given examinations orally or given examinations that are tailored for specific situations. Interpreters may not accompany candidates during examinations.

An examiner may request medical evidence from a practicing medical physician before accommodating an oral or tailored examination.

SUPPLEMENT

There are no age or citizenship restrictions for writing Amateur Radio Operator Certificate examinations in Canada.

A list of accredited examiners can be found at the Radio Amateurs of Canada web site. Contact an examiner from this list to schedule an examination. Accredited examiners are free to negotiate the payment of a fee with candidates in order to recover the cost of administering an examination.

There is no remittance to the Amateur Radio Service Center required. Disputes between candidates and examiners will not be arbitrated.

Examinations are based on the current version of RIC-7 & RIC-8 question banks. The Basic qualification examination comprises of one question drawn from each of the one hundred topics.

RIC-1 "Guide for Examiners Accredited to Conduct Examinations for Amateur Radio Operator Certificates" outlines the policies and procedures for examiners.

QUESTIONS

B-001-22-1.... Which of these statements is NOT correct?

1. An accredited examiner may recover the cost of administering an examination
2. *the fee for taking an examination for an Amateur Radio Operator Certificate at an Industry Canada office is $5 per qualification*
3. an accredited volunteer examiner must hold an Amateur Radio Operator Certificate with Basic, Advanced, and Morse Code qualifications
4. the fee for taking an examination for an Amateur Radio Operator Certificate at an Industry Canada office is $20 per qualification

B-001-22-2.... Which of the following statements is NOT correct?

1. a disabled candidate, taking a Morse code sending test, may be allowed to recite the examination text in Morse code sounds
2. examinations for disabled candidates may be given orally, or tailored to the candidate's ability to complete the examination
3. *a disabled candidate must pass a normal amateur radio certificate examination before being granted any qualification*
4. an accredited examiner may recover the cost of administering an examination

B-001-22-3.... The fee for taking examinations for amateur radio operator certificates by an accredited volunteer examiner is:

1. *to be negotiated between examiner and candidate*
2. always $20 per qualification
3. always free of charge
4. always $20 per visit regardless of the number of examinations

B-001-22-4.... The fee for taking amateur radio certificate examinations at an Industry Canada office is:

1. $20 per visit, regardless of the number of qualification examinations
2. no charge for qualification examinations
3. $5 per qualification examination
4. *$20 per qualification*

B-001-22-5.... Which of the following statements is false?

1. a candidate who fails a written examination for lack of reading skills may be given an oral examination
2. a candidate who fails a written examination due to not usually speaking English or French may be given an oral examination
3. an examiner may request medical evidence from a practicing medical physician before accommodating testing
4. *a candidate with insufficient knowledge of English or French may be accompanied by an interpreter*

COURTEOUS OPERATING

INTRODUCTION

Courteous operating procedures include:

- listening before transmitting so as not to interrupt communications already in progress

- reducing power output to the minimum necessary

- tuning transmitters with a dummy load

- if a regular net frequency is already in use, the net control stations can call and ask the occupants to relinquish the frequency for the scheduled net. If the occupants are not agreeable, the net could be conducted on a frequency 3 or 5 kHz away from the regular frequency. The other option is for the existing frequency users to move to a different frequency as a courtesy to the net.

A dummy load is a device that is capable of dissipating your transmitter's radio frequency output power for a short period of time to allow the operator to make equipment adjustments without causing interference to other amateur stations.

SUPPLEMENT

Learn good radio operating procedures. Very few people like to listen to, or communicate with, amateurs using poor operating procedures.

Remember, conversations on the ham bands are not private. It is likely that there will be a listening audience.

Avoid the subjects of politics, race, religion, sex or any topic which may be offensive to the person you are in communications with or to anyone listening.

Don't butt into the conversations of others.

Single-sideband operators should allow for 3 kHz frequency separation to minimize interference.

Most dummy loads are built with in impedance of 50 ohms, the impedance of most modern transmitters. These devices have been designed for a particular power and time limits.

QUESTIONS

B-002-4-1.... What should you do before you transmit on any frequency?

1. check your antenna for resonance at the selected frequency
2. *listen to make sure others are not using the frequency*
3. make sure the SWR on your antenna transmission line is high enough
4. listen to make sure that someone will be able to hear you

B-002-4-2.... If you contact another station and your signal is extremely strong and perfectly readable, what adjustment should you make to your transmitter?

1. turn on your speech processor
2. reduce your SWR
3. continue with your contact, making no changes
4. *turn down your power output to the minimum necessary*

B-002-4-3.... What is one way to shorten transmitter tune-up time on the air to cut down on interference?

1. use a long wire antenna
2. tune up on 40 metres first, then switch to the desired band
3. use twin lead instead of coaxial cable transmission lines
4. *tune the transmitter into a dummy load*

B-002-4-4.... How can on the air interference be minimized during a lengthy transmitter testing or tuning procedure?

1. choose an unoccupied frequency
2. use a non-resonant antenna
3. use a resonant antenna that requires no loading-up procedure
4. *use a dummy load*

B-002-4-5.... Why would you use a dummy load?

1. to give comparative signal reports
2. *to test or adjust your transceiver without causing interference*
3. it is faster to tune
4. to reduce output power

B-002-4-6.... If you are the net control station of a daily HF net, what should you do if the frequency on which you normally meet is in use just before the net begins?

1. *call and ask occupants to relinquish the frequency for the scheduled net operations, but if they are not agreeable, conduct the net on a frequency 3 to 5 kHz away from the regular net frequency*
2. reduce your output power and start the net as usual
3. increase your power output so that net participants will be able to hear you over the existing activity
4. cancel the net for that day

B-002-4-7.... If a net is about to begin on a frequency which you and another station are using, what should you do?

1. *as a courtesy to the net, move to a different frequency*
2. increase your power output to ensure that all net participants can hear you
3. transmit as long as possible on the frequency so that no other stations may use it
4. turn off your radio

B-002-4-8.... If propagation changes during your contact and you notice increasing interference from other activity on the same frequency, what should you do?

1. tell the interfering stations to change frequency, since you were there first
2. report the interference to your local Amateur Auxiliary Coordinator
3. increase the output power of your transmitter to overcome the interference
4. *move your contact to another frequency*

Finish question section on page 227

PHONETIC ALPHABET

INTRODUCTION

Standard International Phonetic Alphabet

A - Alpha	J - Juliet	S - Sierra
B - Bravo	K - Kilo	T - Tango
C - Charlie	L - Lima	U - Uniform
D - Delta	M - Mike	V - Victor
E - Echo	N - November	W - Whiskey
F - Foxtrot	O - Oscar	X - X-ray
G - Golf	P - Papa	Y - Yankee
H - Hotel	Q - Quebec	Z - Zulu
I - India	R - Romeo	

SUPPLEMENT

Use these internationally recognized phonetics if your callsign is hard to understand or if radiocommunication conditions are difficult.

For example, the callsign VE7AV would be spoken as "Victor Echo Seven Alpha Victor".

During local communications, amateurs commonly use phonetics only for the callsign suffix. For example, VE7XYL would say " V E 7 X-ray Yankee Lima".

QUESTIONS

B-002-2-1.... To make your call sign better understood when using voice transmissions, what should you do?

1. use any words which start with the same letters as your call sign for each letter of your call
2. talk louder
3. turn up your microphone gain
4. use Standard International Phonetics for each letter of your call sign

B-002-2-2.... What can you use as an aid for correct station identification when using phone?

1. Q signals
2. the Standard International Phonetic alphabet
3. unique words of your choice
4. a speech compressor

B-002-2-3.... What is the Standard International Phonetic for the letter A?

1. Alpha
2. Able
3. Adam
4. America

B-002-2-4.... What is the Standard International Phonetic for the letter B?

1. Brazil
2. Bravo
3. Borneo
4. Baker

B-002-2-5.... What is the Standard International Phonetic for the letter D?

1. Dog
2. Denmark
3. David
4. Delta

B-002-2-6.... What is the Standard International Phonetic for the letter E?

1. Easy
2. Edward
3. England
4. Echo

B-002-2-7.... What is the Standard International Phonetic for the letter G?

1. Golf
2. George
3. Germany
4. Gibraltar

B-002-2-8.... What is the Standard International Phonetic for the letter I?

1. Iran
2. Italy
3. India
4. Item

B-002-2-9.... What is the Standard International Phonetic for the letter L?

1. Love
2. London
3. Luxembourg
4. Lima

B-002-2-10.... What is the Standard International Phonetic for the letter P?

1. Portugal
2. Papa
3. Paris
4. Peter

B-002-2-11.... What is the Standard International Phonetic for the letter R?

1. Romeo
2. Roger
3. Radio
4. Romania

SIMPLEX & HF OPERATING PROCEDURES

INTRODUCTION

Simplex means transmitting and receiving on the same frequency.

Simplex operation is used where it is possible to make contact without using a repeater station. This prevents repeater stations from being tied up unnecessarily.

When talking to a station on a repeater, a quick listen for the other station on the repeater input frequency will let one know if it is possible to communicate on a simplex channel. Simplex operation using repeater frequencies should be avoided since changing repeater frequencies is not practical.

It is desirable that VHF/UHF bands be used for local communications. This helps minimize interference on HF bands which are capable of supporting long distance communications.

SUPPLEMENT

Download the appropriate recommended band plans from the RAC web site. These incorporate the recommendations from IARU (International Amateur Radio Union) Region 2. Operating your Amateur station in accordance with these band plans will minimize conflicts between users.

Some common designations of radio spectrum frequencies follow. Most amateur operations occur in the MF and higher frequency ranges. Note that the bandwidth of these frequency ranges differs by a factor of 10.

VLF	Very Low Frequency	3 kHz to 30 kHz
LF	Low Frequency	30 kHz to 300 kHz
MF	Medium Frequency	300 kHz to 3 MHz
HF	High Frequency	3 MHz to 30 MHz
VHF	Very High Frequency	30 MHz to 300 MHz
UHF	Ultra High Frequency	300 MHz to 3 GHz

QUESTIONS

B-002-3-3.... What is simplex operation?

1. transmitting and receiving over a wide area
2. transmitting on one frequency and receiving on another
3. transmitting one-way communications
4. *transmitting and receiving on the same frequency*

B-002-3-4.... When should you consider using simplex operation instead of a repeater?

1. *when signals are reliable between communicating parties without using a repeater*
2. when the most reliable communications are needed
3. when an emergency telephone call is needed
4. when you are travelling and need some local information

B-002-3-5.... Why should local amateur communications use VHF and UHF frequencies instead of HF frequencies?

1. *to minimize interference on HF bands capable of long distance communications*
2. because greater output power is permitted on VHF and UHF
3. because HF transmissions are not propagated locally
4. because signals are stronger on VHF and UHF frequencies

B-002-3-6.... Why should we be careful in choosing a simplex frequency when operating VHF or UHF-FM?

1. some frequencies are designated for narrow band FM and others for wideband FM
2. interference may be caused to unlicensed devices operating in the same band
3. *you may inadvertently choose a channel that is the input to a local repeater*
4. implanted medical devices share the same spectrum

B-002-3-7.... If you are talking to a station using a repeater, how would you find out if you could communicate using simplex instead?

1. see if a third station can clearly receive both of you
2. see if you can clearly receive a more distant repeater
3. *see if you can clearly receive the station on the repeater's input frequency*
4. see if you can clearly receive the station on a lower frequency band

B-002-3-8.... If you are operating simplex on a repeater frequency, why would it be good amateur practice to change to another frequency?

1. *changing the repeater's frequency is not practical*
2. the repeater's output power may ruin your station's receiver
3. there are more repeater operators than simplex operators
4. changing the repeater's frequency requires the authorization of Industry Canada

SIMPLEX & HF OPERATING PROCEDURES continued

INTRODUCTION

Single sideband transmissions above the 40 meter band (7 MHz) are normally upper side band (USB). Transmissions in the 40 meter and lower bands generally utilize lower sideband (LSB).

CQ is the signal used to indicate a general call and a reply by any station is requested. An example of such a general call is:

      CQ CQ CQ this is VE7AV VE7AV VE7AV

A reply could be:

      VE7AV this is VE7XYL

The phonetic alphabet could be used for expressing the call signs, especially if communications are difficult.

When contact is made, amateurs usually exchange signal reports, names and locations. After that, the conversation may turn to description of equipment, weather and other topics of interest.

INTRODUCTION continued

There are three main ways of making contacts on HF.

- responding to a CQ - While tuning across ham bands you may hear one or more stations calling CQ. This is an invitation for any other amateur to respond. If you hear for example "CQ Vancouver", this indicates the transmitting station is asking for a response from any station in Vancouver.

- calling CQ - An example of a general call using single sideband would be " CQ CQ CQ this is Victor Echo Seven Alpha Victor VE7AV". Any amateur may respond.

- tail-ending - Listen to someone else's contact. When that contact ends, immediately call the station you want to contact. Timing is important. Keep it short. Example: "VE7XYL this is Victor Echo Seven Alpha Victor".

QUESTIONS

B-002-3-1.... What is the correct way to call CQ when using voice?

1. *say "CQ" three times, followed by "this is," followed by your call sign spoken three times*
2. say "CQ" once, followed by "this is," followed by your call sign spoken three times
3. say "CQ" at least five times, followed by "this is," followed by your call sign spoken once
4. say "CQ" at least ten times, followed by "this is," followed by your call sign spoken once

B-002-3-2.... How should you answer a voice CQ call?

1. say the other station's call sign at least five times phonetically, followed by "this is", then your call sign twice
2. *say the other station's call sign once, followed by "this is", then your call sign given phonetically*
3. say the other station's call sign at least three times, followed by "this is", and your call sign at least five times phonetically
4. say the other station's call sign at least ten times, followed by "this is", then your call sign at least twice

B-002-3-9.... Which sideband is commonly used for 20 metre phone operation?

1. *upper*
2. lower
3. FM
4. double

B-002-3-10.... Which sideband is commonly used on 3755 kHz for phone operation?

1. FM
2. *lower*
3. double
4. upper

B-002-3-11.... What is the best method to tell if a band is "open" for communication with a particular distant location?

1. ask others on your local 2 metre FM repeater
2. telephone an experienced local amateur
3. look at the propagation forecasts in an amateur radio magazine
4. *listen for signals from that area from an amateur beacon station or a foreign broadcast or television station on a nearby frequency*

REPEATER OPERATING PROCEDURES

INTRODUCTION

The primary purpose of a repeater is to increase the distance range for operating portable and mobile stations. Some repeaters also have an autopatch which is a device that allows repeater users to make telephone calls from their stations.

Amateur repeater stations have time-out-timers. The purpose of these is to interrupt lengthy transmissions without pauses.

Some repeaters also use CTCSS (continuous tone controlled squelch system) or PL (private line) tones. These sub-audible tones activates a receiver audio output when a specific predetermined code is present.

To call another amateur station on a repeater, say the call sign of the station you want to contact, then your call sign. It is preferable to use the standard international phonetic alphabet.

Pause briefly between transmissions when using a repeater. This allows others to join in or to become aware of possible emergency situations requiring repeater access. To join in a conversation, it is best to just say your call sign once during a break between transmissions.

SUPPLEMENT

Additional recommendations:

- Move from repeater channels to simplex channels (same transmit/receive) where possible.
- Watch your manners and do not use profane language.
- Keep transmissions short.
- Support the clubs and organizations that operate repeaters. They make considerable financial investments to make repeater systems happen.

In North America, many repeaters operate in the 2 metre band and use transmit and receive frequencies which are separated by 600 kHz.

Radio Amateurs of Canada and the American Radio Relay League publish information on the topic of repeater operating procedures.

QUESTIONS

B-002-1-1.... What is a good way to make contact on a repeater?

1. say the other operator's name, then your call sign three times
2. *say the call sign of the station you want to contact, then your call sign*
3. say, "Breaker, breaker", then your call sign
4. say the call sign of the station you want to contact three times

B-002-1-2.... What is the main purpose of a repeater?

1. to link amateur stations with the telephone system
2. *to increase the range of portable and mobile stations*
3. to retransmit weather information during severe storm warnings
4. to make local information available 24 hours a day

B-002-1-3.... What is frequency coordination on VHF and UHF bands

1. the selection of simplex frequencies by individual operators
2. *a process which seeks to carefully assign frequencies so as to minimize interference with neighbouring repeaters*
3. a part of the planning prior to a contest
4. a band plan detailing modes and frequency segments within a band

B-002-1-4.... What is the purpose of a repeater time-out timer?

1. it lets a repeater have a rest period after heavy use
2. it logs repeater transmit time to predict when a repeater will fail
3. it tells how long someone has been using a repeater
4. *it interrupts lengthy transmissions without pauses*

B-002-1-6.... How do you call another station on a repeater if you know the station's call sign?

1. *say the station's call sign, then identify your own station*
2. say "break break 79", then say the station's call sign
3. say "CQ" three times, then say the station's call sign
4. wait for the station to call "CQ", then answer it

B-002-1-5.... What is a CTCSS tone? ?? Do what?

1. a tone used by repeaters to mark the end of a transmission
2. *a sub-audible tone that activates a receiver audio output when present*
3. a special signal used for telemetry between amateur space stations and earth stations
4. a special signal used for radio control of model craft

B-002-1-7.... Why should you pause briefly between transmissions when using a repeater?

1. to check the SWR of the repeater
2. to reach for pencil and paper for third-party communications
3. to dial up the repeater's autopatch
4. *to listen for anyone else wanting to use the repeater*

B-002-1-8.... Why should you keep transmissions short when using a repeater?

1. to keep long-distance charges down
2. to give any listening non-hams a chance to respond
3. *a long transmission may prevent someone with an emergency from using the repeater*
4. to see if the receiving station operator is still awake

B-002-1-9.... What is the proper way to join into a conversation on a repeater?

1. wait for the end of a transmission and start calling the desired party
2. shout "break, break!" to show that you're eager to join the conversation
3. turn on an amplifier and override whoever is talking
4. *say your call sign during a break between transmissions*

B-002-1-10.... What is the accepted way to ask someone their location when using a repeater?

1. what is your 20?
2. *where are you ?*
3. locations are not normally told by radio
4. what is your 12?

Finish question section on page 227

56

EMERGENCY PROCEDURES

INTRODUCTION

The internationally recognized priority for emergency communications is:

(1) distress (2) urgency (3) safety.

Distress communications involves the immediate safety of life of individuals or the immediate protection of property. The distress signal in radiotelephony is MAYDAY and in Morse code the distress signal is SOS. Distress signals are used if it is necessary to attract attention.

The best way to interrupt a repeater conversation to signal a distress call is to break-in immediately following the transmission of the active party and state your situation and call sign.

Should stations communicating with each other hear an emergency call for help on the frequency they are using, they must acknowledge the emergency call and act accordingly.

If distress traffic is heard but the receiving operator is not in a position to render assistance, contact authorities and then maintain a listening watch until it is certain that assistance is forthcoming.

SUPPLEMENT

Amateur operators are known for their interest and participation in disasters and emergencies. Some important considerations for amateurs:

- have equipment that is capable of being operated without requiring the use of AC power
- keep several sets of charged batteries on hand for hand-held transceivers
- have dipole antennas prepared for portable HF operation

The urgency signal is used when the distress signal is not fully justified. In radiotelephony, the urgency signal is the group of words PAN PAN repeated three times. In radiotelegraphy it is three repetitions of the group XXX.

The safety signal is used for messages concerned with the safety of ships (e.g. meteorological & navigation warnings). In radiotelephony, the safety signal consists of the word SECURITY and in radiotelegraphy it consists of three repetitions of the group TTT.

QUESTIONS

B-002-8-1.... When may you use your amateur station to transmit an "SOS" or "MAYDAY"?

1. never
2. only at specific times (at 15 and 30 minutes after the hour)
3. only in case of a severe weather watch
4. in a life-threatening distress situation

B-002-8-2.... If you are in contact with another station and you hear an emergency call for help on your frequency, what should you do?

1. immediately stop your contact and acknowledge the emergency call
2. tell the calling station that the frequency is in use
3. direct the calling station to the nearest emergency net frequency
4. call your local police station and inform them of the emergency call

B-002-8-3.... What is the proper distress call to use when operating phone?

1. say "SOS" several times
2. say "EMERGENCY" several times
3. say "MAYDAY" several times
4. say "HELP" several times

B-002-8-4.... What is the proper distress call to use when operating CW?

1. CQD
2. QRRR
3. SOS *Morriscode*
4. MAYDAY

B-002-8-5.... What is the proper way to interrupt a repeater conversation to signal a distress call?

1. say "EMERGENCY" three times
2. say "SOS," then your call sign
3. break-in immediately following the transmission of the active party and state your situation and call sign
4. say "HELP" as many times as it takes to get someone to answer

B-002-8-6.... Why is it a good idea to have a way to operate your amateur station without using commercial AC power lines?

1. so you will comply with rules
2. so you may operate in contests where AC power is not allowed
3. so you may provide communications in an emergency
4. so you may use your station while mobile

B-002-8-7.... What is the most important accessory to have for a hand-held radio in an emergency?

1. several sets of charged batteries
2. an extra antenna
3. a portable amplifier
4. a microphone headset for hands-free operation

B-002-8-8.... Which type of antenna would be a good choice as part of a portable HF amateur station that could be set up in case of an emergency?

1. a parabolic dish
2. a three-element Yagi
3. a dipole ———— *Look up*
4. a three-element quad

B-002-8-9.... If you are communicating with another amateur station and hear a station in distress break in, what should you do?

1. continue your communication because you were on frequency first
2. change to a different frequency so that the station in distress may have a clear channel to call for assistance
3. immediately cease all transmissions because stations in distress have emergency rights to the frequency
4. acknowledge the station in distress and determine its location and what assistance may be needed

Finish question section on page 228.

OPERATING CW

INTRODUCTION

Examples of transmissions in Morse code are:

- CQ CQ CQ DE VE7AV VE7AV VE7AV K (a call to any station)
- VE7AV VE7AV DE VE7XYL VE7XYL K (a response to a call to any station)
- CQ DX CQ DX CQ DX DE VE7AV VE7AV VE7AV K (a call to any distant station)
- 73 DE VE7AV SK (best regards - end of contact)

The meaning of common procedural signals included in the above examples are:

CQ means "calling any station"   DX means "distant station"
DE means "from"   K means "any station please reply"
73 means "best regards"   SK means "end of contact"

CQ transmissions are transmitted at any Morse code speed which the operator can reliably receive. Equipment capable of full break-in telegraphy, permits the operator to receive incoming signals in between transmitted Morse dots and dashes. For CW operation , a separation of 150 to 500 Hz is the frequency separation range required to avoid interfering with a Morse code contact in progress.

SUPPLEMENT

Morse code was used in the first radio communications and still survives as a mode of operation in common use by amateur radio operators.

Although there is a current world wide trend to eliminate Morse code requirements for licensing or certification processes, it is expected that Morse code will continue to be used by amateur radio operators for decades to come.

New amateur radio operators should consider learning Morse code. It is a fun mode of operation. It takes some effort to learn, but the rewards are worth it.

QUESTIONS

B-002-5-1.... What is the correct way to call CQ when using Morse code?

1. send the letters "CQ" three times, followed by "DE", followed by your call sign sent once
2. send the letters "CQ" ten times, followed by "DE", followed by your call sign sent once
3. send the letters "CQ" over and over
4. *send the letters "CQ" three times, followed by "DE", followed by your call sign sent three times*

B-002-5-2.... How should you answer a routine Morse code CQ call?

1. send your call sign four times
2. send the other station's call sign once, followed by "DE", followed by your call sign four times
3. send your call sign followed by your name, station location and a signal report
4. *send the other station's call sign twice, followed by "DE", followed by your call sign twice*

B-002-5-3.... At what speed should a Morse code CQ call be transmitted?

1. *at any speed which you can reliably receive*
2. at any speed below 5 WPM
3. at the highest speed your keyer will operate
4. at the highest speed at which you can control the keyer

B-002-5-4.... What is the meaning of the procedural signal "CQ"?

1. *calling any station*
2. call on the quarter hour
3. an antenna is being tested
4. only the station CQ should answer

B-002-5-5.... What is the meaning of the procedural signal "DE"?

1. received all correctly
2. *from*
3. calling any station
4. directional emissions

B-002-5-6.... What is the meaning of the procedural signal "K"?

1. end of message
2. *any station please reply*
3. called station only transmit
4. all received correctly

B-002-5-7.... What is meant by the term "DX"?

1. calling any station
2. *distant station*
3. go ahead
4. best regards

B-002-5-8.... What is the meaning of the term "73"?

1. long distance
2. love and kisses
3. go ahead
4. *best regards*

B-002-5-9.... Which of the following describes full break-in telegraphy (QSK)?

1. automatic keyers are used to send Morse code instead of hand keys
2. *incoming signals are received between transmitted Morse code dots and dashes*
3. an operator must activate a manual send/receive switch before and after every transmission
4. breaking stations send the Morse code prosign "BK"

B-002-5-10.... When selecting a CW transmitting frequency, what minimum frequency separation from a contact in progress should you allow to minimize interference?

1. *150 to 500 Hz*
2. 5 to 50 Hz
3. 1 to 3 kHz
4. 3 to 6 kHz

Finish question section on page 227.

RST SYSTEM

INTRODUCTION

The RST system is a method of describing signal reception. R is for readability, S is for signal strength and T is for tone. Readability is rated from 1 (unreadable) to 5 (perfectly readable). Signal Strength is rated from 1 (barely perceptible) to 9 (extremely strong). Tone is rated from 1 (very rough) to 9 (perfect).

The S meter is built into receivers to give an indication of relative signal strength. Generally, the first half of the meter scale is marked between 1 to 9 and the second half of the meter is marked in DB's, frequently up to 40 or 60. S meters do not give precise readings. However, most are designed so when a transmitter increases the output power by 4 times, the receiver's S meter reading will increase one S unit higher (e.g. S8 to S9). Some RST examples are:

1-1 indicates the received signal is unreadable and barely perceptible
3-3 indicates the received signal is readable with considerable difficulty and weak in strength
5-7 indicates the received signal is perfectly readable and moderately strong
5-9 plus 20 dB   indicates the received signal is perfectly readable and the relative signal strength
        meter reading is 20 decibels greater than strength 9
4-5-9 indicates the Morse code signal is perfectly readable, fair strength with a perfect tone
5-7-9 indicates the Morse code signal is perfectly readable, moderately strong with a perfect tone

INTRODUCTION continued

A sample Morse code transmission:

VE7XYL DE VE7AV TNX QSO UR 579 QTH PRINCE GEORGE HW COPY? BK

This means: VE7XYL from VE7AV. Thanks for the contact. Your signal is RST 579 (perfectly readable, signal strength 7 with perfect tone). My location is Prince George. How do you receive me? Break.

A sample Radiotelephone transmission:

VE7XYL from VE7AV. Thanks for the contact. Your signal is very strong, 20 dB over S9. I am located in Prince George B.C. How do you copy me. OVER.

QUESTIONS

B-002-6-1.... What are "RST" signal reports?

1. a short way to describe transmitter power
2. a short way to describe signal reception
3. a short way to describe sunspot activity
4. a short way to describe ionospheric conditions

B-002-6-2.... What does "RST" mean in a signal report?

1. recovery, signal strength, tempo
2. recovery, signal speed, tone
3. readability, signal speed, tempo
4. readability, signal strength, tone

B-002-6-5.... What is meaning of: "You are 5 9 plus 20 dB"?

1. the bandwidth of your signal is 20 decibels above linearity
2. repeat your transmission on a frequency 20 kHz higher
3. you are perfectly readable with a signal strength 20 decibels greater than S 9
4. your signal strength has increased by a factor of 100

B-002-6-6.... A distant station asks for a signal report on a local repeater you monitor. Which fact affects your assessment?

1. signal reports are only useful on simplex communications
2. the repeater gain affects your S-meter reading
3. the other operator needs to know how well he is received at the repeater, not how well you receive the repeater
4. you need to listen to the repeater input frequency for an accurate signal report

B-002-6-7.... If the power output of a transmitter is increased by four times, how might a nearby receiver's S meter reading change?

1. increase by approximately four S units
2. increase by approximately one S unit
3. decrease by approximately four S units
4. decrease by approximately one S unit

B-002-6-8.... By how many times must the power output of a transmitter be increased to raise the S meter reading on a nearby receiver from S8 to S9?

1. approximately 5 times
2. approximately 3 times
3. approximately 4 times
4. approximately 2 times

RST SYSTEM continued

INTRODUCTION

RST READABILITY

1 - unreadable
2 - barely readable, occasional words distinguishable
3 - readable with considerable difficulty
4 - readable with practically no difficulty
5 - perfectly readable

RST STRENGTH

1 - faint signals barely perceptible
2 - very weak signals
3 - weak signals
4 - fair signals
5 - fairly good signals
6 - good signals
7 - moderately strong signals
8 - strong signals
9 - extremely strong signals

INTRODUCTION continued

RST TONE

1 - sixty cycle ac or less, very rough and broad
2 - very rough ac, very harsh and broad
3 - rough ac tone, rectified but not filtered
4 - rough note, some trace of filtering
5 - filtered rectified ac but strongly ripple modulated
6 - filtered tone, trace of ripple modulation
7 - near pure tone, trace of ripple modulation
8 - near perfect tone, slight trace of modulation
9 - perfect tone, no trace of ripple or modulation of any kind

QUESTIONS

B-002-6-3.... What is the meaning of "Your signal report is 5 7"?

1. your signal is readable with considerable difficulty
2. *your signal is perfectly readable and moderately strong*
3. your signal is perfectly readable with near pure tone
4. you signal is perfectly readable, but weak

B-002-6-4.... What is the meaning of: "Your signal report is 3 3"?

1. your signal is unreadable, very weak in strength
2. the station is located at latitude 33 degrees
3. *your signal is readable with considerable difficulty and weak in strength*
4. the contact is serial number 33

B-002-6-9.... What does "RST 579" mean in a Morse code contact?

1. *your signal is perfectly readable, moderately strong, and with perfect tone*
2. your signal is perfectly readable, weak strength, and with perfect tone
3. your signal is fairly readable, fair strength, and with perfect tone
4. your signal is barely readable, moderately strong, and with faint ripple

B-002-6-10.... What does "RST 459" mean in a Morse code contact?

1. your signal is very readable, very strong, and with perfect tone
2. your signal is barely readable, very weak, and with perfect tone
3. your signal is moderately readable, very weak, and with hum on the tone
4. *your signal is quite readable, fair strength, and with perfect tone*

B-002-6-11.... What is the meaning of: "Your signal report is 1 1"?

1. *your signal is unreadable, and barely perceptible*
2. your signal is 11 dB over S9
3. your signal is first class in readability and first class in strength
4. your signal is very readable and very strong

Q SIGNALS

INTRODUCTION

Some commonly used Q signals for Morse code communications follows. Adding a question mark immediately after the Q signal changes the meaning to a question.

QRL - frequency is in use
QRM - I am being interfered with
QRN - I am troubled by static
QRS - send more slowly
QRX - I will call you again
QRZ - who is calling
QSB - your signal is fading
QSO - contact is in progress
QSY - change frequency
QTH - my location is

SUPPLEMENT

Some other commonly used Q signals to be aware of are listed below.

QRA - name of my station is
QRK - the intelligibility of your signal is (1 through 5) (bad to excellent)
QRO - increase transmitter power
QRP - decrease transmitter power
QRQ - send faster
QRU - no traffic
QRT - stop sending
QSA - signal strength is (1 through 5) (barely perceptible to excellent)
QSK - reception between transmitted signals
QSP - relay to
QSL - confirm receipt
QSV - send a series of the letter "V"

QUESTIONS

B-002-7-1.... What is the meaning of the Q signal "QRS"?

1. interference from static
2. send RST report
3. radio station location is
4. *send more slowly*

B-002-7-2.... What is one meaning of the Q signal "QTH"?

1. stop sending
2. my name is
3. *my location is*
4. time here is

B-002-7-3.... What is the proper Q signal to use to see if a frequency is in use before transmitting on CW?

1. *QRL?*
2. QRV?
3. QRU?
4. QRZ?

B-002-7-4.... What is one meaning of the Q signal "QSY"?

1. use more power
2. send faster
3. *change frequency*
4. send more slowly

B-002-7-5.... What is the meaning of the Q signal "QSB"?

1. I am busy
2. *your signal is fading*
3. I have no message
4. a contact is confirmed

B-002-7-6.... What is the proper Q signal to ask who is calling you on CW?

1. *QRZ?*
2. QSL?
3. QRL?
4. QRT?

B-002-7-7.... The signal "QRM" signifies:

1. I am troubled by static
2. your signals are fading
3. is my transmission being interfered with
4. *I am being interfered with*

B-002-7-8.... The signal "QRN" means:

1. I am busy
2. are you troubled by static
3. I am being interfered with
4. *I am troubled by static*

B-002-7-9.... The "Q signal" indicating that you want the other station to send slower is:

1. QRM
2. *QRS*
3. QRL
4. QRN

B-002-7-10.... "Who is calling me" is denoted by the "Q" signal:

1. QRK?
2. QRP?
3. *QRZ?*
4. QRM?

B-002-7-11.... The "Q signal" which signifies "I will call you again" is:

1. *QRX*
2. QRZ
3. QRS
4. QRT

OPERATOR AIDS

INTRODUCTION

LOG BOOKS are optional in Canada. These are not required by regulation. Log books are desirable for tracking awards, recording fondest memories and may also be useful for handling interference complaints. Computer logging programs are numerous and used by many amateur operators.

AZIMUTHAL MAP centered on the operator's country graphically shows the direction of the shortest path to other locations. Sometimes the best path to communicate is the long path which is 180 degrees from the short path heading.

QSL CARD is a written confirmation of communication between two amateur stations and contains the date, time, frequency, mode of operation and signal report.

UTC (Universal Time Coordinated) is the time system used for log books and for QSL cards. This time was formerly known as GMT (Greenwich Mean Time). This is the time along the prime meridian of the world - 0 degrees longitude. The prime meridian passes through Greenwich, England. CHU, WWV and WWVH are UTC time signal stations that can be readily heard on the short wave bands in North America. CHU is located in Ottawa, WWV in Colorado and WWVH in Hawaii.

SUPPLEMENT

LOG BOOKS and log keeping is still very much a common part of HF operation. The trend is towards using computers for this function. Numerous commercial software logging packages are available.

AZIMUTHAL MAPS are frequently distributed freely by ham equipment manufacturers. Contact a ham radio equipment dealer and you may be able to get a free map. The ARRL, CQ Magazine and Callbook are some of the organizations that also publish this type of map.

QSL CARDS are mainly distributed to confirm long distance (DX) communications. The bulk of these are distributed through QSL Bureaus. In Canada, Radio Amateurs of Canada operates QSL Bureaus throughout the country. It is a great way to distribute large numbers of QSL cards and saves the costs associated with direct mailing. Some SWL's (short wave listeners) also send out QSL cards which report reception of your signals and ask for a confirmation QSL card in return.

TIME SIGNAL FREQUENCIES - CHU - Ottawa 3.33, 7.85, 14.67 Mhz.
WWV - Colorado 2.5, 5, 10, 15, 20 Mhz. - WWVH - Hawaii 2.5, 5, 10, 15 Mhz.

B-002-9-1.... What is a QSL card?

1. a Notice of Violation from Industry Canada
2. *a written proof of communication between two amateurs*
3. a postcard reminding you when your certificate will expire
4. a letter or postcard from an amateur pen pal

B-002-9-2.... What is an azimuthal map?

1. a map projection cantered on the North Pole
2. a map that shows the angle at which an amateur satellite crosses the equator
3. a map that shows the number of degrees longitude that an amateur satellite appears to move westward at the equator
4. *a map projection cantered on a particular location, used to determine the shortest path between points on the earth's surface*

B-002-9-8.... Why would it be useful to have a azimuthal world map centered on the location of your station?

1. *because it shows the compass bearing from your station to any place on earth, for antenna planning and pointing*
2. because it looks impressive
3. because it shows the angle at which an amateur satellite crosses the equator
4. because it shows the number of degrees longitude that an amateur satellite moves west

B-002-9-6.... You hear other local stations talking to radio amateurs in New Zealand but you don't hear those stations with your beam aimed on the normal compass bearing to New Zealand. What should you try?

1. point your antenna toward Newington, Connecticut
2. point your antenna to the north
3. *point your beam 180 degrees away from that bearing and listen for the stations arriving on the "long-path"*
4. point your antenna to the south

B-002-9-3.... What is the most useful type of map to use when orienting a directional HF antenna toward a distant station?

1. Mercator
2. polar projection
3. topographical
4. *azimuthal*

B-002-9-4.... A directional antenna pointed in the long-path direction to another station is generally oriented how many degrees from its short-path heading?

1. 45 degrees
2. 90 degrees
3. 270 degrees
4. *180 degrees*

B-002-9-5.... What method is used by radio amateurs to provide written proof of communication between two amateur stations?

1. *a signed post card listing contact date, time, frequency, mode and power, called a "QSL card"*
2. a two page letter containing a photograph of the operator
3. a radiogram sent over the CW traffic net
4. a packet message

B-002-9-7.... Which statement about recording all contacts and unanswered CQ calls in a station log book or computer log is NOT correct?

1. a log is important for recording contacts for operating awards
2. *a logbook is required by Industry Canada*
3. a well kept log preserves your fondest amateur radio memories for years
4. a log is important for handling neighbour interference complaints

Finish question section on page 228

BATTERIES

INTRODUCTION

Primary batteries or cells cannot be recharged. The flashlight (carbon-zinc) battery is this type. When current is drawn, the chemical process that takes place produces electricity. Eventually this chemical process slows down and stops when this material is depleted. The nominal voltage of new cells is 1.5V.

Secondary batteries or storage cells can be recharged. Lead-acid cells are this type and have a nominal voltage of 2 volts. The chemical reaction in these type of batteries is reversed by passing current through them in the reverse direction. In a car battery, six cells are connected in series to provide 12 volts.

The lithium-ion battery is rapidly becoming the most common small-storage battery and is replacing the nickel-cadmium (NiCd) generation of batteries. The nominal cell voltage of the NiCd is 1.2 volts. For long life and many recharges, the NiCd battery should not be allowed to discharge below 1.0 volts. Never short circuit this type of battery as these have extremely low internal resistance. The high currents that would result from a short circuit may cause severe damage.

Connecting batteries in series increases voltage. Connecting batteries in parallel increases current capacity. Batteries are a source of electromotive force (EMF). The potential difference causes electrons (current) to flow.

SUPPLEMENT

The circuit symbol for the battery is: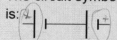

The long bar represents the positive terminal and the short bar the negative terminal. This shows two batteries connected in series.

Rechargeable Nickel Metal Hydride batteries (NiMH) are now used more frequently than Nickel Cadmium (NiCd) types.

The top row shows non-rechargeable batteries. A long life lithium battery is shown bottom left. The other batteries are re-chargeable NiMH types.

QUESTIONS

B-003-16-1.... How much voltage does a standard automobile battery usually supply?

1. about 240 volts
2. about 120 volts
3. *about 12 volts*
4. about 9 volts

B-003-16-2.... Which component has a positive and a negative side?

1. a potentiometer
2. a fuse
3. a resistor
4. *a battery*

B-003-16-3.... A cell, that can be repeatedly recharged by supplying it with electrical energy, is known as a:

1. low leakage cell
2. memory cell
3. *storage cell*
4. primary cell

B-003-16-4.... Which of the following is a source of electromotive force (EMF)?

1. germanium diode
2. *lithium-ion battery*
3. P channel FET
4. carbon resistor

B-003-16-5.... An important difference between a conventional flashlight battery and a lead acid battery is that only the lead acid battery:

1. has two terminals
2. *can be repeatedly recharged*
3. can be completely discharged
4. contains an electrolyte

B-003-16-6.... An alkaline cell has a nominal voltage of 1.5 volts. When supplying a great deal of current, the voltage may drop to 1.2 volts. This is caused by the cell's:

1. electrolyte becoming dry
2. *internal resistance*
3. current capacity
4. voltage capacity

B-003-16-7.... An inexpensive primary cell in use today is the carbon-zinc or flashlight cell. This type of cell can be recharged:

1. *never*
2. twice
3. many times
4. once

B-003-16-8.... Battery capacity is commonly stated as a value of current delivered over a specified period of time. What is the effect of exceeding that specified current?

1. the internal resistance of the cell is short-circuited
2. the battery will accept the subsequent charge in shorter time
3. the voltage delivered will be higher
4. *a battery charge will not last as long*

B-003-16-9.... To increase the current capacity of a cell, several cells should be connected in:

1. *parallel*
2. series
3. parallel resonant
4. series resonant

B-003-16-10.... To increase the voltage output, several cells are connected in:

1. parallel
2. series-parallel
3. resonance
4. *series*

Finish question section on page 229

RESISTANCE & CONDUCTANCE

INTRODUCTION

Conductors are made from materials in which electrons are easily moved. Copper, silver, aluminum and gold make good conductors.

Materials that do not conduct current are called insulators. Glass, porcelain, rubber and some plastics make good insulators.

Resistance is that property of a material which restricts the flow of current. Resistors are manufactured to provide for specific values of resistance. Carbon is the most common material used for making resistors. When resistors restrict the flow of current, heat is generated. Heat can also change values of resistance. The unit of resistance is the ohm.

The reciprocal of resistance is conductance. A circuit with high conductance has low resistance and vice versa.

The voltage drop across a resistance can be measured with a volt meter across the terminals. If the current and resistance is known, voltage drop can be calculated using Ohms law: $E = I\,R$. That is: voltage = amperes x ohms

SUPPLEMENT

In your house, drinking water travels through pipes and valves. The water is under pressure. When considering an electronic circuit, You can think of the water being analogous to current, the pressure to voltage and resistance to the valves and pipe size.

The picture shows a roll of common electrical insulating tape. This type of tape is used for lower voltage situations. The porcelain insulators shown are suitable for use with wire type antennas.

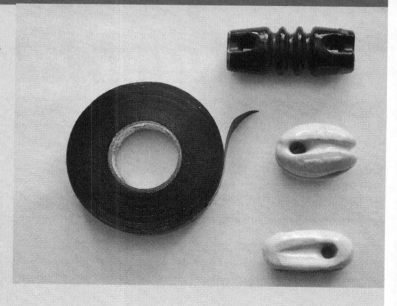

QUESTIONS

B-005-2-1.... Name three good electrical conductors.

1. gold, silver, wood
2. *gold, silver, aluminium*
3. copper, aluminum, paper
4. copper, gold, mica

B-005-2-2.... Name four good electrical insulators.

1. plastic, rubber, wood, carbon
2. paper, glass, air, aluminum
3. *glass, air, plastic, porcelain*
4. glass, wood, copper, porcelain

B-005-2-3.... Why do resistors sometimes get hot when in use?

1. their reactance makes them heat up
2. hotter circuit components nearby heat them up
3. they absorb magnetic energy which makes them hot
4. *some electrical energy passing through them is lost as heat*

B-005-2-4.... What is the best conductor among the following materials?

1. carbon
2. silicon
3. aluminum
4. *copper*

B-005-2-5.... Which type of material listed will most readily allow an electric current to flow?

1. *a conductor*
2. an insulator
3. a semi conductor
4. a dielectric

B-005-2-11.... The most common material used to make a resistor is:

1. *carbon*
2. gold
3. mica
4. lead

B-005-2-6.... A length of metal is connected in a circuit and is found to conduct electricity very well. It would be best described as having a:

1. high resistance
2. high wattage
3. low wattage
4. *low resistance*

B-005-2-7.... The letter "R" is the symbol for:

1. impedance
2. *resistance*
3. reluctance
4. reactance

B-005-2-8.... The reciprocal of resistance is:

1. *conductance*
2. reactance
3. reluctance
4. permeability

B-005-2-9.... Voltage drop means:

1. *the voltage developed across the terminals of a component*
2. any point in a radio circuit which has zero voltage
3. the difference in voltage at output terminals of a transformer
4. the voltage which is dissipated before useful work is accomplished

B-005-2-10.... The resistance of a conductor changes with:

1. voltage
2. *temperature*
3. current
4. humidity

Finish question session on page 231

RESISTORS

INTRODUCTION

Components known as resistors introduce a reduction of circuit current. Resistors are rated for their resistance which is measured in ohms. The accuracy of that resistance is a percentage of the ohmic resistance which is the tolerance.

Resistors are also rated for power dissipation in watts. Size is the main determining factor for power dissipation. The voltage rating of a resistor should also be considered.

Temperature can affect a resistor's resistance. The temperature coefficient rating of the resistive material used to construct the resistor affects this.

Most resistors are identified by colored bands. Resistance values can be decoded in accordance with the following:

First band - 1st digit of the resistance
Second band - 2nd digit of the resistance
Third band - add these number of zeros
Fourth band - tolerance - assume 20% if there is no fourth band

INTRODUCTION continued

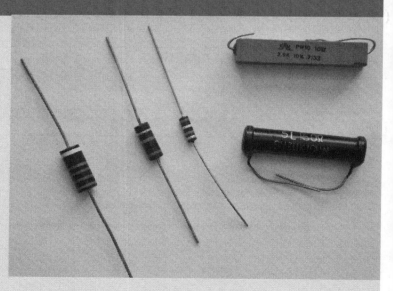

Colour	Value	Tolerance
Black	0	-
Brown	1	-
Red	2	2%
Orange	3	-
Yellow	4	-
Green	5	-
Blue	6	-
Violet	7	-
Grey	8	-
White	9	-
Silver	-	10%
Gold	-	5%

Ω is the symbol for ohm. 1,000 ohms can also be written as 1K. 1,000,000 ohms would be written as 1M.

QUESTIONS

B-004-6-1.... How do you find a resistor's tolerance rating?

1. by using Thevenin's theorem for resistors
2. *by reading the resistor's color code*
3. by reading its Baudot code
4. by using a voltmeter

B-004-6-2.... What do the first three color bands on a resistor indicate?

1. the resistance material
2. the power rating in watts
3. *the value of the resistor in ohms*
4. the resistance tolerance in percent

B-004-6-3.... What would the fourth color band on a 47 ohm resistor indicate?

1. the value of the resistor in ohms
2. the power rating in watts
3. the resistance material
4. *the resistance tolerance in percent*

B-004-6-4.... What are the possible values of a 100 ohm resistor with a 10% tolerance?

1. *90 to 110 ohms*
2. 90 to 100 ohms
3. 10 to 100 ohms
4. 80 to 120 ohms

B-004-6-5.... How do you find a resistor's value?

1. *by using the resistor's color code*
2. by using a voltmeter
3. by using Thevenin's theorem for resistor
4. by using the Baudot code

B-004-6-8.... If a carbon resistor's temperature is increased, what will happen to the resistance?

1. it will stay the same
2. *it will change depending on the resistors temperature coefficient rating*
3. it will become time dependent
4. it will increase by 20% for every 10 degrees centigrade

B-004-6-6.... A club project requires that a resistive voltage divider provide a very accurate and predictable ratio. Out of the list below, which resistor tolerance would you select?

1. 5%
2. 10%
3. 20%
4. *0.1%*

B-004-6-7.... You need a current limiting resistor for a light-emitting diode (LED). The actual resistance is not critical at all. Out of the list below, which resistor tolerance would you select?

1. *20%*
2. 0.1%
3. 5%
4. 10%

B-004-6-9.... A gold tolerance band on a resistor indicates the tolerance is:

1. 20%
2. 10%
3. *5%*
4. 1%

B-004-6-10.... Which colour band would differentiate a 120-ohm from a 1200-ohm resistor?

1. *third band*
2. fourth band
3. second band
4. first band

B-004-6-11.... Given that red=2, violet=7 and yellow=4, what is the nominal value of a resistor whose colour code reads "red", "violet" and "yellow"?

1. 274 ohms
2. 72 kilohms
3. 27 megohms
4. *270 kilohms*

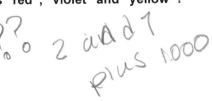

OHM'S LAW

INTRODUCTION

German scientist Ohm discovered the relationship that exists between voltage, current and resistance in a circuit. This relationship has become known as OHM's LAW.

Ohm's law can be stated as follows:

$E = I R$ (voltage = current multiplied by resistance)

$I = E / R$ (current = voltage divided by resistance)

$R = E / I$ (resistance = voltage divided by current)

E = electromotive force in volts
I = current in amperes
R = resistance in ohms

Cover any one of the letters
and the Ohms law formula
is revealed

SUPPLEMENT

How to solve for the following series of questions:

B-005-4-1   2 amps x 50 ohms = 100 volts

B-005-4-5   12 volts ÷ .25 amps = 48 ohms

B-005-4-6   100 volts ÷ .0008 amps = 125,000 ohms (125K ohms)

B-005-4-7   4.4 amps x 50 ohms = 220 volts

B-005-4-8   6 volts ÷ 30 ohms = 0.2 amps

B-005-4-9   0.2 amps x 25 ohms = 5 volts

B-005-4-11   3 volts ÷ 0.3 amps = 10 ohms

QUESTIONS

B-005-4-1.... If a current of 2 amperes flows through a 50 ohm resistor, what is the voltage across the resistor?

1. 48 volts
2. 52 volts
3. 100 volts
4. 25 volts

B-005-4-2.... How is the current in a DC circuit calculated when the voltage and resistance are known?

1. current equals voltage divided by resistance
2. current equals resistance multiplied by voltage
3. current equals resistance divided by voltage
4. current equals power divided by voltage

B-005-4-3.... How is the resistance in a DC circuit calculated when the voltage and current are known?

1. resistance equals current multiplied by voltage
2. resistance equals voltage divided by current
3. resistance equals power divided by voltage
4. resistance equals current divided by voltage

B-005-4-4.... How is the voltage in a DC circuit calculated when the current and resistance are known?

1. voltage equals current divided by resistance
2. voltage equals resistance divided by current
3. voltage equals power divided by current
4. voltage equals current multiplied by resistance

B-005-4-5.... If a 12 volt battery supplies 0.25 amp to a circuit, what is the circuit resistance?

1. 3 ohms
2. 48 ohms
3. 12 ohms
4. 0.25 ohm

B-005-4-6.... Calculate the value of resistance necessary to drop 100 volts with current flow of 0.8 milliamperes:

1. 125 kilohms
2. 125 ohms
3. 1250 ohms
4. 0.25 ohm

How to know kilohms

B-005-4-7.... The voltage required to force a current of 4.4 amperes through a resistance of 50 ohms is:

1. 220 volts
2. 2220 volts
3. 22.0 volts
4. 0.220 volt

B-005-4-8.... A lamp has a resistance of 30 ohms and a 6 volt battery is connected. The current flow will be:

1. 2 amperes
2. 0.5 ampere
3. 0.005 ampere
4. 0.2 amperes

B-005-4-9.... What voltage would be needed to supply a current of 200 milliamperes to operate an electric lamp which has a resistance of 25 ohms?

1. 5 volts
2. 8 volts
3. 175 volts
4. 225 volts

B-005-4-10.... The resistance of a circuit can be found by using one of the following:

1. R = E / I
2. R = I / E
3. R = E / R
4. R = E x I

Finish question section on page 231

POWER

INTRODUCTION

The formula for calculating power is:

P = E I (power = voltage x current)

P = power in watts
E = electromotive force in volts
I = current in amperes

For example, if a lamp draws 2 ampere of current when connected across a 12 volt battery, the power dissipated by the lamp is calculated as follows. 12 volts x 2 amperes = 24 watts of power.

The power handling rating of resistors is expressed in watts and is determined by the heat dissipation qualities of the resistor.

The power rating of two or more resistors connected in series or in parallel can be be added to determine the total power dissipation capability.

SUPPLEMENT

To do work or expend power, there has to be an electrical pressure (voltage) and a movement of electrons (current). There are two more ways of calculating power. These are:

P = I(squared) * R   Power = current squared multiplied by resistance

P= E(squared) / R   Power = voltage squared divided by resistance

B-005-6-2   12 volts x 0.2 amps = 2.4 amps
B-005-6-3   12 volts x 0.5 amps = 6 watts
B-005-6-4   2 x 1 watt = 2 watts
B-005-6-5   2 x 1 watt = 2 watts
B-005-6-9   10 volts ÷ (2x10 ohms) = 0.5 amps - then 10 volts x 0.5 amps = 5 watts

B-005-6-1.... Why would a large size resistor be used instead of a smaller one of the same resistance?

1. for better response time
2. for a higher current gain
3. for less impedance in the circuit
4. for greater power dissipation *More surface area?*

B-005-6-2.... How many watts of electrical power are used by a 12 volt DC light bulb that draws 0.2 amperes?

1. 2.4 watts
2. 60 watts
3. 24 watts
4. 6 watts

B-005-6-3.... The DC input power of a transmitter operating at 12 volts and drawing 500 milliamperes would be:

1. 20 watts
2. 6 watts
3. 500 watts
4. 12 watts

B-005-6-4.... When two 500 ohm 1 watt resistors are connected in series, the maximum total power that can be dissipated by the resistors is:

1. 1 watt
2. 2 watts
3. 1/2 watt
4. 4 watts

B-005-6-5.... When two 500 ohm 1 watt resistors are connected in parallel, they can dissipate a maximum total power of:

1. 1/2 watt
2. 1 watt
3. 2 watts
4. 4 watts

B-005-6-6.... If the voltage applied to two resistors in series is doubled, how much will the total power change? *x4*

1. increase four times
2. decrease to half
3. double
4. no change

B-005-6-7.... Which combination of resistors could make up a 50 ohms dummy load capable of safely dissipating 5 watts?

1. two 2-watt 25 ohms resistors in series
2. ten quarter-watt 500 ohms resistors in parallel
3. two 5-watt 100 ohms resistors in series
4. four 2-watt 200 ohms resistors in parallel

B-005-6-8.... A 12 volt light bulb is rated at a power of 30 watts. The current drawn would be:

1. 30/12 amperes *AMPS Same as watts over volts*
2. 18 amperes
3. 360 amperes
4. 12/30 amperes

B-005-6-9.... If two 10 ohm resistors are connected in series with a 10 volt battery, the power consumption would be:

1. 5 watts
2. 10 watts
3. 20 watts
4. 100 watts

B-005-6-10.... One advantage of replacing a 50 ohm resistor with a parallel combination of two similarly rated 100 ohm resistors is that the parallel combination will have:

1. the same resistance but lesser power rating
2. greater resistance and similar power rating
3. the same resistance but greater power rating
4. lesser resistance and similar power rating

Finish question section on page 231

POWER & CIRCUITS

INTRODUCTION

Power is rate of doing work. If there is no voltage, there can be no current and therefore no power. The unit of power is watt. The formula for calculating power is: $P = E\,I$ (P = power, E = voltage and I = current).

In a resistance, power is converted to heat. Physically larger resistors are capable of dissipating much more heat to the air than small resistors with the same resistance value. For example, 20 watts of energy dissipated in a resistor designed for 50 watts will probably cause the resistor to become only mildly warm. Allowing a resistor designed to handle 1/2 watt to dissipate 20 watts of power will cause the resistor to burn-up and be destroyed.

A circuit is a connection of electronic components designed to accomplish specific tasks. In an open circuit, no current can flow and no power is used. Current can flow in a completed circuit in which case power is consumed. An on/off switch is a device that creates an open circuit in the off position and a completed circuit in the on position.

A short circuit is usually an unintentional circuit that causes current to flow in unwanted directions.

INTRODUCTION continued

To calculate the total power dissipating capability of resistors connected in series or in parallel, just add the dissipation rating of each resistor.

Resistors also have maximum voltage ratings. This information is not color coded. Refer to the manufacturer's specifications.

QUESTIONS

B-005-3-1.... What is the word used to describe the rate at which electrical energy is used?

1. current
2. power
3. voltage
4. resistance

B-005-3-2.... If you have light bulbs marked 40 watts, 60 watts and 100 watts, which one will use electrical energy the fastest?

1. they will all be the same
2. the 40 watt bulb
3. the 100 watt bulb
4. the 60 watt bulb

B-005-3-3.... What is the basic unit of electrical power?

1. the ampere
2. the volt
3. the watt
4. the ohm

B-005-3-4.... Which electrical circuit will have no current?

1. a short circuit
2. an open circuit
3. a complete circuit
4. a closed circuit

B-005-3-5.... Which electrical circuit draws too much current?

1. a dead circuit
2. a short circuit
3. a closed circuit
4. an open circuit

B-005-3-6.... Power is expressed in:

1. volts
2. amperes
3. watts
4. ohms

B-005-3-7.... Which of the following two quantities should be multiplied together to find power?

1. inductance and capacitance
2. voltage and inductance
3. voltage and current
4. resistance and capacitance

B-005-3-8.... Which two electrical units multiplied together give the unit "watts"?

1. volts and farads
2. farads and henrys
3. amperes and henrys
4. volts and amperes

B-005-3-9.... A resistor in a circuit becomes very hot and starts to burn. This is because the resistor is dissipating too much:

1. voltage
2. resistance
3. current
4. power

B-005-3-10.... High power resistors are usually large with heavy leads. The size aids the operation of the resistor by:

1. allowing higher voltage to be handled
2. increasing the effective resistance of the resistor
3. allowing heat to dissipate more readily
4. making it shock proof

B-005-3-11.... The resistor that could dissipate the most heat would be marked:

1. 100 ohms
2. 2 ohms
3. 20 watts
4. 0.5 watt

SERIES & PARALLEL CIRCUITS

INTRODUCTION

Series Circuits:

- the applied voltage is equal to the sum of voltage drops across each component
- the current is the same through each component
- the total resistance is greater than the largest resistance
- to calculate for total resistance, add the value of each resistor

Parallel Circuits:

- the voltage drop across each component is equal to the applied voltage
- total current is equal to the sum of the currents in each component
- the total resistance is less than the smallest resistance
- to calculate for total resistance where resistors are of equal value, divide the resistance of one resistor by the number of resistors

Some circuits may use a combination of series and parallel connections. Analysis of such circuits is done by breaking them down into individual series or parallel segments.

SUPPLEMENT

How to solve for the following series of questions:

Series connected resistors

B-005-5-4   1000 ohms ÷ 2 = 500 ohms
             40 volts ÷ 500 ohms = .08 amps
             .08 amps = 80 milliamps

B-005-5-6   10 + 10 + 10 + 10 + 10 = 50 ohms

B-005-5-7   120 ÷ 5 = 24 ohms

B-005-5-9   68 ohms ÷ 4 = 17 ohms

Parallel connected resistors

QUESTIONS

B-005-5-1.... In a parallel circuit with a voltage source and several branch resistors, how is the total current related to the current in the branch resistors?

1. it equals the sum of the branch current through each resistor
2. it equals the average of the branch current through each resistor
3. it decreases as more parallel resistors are added to the circuit
4. it is the sum of each resistors voltage drop multiplied by the total number of resistors

B-005-5-2.... Three resistors, respectively rated at 10, 15, and 20 ohms are connected in parallel across a 6 volt battery. Which statement is true?

1. the current through the 10 ohms, 15 ohms and 20 ohms separate resistances, when added together, equals the total current drawn from the battery
2. the current flowing through the 10 ohm resistance is less than that flowing through the 20 ohm resistance
3. the voltage drop across each resistance added together equals 6 volts
4. the voltage drop across the 20 ohm resistance is greater than the voltage across the 10 ohm resistance

B-005-5-3.... Total resistance in a parallel circuit:

1. is always less than the smallest resistance
2. depends upon the voltage drop across each branch
3. could be equal to the resistance of one branch
4. depends upon the applied voltage

B-005-5-4.... Two resistors are connected in parallel and are connected across a 40 volt battery. If each resistor is 1000 ohms, the total current is:

1. 80 milliamperes
2. 40 milliamperes
3. 80 amperes
4. 40 amperes

B-005-5-5.... The total resistance of resistors connected in series is:

1. greater than the resistance of any one resistor
2. less than the resistance of any one resistor
3. equal to the highest resistance present
4. equal to the lowest resistance present

B-005-5-6.... Five 10 ohm resistors connected in series equals:

1. 50 ohms
2. 5 ohms
3. 10 ohms
4. 1 ohm

B-005-5-7.... Which series combination of resistors would replace a single 120 ohm resistor?

1. six 22 ohm
2. two 62 ohm
3. five 100 ohm
4. five 24 ohm

B-005-5-8.... If ten resistors of equal value were wired in parallel, the total resistance would be:

1. 10 / R
2. R / 10
3. 10 x R
4. 10 + R

B-005-5-9.... The total resistance of four 68 ohm resistors wired in parallel is:

1. 12 ohms
2. 34 ohms
3. 272 ohms
4. 17 ohms

Finish question section on page 231.

ALTERNATING CURRENT

INTRODUCTION

In alternating current (AC), the current first flows in one direction and then at periodic intervals current flows in the opposite direction. If this complete cycle were to occur during a 1 second period, the frequency would be 1 Hz. In direct current (DC), electron flow is only in one direction.

Canadian power companies provide 60 Hz alternating current. One cycle is completed every 1/60th of a second. Much higher frequency rates are referred to radio frequencies.

The distance that is travelled during one cycle is called the wavelength. Wavelength is the speed of light in metres divided by the frequency in Hertz or:

$$\text{Wavelength} = 300 / F \text{ (MHz)}$$

The longer the wavelength, the lower the frequency. The shorter the wavelength, the higher the frequency.

Human ears sense sound frequencies in the 20 to 20 000 Hz range. Ears detect air pressure changes and not electromagnetic waves that occur in the same frequency range.

SUPPLEMENT

The original frequency of a signal is the fundamental frequency. Slight distortions of the original signal may also cause harmonic signals to be present. For example, if the fundamental frequency is 2 kHz, then the second harmonic signal would be 4 kHz and the third harmonic signal would be 6 kHz. etc.

One cycle of alternating current can be plotted as shown in the diagram. The horizontal line is broken up into degrees and represents the absence of current.

The time period of 0 to 180 degrees is 1/2 cycle during which current flows in the positive direction. Between 180 and 360 degrees, current flows in the opposite direction.

The diagram for voltage is the same as one for current.

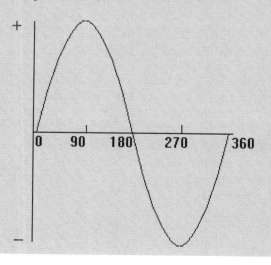

QUESTIONS

B-005-7-1.... What term means the number of times per second that an alternating current flows back and forth?

1. speed
2. pulse rate
3. *frequency*
4. inductance

B-005-7-2.... Approximately what frequency range can most humans hear?

1. 20 000 - 30 000 Hz
2. 200 - 200 000 Hz
3. *20 - 20 000 Hz*
4. 0 - 20 Hz

B-005-7-3.... Why do we call signals in the range 20 Hz to 20 000 Hz, audio frequencies?

1. because the human ear cannot sense anything in this range
2. because this range is too low for radio energy
3. because the human ear can sense radio waves in this range
4. *because the human ear can sense sounds in this range*

B-005-7-4.... Electrical energy at a frequency of 7125 kHz is in what frequency range?

1. *radio*
2. audio
3. hyper
4. super-high

B-005-7-11.... A signal is composed of a fundamental frequency of 2 kHz and another of 4 kHz. This 4 kHz signal is referred to as:

1. a fundamental of the 2 kHz signal
2. the DC component of the main signal
3. a dielectric signal of the main signal
4. *a harmonic of the 2 kHz signal*

Finish question section on page 231

B-005-7-5.... What is the name for the distance an AC signal travels during one complete cycle?

1. *wavelength*
2. wave speed
3. waveform
4. wave spread

B-005-7-6.... What happens to a signal's wavelength as its frequency increases?

1. it gets longer
2. it stays the same
3. it disappears
4. *it gets shorter*

B-005-7-7.... What happens to a signal's frequency as its wavelength gets longer?

1. it disappears
2. it stays the same
3. *it goes down*
4. it goes up

B-005-7-8.... What does 60 hertz (Hz) mean?

distance

1. 6000 metres per second
2. *60 cycles per second*
3. 60 metres per second
4. 6000 cycles per second

B-005-7-9.... If the frequency of the waveform is 100 Hz, the time for one cycle is:

Time

0.01

1. 10 seconds
2. 0.0001 second
3. *0.01 second*
4. 1 second

B-005-7-10.... Current in an AC circuit goes through a complete cycle in 0.1 second. This means the AC has a frequency of:

1. *10 Hz*
2. 1 Hz
3. 100 Hz
4. 1000 Hz

MEASUREMENTS

INTRODUCTION

Frequency = Hz (hertz - previously called cycles)

- Kilohertz - kHz = 1 000 Hz
- Megahertz - MHz = 1 000 000 Hz
- Gigahertz - GHz = 1 000 000 000 Hz

Current - Ampere

- Milliampere - mA = .001 ampere
- Microampere - uA = .000 001 ampere

EMF - volt

- Kilovolt - KV - 1 000 volts
- Millivolt - mV = .001 volts
- Microvolt - uV = .000 001 volts

INTRODUCTION continued

Resistance - Ohms

- Kilohm = 1 000 ohms
- Megohm = 1 000 000 ohms

Capacitance - Farad

- Microfarad = .000 001 farads
- Picofarad = .000 000 000 001 farads

Power - Watts

- Kilowatt = 1 000 watts
- Milliwatt = .001 watts
- Microwatt = .000 001 watts

Inductance - Henry

- Millihenry = .001 Henry
- Microhenry = .000 001 Henry

NEED PRACTICE

 RAC

QUESTIONS

B-005-1-1.... If a dial marked in megahertz shows a reading of 3.525 MHz., what would it show if it were marked in kilohertz?

1. 35.25 kHz
2. 3 525 kHz
3. 3 525 000 kHz
4. 0.003 525 kHz

decimal moved three →

B-005-1-2.... If an ammeter marked in amperes is used to measure a 3 000 milliampere current, what reading would it show?

1. 3 amperes
2. 0.003 ampere
3. 0.3 ampere
4. 3 000 000 amperes

moved three ←

B-005-1-3.... If a voltmeter marked in volts is used to measure a 3 500 millivolt potential, what reading would it show?

1. 3.5 volts
2. 0.35 volt
3. 35 volts
4. 350 volts

Move three ←

B-005-1-4.... How many microfarads is 1 000 000 picofarads?

1. 1 000 000 000 microfarads
2. 1 000 microfarads
3. 1 microfarad
4. 0.001 microfarad

Moved 6 ←

B-005-1-5.... If you have a hand-held transceiver which puts out 500 milliwatts, how many watts would this be?

1. 5
2. 0.5
3. 50
4. 0.02

B-005-1-6.... A kilohm is:

1. 0.1 ohm
2. 0.001 ohm
3. 10 ohms
4. 1 000 ohms

B-005-1-7.... 6.6 kilovolts is equal to:

1. 6 600 volts
2. 660 volts
3. 66 volts
4. 66 000 volts

B-005-1-8.... A current of one quarter ampere may be written as:

1. 0.5 ampere
2. 0.25 milliampere
3. 250 microamperes
4. 250 milliamperes

B-005-1-9.... How many millivolts are equivalent to two volts?

1. 0.000 002
2. 2 000
3. 2 000 000
4. 0.002

B-005-1-10.... One megahertz is equal to:

1. 1 000 kHz
2. 100 kHz
3. 0.001 Hz
4. 10 Hz

B-005-1-11.... An inductance of 10 000 microhenrys may be stated correctly as:

1. 100 millihenrys
2. 10 henrys
3. 1 000 henrys
4. 10 millihenrys

METERS

INTRODUCTION

Voltmeters measure electromotive force. The unit of measurement is the volt. The meter leads are connected in parallel to the circuit or component. Voltmeters have a multiplier resistor in series with the meter movement. Only a tiny portion of the available circuit current is used by voltmeters. The terms voltage drop and potential difference are also used to describe the voltage between the terminals of a component.

Ammeters measure current. The unit of measurement is ampere. The meter leads are connected in series with the circuit or component. Ammeters have a shunt resistor in parallel with the meter. Most of the current flows through the shunt and only a tiny portion of the available circuit current is used by ammeters.

Ohmmeters measure resistance. The unit of measurement is ohm. The meter leads are connected in parallel with the circuit or component. Ohmmeters use an internal battery source and resistors to operate a calibrated meter.

Multimeters are capable of measuring voltage, current and resistance.

SUPPLEMENT

The picture displays a digital multimeter or VOM (Volt Ohm Meter). These have replaced analog meters for most measuring purposes. Very accurate readings are possible.

In circuit diagrams, the symbols for voltmeters and ammeters are:

QUESTIONS

B-005-13-1.... How is a voltmeter usually connected to a circuit under test?

1. in series with the circuit
2. in quadrature with the circuit
3. in phase with the circuit
4. *in parallel with the circuit*

B-005-13-2.... How is an ammeter usually connected to a circuit under test?

1. in quadrature with the circuit
2. *in series with the circuit*
3. in phase with the circuit
4. in parallel with the circuit

B-005-13-3.... What does a multimeter measure?

1. resistance, capacitance and inductance
2. *voltage, current and resistance*
3. resistance and reactance
4. SWR and power

B-005-13-4.... The correct instrument to measure plate current or collector current of a transmitter is:

1. an ohmmeter
2. a wattmeter
3. *an ammeter*
4. a voltmeter

B-005-13-8.... Potential difference is measured by means of:

1. a wattmeter
2. an ohmmeter
3. *a voltmeter*
4. an ammeter

B-005-13-10.... In measuring volts and amperes, the connections should be made with:

1. both voltmeter and ammeter in series
2. both voltmeter and ammeter in parallel
3. *the voltmeter in parallel and ammeter in series*
4. the voltmeter in series and ammeter in parallel

B-005-13-5.... Which of the following meters would you use to measure the power supply current drawn by a small hand-held transistorized receiver?

1. *a DC ammeter*
2. an RF ammeter
3. an RF power meter
4. an electrostatic voltmeter

B-005-13-6.... When measuring current drawn from a DC power supply, it is true to say that the meter will act in circuit as:

1. a perfect conductor
2. *a low value resistance*
3. an extra current drain
4. an insulator

B-005-13-7.... When measuring the current drawn by a receiver from a power supply, the current meter should be placed:

1. in series with both receiver power leads
2. *in series with one of the receiver power leads*
3. in parallel with both receiver power supply leads
4. in parallel with one of the receiver power leads

B-005-13-9.... The instrument used for measuring the flow of electrical current is the:

1. voltmeter
2. wattmeter
3. *ammeter*
4. faradmeter

DECIBEL

INTRODUCTION

Decibels can be used to express the ratio of one power to another.

1 dB = a power gain of 1.26 (26%)
3 dB = a power gain of 2
6 dB = a power gain of 4
10 dB = a power gain of 10
20 dB = a power gain of 100
30 dB = a power gain of 1000

Examples:

Increasing a 100 watt transmitter power by 3 dB (100 x 2 = 200 watts)

Decreasing a 200 watt transmitter power by 6 dB (200 / 4= 50 watts)

Using a 10 dB gain antenna with a 50 watt transmitter (effective radiated power = 50 x 10 = 500 watts)

Using a 20 dB gain power amplifier with a 10 watt transmitter (power output = 10 x 100 = 1000 watts)

SUPPLEMENT

Decibels can also be used to describe relationships between voltages and current. In this case:

1 dB = a gain of 1.12
3 dB = a gain of 1.41
6 dB = a gain of 2
20 dB = a gain of 10
40 dB = a gain of 100
60 dB = a gain of 1000

The decibel is logarithmic. It is used because the decibel makes it is easier to visualize huge changes in quantities.

QUESTIONS

B-005-8-1.... A two-times increase in power results in a change of how many dB?

1. 6 dB higher
2. 3 dB higher
3. 12 dB higher
4. 1 dB higher

B-005-8-2.... How can you decrease your transmitter's power by 3 dB?

1. divide the original power by 1.5
2. divide the original power by 3
3. divide the original power by 4
4. divide the original power by 2

B-005-8-3.... How can you increase your transmitter's power by 6 dB?

1. multiply the original power by 3
2. multiply the original power by 2
3. multiply the original power by 4
4. multiply the original power by 1.5

B-005-8-4.... If a signal-strength report is "10 dB over S9", what should the report be if the transmitter power is reduced from 1500 watts to 150 watts?

1. S9 plus 3 dB
2. S9 minus 10 dB
3. S9 plus 5 dB
4. S9

B-005-8-5.... If a signal-strength report is "20 dB over S9", what should the report be if the transmitter power is reduced from 1500 watts to 150 watts?

1. S9 plus 10 dB
2. S9 plus 5 dB
3. S9 plus 3 dB
4. S9

B-005-8-6.... The unit "decibel" is used to indicate:

1. an oscilloscope wave form
2. a mathematical ratio
3. certain radio waves
4. a single side band signal

B-005-8-7.... The power output from a transmitter increases from 1 watt to 2 watts. This is a db increase of:

1. 30
2. 6
3. 3
4. 1

B-005-8-8.... The power of a transmitter is increased from 5 watts to 50 watts by a linear amplifier. The power gain, expressed in dB, is:

1. 30 dB
2. 10 dB
3. 40 dB
4. 20 dB

B-005-8-9.... You add a 9 dB gain amplifier to your 2 watt handheld. What is the power output of the combination?

1. 11 watts
2. 16 watts
3. 20 watts
4. 18 watts

B-005-8-10.... The power of a transmitter is increased from 2 watts to 8 watts. This is a power gain of _____ dB.

1. 6 dB
2. 3 dB
3. 8 dB
4. 9 dB

Finish question section on page 231.

INDUCTANCE & CAPACITANCE

INTRODUCTION

Inductors are conductors usually in the form of a coil. The factors that affect inductance are the number of turns, diameter of turns, length of coil and core material.

Current through inductors causes electromagnetic fields to form around the inductor. With AC, the induction from the changing electromagnetic field causes the inductor to oppose changes in current.

Inductance is measured in henrys.

When two inductors of equal value are connected in parallel, the total inductance is half the value of one inductor. When two inductors of equal value are connected in series, the total inductance is twice the value of one inductor.

In circuits designed for lower frequencies, larger values of inductance are more common than smaller values.

The symbol for an inductor is:

SUPPLEMENT

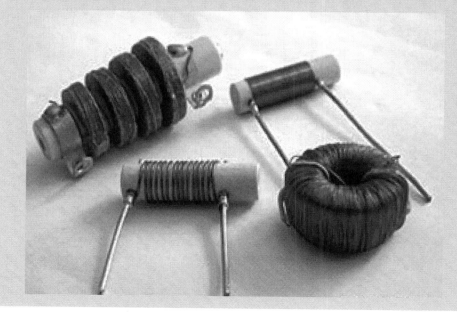

QUESTIONS

B-005-9-1.... If two equal-value inductors are connected in series, what is their total inductance?

1. half the value of one inductor
2. the same as the value of either inductor
3. the value of one inductor times the value of the other
4. *twice the value of one inductor*

B-005-9-2.... If two equal-value inductors are connected in parallel, what is their total inductance?

1. twice the value of one inductor
2. the same as the value of either inductor
3. the value of one inductor times the value of the other
4. *half the value of one inductor*

B-005-9-5.... What determines the inductance of a coil?

1. the core material, the number of turns used to wind the coil and the frequency of the current through the coil
2. the coil diameter, the number of turns of wire used to wind the coil and the type of metal used for the wire
3. *the core material, the coil diameter, the length of the coil and the number of turns of wire used to wind the coil*
4. the core material, the coil diameter, the length of the coil and whether the coil is mounted horizontally or vertically

B-005-9-8.... To replace a faulty 10 millihenry choke, you could use two:

1. 20 millihenry chokes in series
2. *5 millihenry chokes in series*
3. 30 millihenry chokes in parallel
4. 5 millihenry chokes in parallel

INDUCTANCE AND CAPACITANCE continued

INTRODUCTION

Capacitors have the ability to store electron charges. A basic capacitor consists of two metal plates separated by a nonconducting dielectric. The factors that affect capacity are the area of the plates, the number of plates, spacing between the plates and the composition of the nonconducting material (dielectric).

Capacity is measured in farads. Capacitance opposes voltage changes.

When two capacitors of equal value are connected in parallel, the total capacitance is twice the value of one capacitor. For capacitors of unequal values connected in parallel, capacitance is always greater than the largest value.

When two capacitors of equal value are connected in series, the total capacitance is half the value of one capacitor. For capacitors of unequal value connected in series, capacitance is always less than the smallest value.

In circuits designed for lower frequencies, larger values of capacitance are more common than smaller values. The symbol for a capacitor is: ⊣⊢

SUPPLEMENT

QUESTIONS

B-005-9-3.... If two equal-value capacitors are connected in series, what is their total capacitance?

1. twice the value of one capacitor
2. the same as the value of either capacitor
3. the value of one capacitor times the value of the other
4. half the value of either capacitor *(circled)*

B-005-9-4.... If two equal-value capacitors are connected in parallel, what is their total capacitance?

1. the same as the value of either capacitor
2. twice the value of one capacitor *(circled)*
3. the value of one capacitor times the value of the other
4. half the value of one capacitor

B-005-9-6.... What determines the capacitance of a capacitor?

1. the material between the plates, the surface area of the plates, the number of plates and the spacing between the plates *(circled)*
2. the material between the plates, the number of plates and the size of the wires connected to the plates
3. the number of plates, the spacing between the plates and whether the dielectric material is N type or P type
4. the material between the plates, the area of one plate, the number of plates and the material used for the protective coating

B-005-9-7.... If two equal-value capacitors are connected in parallel, what is their capacitance?

1. the same value of either capacitor
2. the value of one capacitor times the value of the other
3. half the value of either capacitor
4. twice the value of either capacitor *(circled)*

B-005-9-9.... Three 15 microfarad capacitors are wired in series. The total capacitance of this arrangement is:

(handwritten: series total goes down)

1. 45 microfarads
2. 12 microfarads
3. 5 microfarads *(circled)*
4. 18 microfarads

B-005-9-10.... Which series combinations of capacitors would best replace a faulty 10 microfarad capacitor?

1. two 10 microfarad capacitors
2. two 20 microfarad capacitors *(circled)*
3. twenty 2 microfarad capacitors
4. ten 2 microfarad capacitors

B-005-9-11.... The total capacitance of two or more capacitors in series is:

1. found by adding each of the capacitors together and dividing by the total number of capacitors
2. found by adding each of the capacitors together
3. always less than the smallest capacitor *(circled)*
4. always greater than the largest capacitor

94

REACTANCE

INTRODUCTION

Capacitance opposes change in voltage. In AC circuits, capacitors exhibit capacitive reactance which is expressed in ohms. Capacitive reactance decreases as frequency increases.

Inductance opposes change in current. In AC circuits, inductors exhibit inductive reactance which is expressed in ohms. Inductive reactance increases as frequency increases.

XL = 2 Pi F L

XC = 1 / (2 Pi F C)

XL = inductive reactance in ohms
XC = capacitive reactance in ohms
Pi = 3.141
F = frequency in hertz
L = inductance in henrys
C = capacitance in farads

SUPPLEMENT

If you were to measure the ohmic resistance of a transformer winding, you would encounter very low values of resistance. It is the inductive reactance and the circuit load which determines how much current will flow in a transformer winding.

If you were to attach a battery to a direct current source such as a battery, current will flow until the capacitor is fully charged to the battery voltage. Current flow will become zero, assuming the dielectric of the capacitor has no loss. If no current flows, the ohmic resistance is infinite.

Connect a capacitor in an alternating current circuit, the capacitor continuously charges and discharges. The ohmic resistance depends on the value of the capacitor and the frequency of the circuit.

High inductive or capacitive reactance rejects signals.
Low inductive or capacitive reactance passes signals.

QUESTIONS

B-005-10-1.... How does a coil react to AC?

1. as the amplitude of the applied AC increases, the reactance decreases
2. as the amplitude of the applied AC increases, the reactance increases
3. *as the frequency of the applied AC increases, the reactance increases*
4. as the frequency of the applied AC increases, the reactance decreases

B-005-10-2.... How does a capacitor react to AC?

1. *as the frequency of the applied AC increases, the reactance decreases*
2. as the frequency of the applied AC increases, the reactance increases
3. as the amplitude of the applied AC increases, the reactance increases
4. as the amplitude of the applied AC increases, the reactance decreases

B-005-10-3.... The reactance of capacitors increases as:

1. applied voltage increases
2. frequency decreases
3. applied voltage decreases
4. frequency increases

B-005-10-4.... In inductances, AC may be opposed by both resistance of winding wire and reactance due to inductive effect. The term which includes resistance and reactance is:

1. resonance
2. inductance
3. impedance
4. capacitance

B-005-10-5.... Capacitive reactance:

1. *decreases as frequency increases*
2. applies only to series RLC circuits
3. increases as frequency increases
4. increases with the time constant

B-005-10-6.... Inductive reactance may be increased by:

1. a decrease in the applied frequency
2. a decrease in the supplied current
3. an increase in the applied voltage
4. *an increase in the applied frequency*

B-005-10-7.... What property allows a coil wound on a ferrite core to mitigate the effects of an offending radio signal?

1. high reactance at audio frequencies
2. *high reactance at radio frequencies*
3. low reactance at radio frequencies
4. low reactance at audio frequencies

B-005-10-8.... What property allows an RF bypass capacitor on an audio circuit to divert an offending radio signal?

1. *low reactance at radio frequencies*
2. high reactance at radio frequencies
3. low reactance at audio frequencies
4. high reactance at audio frequencies

B-005-10-9.... What property allows an RF bypass capacitor to have little effect on an audio circuit?

1. low reactance at high frequencies
2. high reactance at high frequencies
3. low reactance at low frequencies
4. *high reactance at low frequencies*

B-005-10-10.... What property allows an RF choke coil to have little effect on signals meant to flow through the coil?

1. *low reactance at low frequencies*
2. high reactance at low frequencies
3. low reactance at high frequencies
4. high reactance at high frequencies

Finish question section on page 231.

MAGNETISM & TRANSFORMERS

INTRODUCTION

It is possible to align atoms of iron, nickel or cobalt to cause these elements to become permanent magnets. Permanent magnets have north and south poles. Magnets with the "unlike poles" held near each other are attracted to each other. Magnets with the similar or "like poles" held near each other are repelled.

A magnetic field is always present when current flows through a conductor. The stronger the current, the stronger the magnetic field. The magnetic field can be concentrated by forming a coil and choosing material that can easily be magnetized for the coil core.

Induction of an electromotive force in a conductor or coil occurs when magnetic lines of force intersect the conductor. Induction is greatest when the lines of force are perpendicular to the conductor.

Atoms consist of a nucleus of protons surrounded by one or more electrons that encircle the nucleus. For most atoms, the magnetic forces cancel each other out. Only the atoms of elements such as iron, nickel and cobalt can arrange themselves into magnetic entities.

SUPPLEMENT

Transformer symbol

A transformer in a 12 volt, 30 amp, power supply is shown in the photo.

QUESTIONS

B-005-11-5.... The strength of the magnetic field around a conductor in air is:

1. inversely proportional to the diameter of the conductor
2. directly proportional to the diameter of the conductor
3. *directly proportional to the current in the conductor*
4. inversely proportional to the voltage on the conductor

B-005-11-6.... Maximum induced voltage in a coil occurs when:

1. *current is going through its greatest rate of change*
2. the current through the coil is of a DC nature
3. current is going through its least rate of change
4. the magnetic field around the coil is not changing

B-005-11-7.... The voltage induced in a conductor moving in a magnetic field is at a maximum when the movement is:

1. made in a counterclockwise direction
2. parallel to the lines of force
3. *perpendicular to the lines of force*
4. made in a clockwise direction

B-005-11-9.... A force of repulsion exists between two _____ magnetic poles.

1. unlike
2. positive
3. negative
4. *like*

B-005-11-10.... A permanent magnet would most likely be made from:

1. copper
2. aluminum
3. brass
4. *steel*

MAGNETISM & TRANSFORMERS continued

INTRODUCTION

When two coils are in the same magnetic field, we have the makings of a transformer. The changing current in one of the inductors causes an induction of current in the other inductor. This is called mutual inductance.

The coil of a transformer attached to the source of electromotive force (EMF) is called the primary winding. The other coil is the secondary winding. Transformers are very efficient and it can be said that power drawn by the primary winding is almost equal to the power drawn from the secondary winding. There are some small losses, such as wire resistance, which are converted to heat. Even when no current is drawn from the secondary winding, a very small magnetizing current is required to overcome the resisting effect (hysteresis) from constant changing of the magnetic state of the transformer core.

By calculating volts per turn of either the primary or secondary windings, it is possible to calculate the voltage of the other winding. For example, a transformer primary winding has 60 turns of wire and is connected to a 120 volts AC. This computes to be 120 / 60 = 2 volts per turn. If the secondary winding has 6 turns of wire, the secondary output voltage would be 2 volts per turn multiplied by 6 turns = 12 volts.

SUPPLEMENT

On the transformer shown, the primary 120 volt connections are the top 2 soldering lugs. The secondary 18 volt connections are on the bottom. The soldering lug in the middle is the center tap of the secondary winding.

The core of this transformer is made from numerous thin strips of iron which are referred to as laminations. Small internal currents within the laminations cause heat and effect the efficiency of transformers. The amount of heat generated is dependent on the quality of the material and type of construction.

QUESTIONS

B-005-11-1.... If no load is attached to the secondary winding of a transformer, what is current in the primary winding called?

1. *magnetizing current*
2. direct current
3. latent current
4. stabilizing current

B-005-11-2.... A transformer operates a 6.3 volt 2 ampere light bulb from its secondary winding. The input power to the primary winding is approximately:

1. *13 watts*
2. 6 watts
3. 8 watts
4. 3 watts

B-005-11-3.... A transformer has a 240 volt primary that draws a current of 250 milliamperes from the mains supply. Assuming no losses and only one secondary, what current would be available from the 12 volt secondary?

1. 215 amperes
2. 25 amperes
3. 50 amperes
4. *5 amperes*

B-005-11-4.... In a mains power transformer, the primary winding has 250 turns, and the secondary has 500. If the input voltage is 120 volts, the likely secondary voltage is:

1. 480 V
2. *240 V*
3. 610 V
4. 26 V

B-005-11-8.... A 100% efficient transformer has a turns ratio of 1/5. If the secondary current is 50 milliamperes, the primary current is:

1. 2 500 mA
2. 0.01 A
3. *0.25 A*
4. 0.25 mA

B-005-11-11.... The fact that energy transfer from primary to secondary windings in a power transformer is not perfect is indicated by:

1. electrostatic shielding
2. large secondary currents
3. *warm iron laminations*
4. high primary voltages

RESONANCE

INTRODUCTION

Resonance occurs at the frequency for which inductive reactance and capacitive reactance are equal.

In parallel resonant circuits:

- impedance is high
- circuit current is low

In series resonant circuits:

- impedance is low
- circuit current is high

Adding resistance to resonant circuits does not affect the resonant frequency.

Inductors exhibit inductive reactance and capacitors exhibit capacitive reactance. In combination, these components form the resonant circuitry that is used in oscillators, amplifiers and filters, all of which are required to make radio equipment function.

SUPPLEMENT

The coil and capacitor as shown forms a parallel resonant circuit.

Decreasing the size of the inductance or capacitance will increase the resonant frequency.

Increasing the size of the inductance or capacitance will decrease the resonant frequency.

QUESTIONS

B-005-12-1.... Resonance is the condition that exists when:

1. *inductive reactance and capacitive reactance are equal*
2. inductive reactance is the only opposition in the circuit
3. the circuit contains no resistance
4. resistance is equal to the reactance

B-005-12-2.... Parallel tuned circuits offer:

1. low impedance at resonance
2. zero impedance at resonance
3. an impedance equal to resistance of the circuit
4. *high impedance at resonance*

B-005-12-3.... Resonance is an electrical property used to describe:

1. an inductor
2. a set of parallel inductors
3. the results of tuning a varicap (varactor)
4. *the frequency characteristic of a coil and capacitor circuit*

B-005-12-4.... A tuned circuit is formed from two basic components. These are:

1. resistors and transistors
2. directors and reflectors
3. diodes and transistors
4. *inductors and capacitors*

B-005-12-6.... In a parallel resonant circuit at resonance, the circuit has a:

1. low impedance
2. low mutual inductance
3. high mutual inductance
4. *high impedance*

B-005-12-7.... In a series resonant circuit at resonance, the circuit has:

1. *low impedance*
2. high impedance
3. low mutual inductance
4. high mutual inductance

B-005-12-5.... When a parallel coil-capacitor combination is supplied with AC of different frequencies, there will be one frequency where the impedance will be highest. This is the:

1. *resonant frequency*
2. impedance frequency
3. inductive frequency
4. reactive frequency

B-005-12-8.... A coil and an air-spaced capacitor are arranged to form a resonant circuit. The resonant frequency will remain the same if we:

1. increase the area of plates in the capacitor
2. insert Mylar sheets between the plates of the capacitor
3. wind more turns on the coil
4. *add a resistor to the circuit*

B-005-12-9.... Resonant circuits in a receiver are used to:

1. filter direct current
2. *select signal frequencies*
3. increase power
4. adjust voltage levels

B-005-12-10.... Resonance is the condition that exists when:

1. *inductive reactance and capacitive reactance are equal and opposite in sign*
2. inductive reactance is the only opposition in the circuit
3. the circuit contains no resistance
4. resistance is equal to the reactance

B-005-12-11.... When a series LCR circuit is tuned to the frequency of the source, the:

1. line current lags the applied voltage
2. line current leads the applied voltage
3. *line current reaches maximum*
4. impedance is maximum

DIODES

INTRODUCTION

Diodes are semiconductor devices. They are one-way electronic valves. The current can only flow through them in one direction. Current flows when the anode-cathode junction is forward biased. When the anode-cathode junction is reversed biased, there is no current flow.

Rectifier diodes allow current flow in only one direction. In a power supply, a diode converts alternating current (AC) into pulsating direct current (DC). This process is called rectification.

Zener diodes have the unique property of developing a constant voltage drop across the device for a wide range of changing currents. This makes them effective voltage regulators.

Signal diodes can be used to remove information from transmitted signals. This process is called demodulation.

Light-emitting diodes (LED) will glow in different colours when current flows through these devices. The colour is determined by the chemical composition in the manufacturing process.

SUPPLEMENT

A sampling of diodes are shown below. Diodes are rated by voltage, peak inverse voltage and current. Circuit designers must also consider other ratings and parameters, The left bottom diode is an LED.

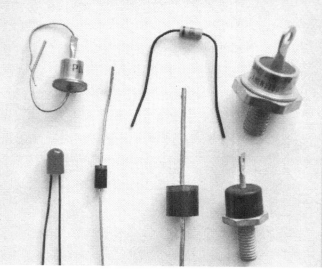

QUESTIONS

B-004-2-1.... Zener diodes are used as:

1. current regulators
2. *voltage regulators*
3. RF detectors
4. AF detectors

B-004-2-2.... One important application for diodes is recovering information from transmitted signals. This is referred to as:

1. regeneration
2. ionization
3. biasing
4. *demodulation*

B-004-2-3.... The primary purpose of a Zener diode is to:

1. provide a voltage phase shift
2. *regulate or maintain a constant voltage*
3. boost the power supply voltage
4. provide a path through which current can flow

B-004-2-4.... The action of changing alternating current to direct current is called:

1. amplification
2. *rectification*
3. transformation
4. modulation

B-004-2-5.... The electrodes of a semiconductor diode are known as :

1. gate and source
2. *anode and cathode*
3. collector and base
4. cathode and drain

B-004-2-6.... If alternating current is applied to the anode of a diode, what would you expect to see at the cathode?

1. no signal
2. steady direct current
3. *pulsating direct current*
4. pulsating alternating current

B-004-2-7.... In a semiconductor diode, electrons flow from:

1. anode to cathode
2. cathode to grid
3. grid to anode
4. *cathode to anode*

B-004-2-8.... What semiconductor device glows different colours, depending upon its chemical composition?

1. *a light-emitting diode*
2. a fluorescent bulb
3. a neon bulb
4. a vacuum diode

B-004-2-9.... Voltage regulation is the principal application of the:

1. junction diode
2. light-emitting diode
3. vacuum diode
4. *zener diode*

B-004-2-10.... In order for a diode to conduct, it must be:

1. close coupled
2. *forward-biased*
3. enhanced
4. reverse-biased

TRANSISTORS

INTRODUCTION

Doping is a manufacturing process of adding impurities to the crystal structure of semiconductors. A semiconductor doped to have extra electrons is N type. A semiconductor doped to have missing electrons is P type.

Bipolar transistors have NPN or PNP junctions. Each of these three doped semiconductor material blocks are connected to a wire. The center block is the base. The outside blocks are the emitter and collector.

A small current through the emitter/base junction can control a much larger emitter/collector current. This is how a transistor amplifies. In comparison to a vacuum tube, the emitter can be compared to a cathode, the base to a control grid and the collector to a plate.

The biggest enemy of transistors is excessive heat. Excessive heat will destroy a transistor.

Circuit symbol for NPN transistor.

Circuit symbol for PNP transistor.

SUPPLEMENT

In circuit diagrams, transistor symbols are generally drawn without identifying the connections.

B= Base   C= Collector   E = Emitter

Sample transistors are shown.

Credit : Transistor symbols by Zedh

QUESTIONS

B-004-3-1.... Which component can amplify a small signal using low voltages?

1. a variable resistor
2. an electrolytic capacitor
3. a multiple-cell battery
4. *a PNP transistor*

B-004-3-2.... The basic semiconductor amplifying device is the:

1. tube
2. P-N junction
3. *transistor*
4. diode

B-004-3-3.... The three leads from a PNP transistor are named:

1. drain, base and source
2. *collector, emitter and base*
3. collector, source and drain
4. gate, source and drain

B-004-3-5.... Bipolar transistors usually have:

1. 2 leads
2. *3 leads*
3. 1 lead
4. 4 leads

B-004-3-6.... A semiconductor is described as a "general purpose audio NPN device". This would be:

1. *a bipolar transistor*
2. a silicon diode
3. a triode
4. an audio detector

B-004-3-7.... The two basic types of bipolar transistors are:

1. diode and triode types
2. *NPN and PNP types*
3. varicap and Zener types
4. P and N channel types

B-004-3-4.... If a low level signal is placed at the input to a transistor, a higher level of signal is produced at the output lead. This effect is known as:

1. detection
2. modulation
3. rectification
4. *amplification*

B-004-3-8.... A transistor can be destroyed in a circuit by:

1. *excessive heat*
2. excessive light
3. saturation
4. cut-off

B-004-3-9.... In a bipolar transistor, the _____ compares closest to the control grid of a triode vacuum tube.

1. emitter
2. *base*
3. source
4. collector

B-004-3-10.... In a bipolar transistor, the _____ compares closest to the plate of a triode vacuum tube.

1. gate
2. emitter
3. *collector*
4. base

B-004-3-11.... In a bipolar transistor, the _____ compares closest to the cathode of a triode vacuum tube.

1. collector
2. base
3. drain
4. *emitter*

FIELD EFFECT TRANSISTORS

INTRODUCTION

Two types of field effect transistors (FET) are:
- JFET - junction field effect transistor
- MOSFET - metal-oxide silicon field effect transistor

An FET with a conduction channel made from N type material is called an N-channel FET. If the channel is made from P type material, it is referred to as an P-channel FET.

Connections to the channel ends are referred to as the source and drain. At some point along the channel, material of the other type is introduced to become the gate. A small voltage difference between the gate and the channel is able to control relatively large currents. A large enough reverse bias will pinch-off the source/drain current.

SOURCE - entry point for charge carriers - corresponds to emitter in a bipolar transistor
DRAIN - exit point for charge carriers - corresponds to the collector in a bipolar transistor
GATE - controls the source/drain conductance - corresponds to the base in a bipolar transistor

The characteristics of a field effect transistor are similar to the characteristics of a triode vacuum tube.

SUPPLEMENT

FIELD EFFECT TRANSISTORS

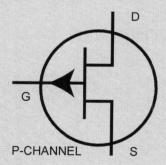

N-CHANNEL   S   P-CHANNEL   S   MOSFET

QUESTIONS

B-004-4-1.... The two basic types of field effect transistors (FET) are:

1. NPN and PNP
2. germanium and silicon
3. inductive and capacitive
4. *N and P channel*

B-004-4-2.... A semiconductor having its leads labeled gate, drain and source is best described as a:

1. gated transistor
2. *field-effect transistor*
3. bipolar transistor
4. silicon diode

B-004-4-3.... In a field effect transistor, the _____ is the terminal that controls the conductance of the channel:

1. *gate*
2. drain
3. source
4. collector

B-004-4-4.... In a field effect transistor, the _____ is the terminal where the charge carriers enter the channel.

1. *source*
2. gate
3. drain
4. emitter

B-004-4-5.... In a field effect transistor, the _____ is the terminal where the charge carriers leave the channel.

1. collector
2. source
3. *drain*
4, gate

B-004-4-6.... Which semiconductor device has characteristics most similar to a triode vacuum tube?

1. junction diode
2. zener diode
3. *field effect transistor*
4. bipolar transistor

B-004-4-7.... The control element in the field effect transistor is the:

1. *gate*
2. source
3. drain
4. base

B-004-4-8.... If you wish to reduce the current flowing in a field effect transistor, you could:

1. *increase the reverse bias voltage*
2. decrease the reverse bias voltage
3. increase the forward bias voltage
4. increase the forward bias gain

B-004-4-9.... The source of a field effect transistor corresponds to the _____ of a bipolar transistor:

1. base
2. *emitter*
3. drain
4. collector

B-004-4-10.... The drain of a field effect transistor corresponds to the _____ of a bipolar transistor:

1. base
2. *collector*
3. source
4. emitter

Finish question section on page 230.

VACUUM TUBES

INTRODUCTION

Vacuum tubes are still popular in high power linear amplifier designs. The elements of a triode vacuum tube are:

- filament or heater   • cathode   • control grid   • plate

The filament or heater is used to raise the cathode temperature which will cause many free electrons to appear on the surface of the cathode. To attract free electrons from the cathode, the plate is made positive in relation to the cathode. In between the plate but closer to the cathode, there is a control grid, which is used to control plate/cathode current. A small control grid voltage is able to control a much larger cathode to plate current. This is amplification.

Vacuum tubes are used today for their higher power capabilities. New advances in the semiconductor industry are eliminating this advantage.

Shown below is a small display of vacuum tubes. The larger tubes are designed for the higher power applications. The small tube is designed to be used in small signal applications.

SUPPLEMENT

hamstudy.com

QUESTIONS

B-004-5-1.... What is one reason a triode vacuum tube might be used instead of a transistor in a circuit?

1. it uses less current
2. *it may be able to handle higher power*
3. it is much smaller
4. it uses lower voltages

B-004-5-2.... Which component can amplify a small signal but must use high voltages?

1. *a vacuum tube*
2. a transistor
3. an electrolytic capacitor
4. a multiple-cell battery

B-004-5-3.... A feature common to triode tubes and transistors is that both:

1. have electrons drifting through a vacuum
2. *can amplify signals*
3. convert electrical energy to radio waves
4. use heat to cause electron movement

B-004-5-4.... In a vacuum tube, the electrode that is operated with the highest positive potential is the _____:

1. filament (heater)
2. *plate*
3. cathode
4. grid

B-004-5-5.... In a vacuum tube, the electrode that is usually a cylinder of wire mesh is the _____:

1. filament (heater)
2. *grid*
3. cathode
4. plate

B-004-5-6.... In a vacuum tube, the electrode that is furthest away from the plate is the _____:

1. grid
2. emitter
3. cathode
4. *filament (heater)*

B-004-5-7.... In a vacuum tube, the electrode that emits electrons is the _____ :

1. *cathode*
2. grid
3. collector
4. plate

B-004-5-8.... What is inside the envelope of a triode tube?

1. argon
2. *a vacuum*
3. air
4. neon

B-004-5-9.... How many grids are there in a triode vacuum tube?

1. two
2. three
3. three plus a filament
4. *one*

AMPLIFIERS

INTRODUCTION

Amplifiers are one of the most common circuits in electronics. Circuitry designed to increase the input level is called an amplifier. The increase in signal level by an amplifier is gain. Amplifiers can be designed to give voltage, current or power gains.

If input waveforms are reproduced faithfully in the output, the amplifier is said to be linear. The linearity of amplifiers is not always perfect. Imperfections in the amplification process appear as distortion.

Some common types of amplifiers are:

AF   - audio frequency amplifier
RF   - radio frequency amplifier
IF   - intermediate frequency amplifier
PA   - power amplifier

Amplifiers can be designed to amplify specific frequencies or ranges of frequencies. For example, an audio frequency amplifier for voice transmissions would be designed to give gain in the 300 to 3000 Hz. frequency range.

SUPPLEMENT

AF amplifiers operate in the human hearing range of 20 to 20,000 Hz. Most AF amplifiers for voice communication are designed to work from 30 to 3000 Hz. Other frequency ranges are filtered out to minimize the transmitter's bandwidth.

IF amplifiers are designed to operate on specific frequencies with bandwidths that accommodate the chosen mode of operation. The most used IF center frequencies are 455 kHz. and 10.7 MHz.

QUESTIONS

B-004-1-1.... A circuit designed to increase the level of its input signal is called:

1. an amplifier
2. a modulator
3. an oscillator
4. a receiver

B-004-1-2.... If an amplifier becomes non-linear, the output signal would:

1. become distorted
2. be saturated
3. cause oscillations
4. overload the power supply

B-004-1-3.... To increase the level of very weak radio signals from an antenna, you would use:

1. an RF oscillator
2. an audio oscillator
3. an RF amplifier
4. an audio amplifier

B-004-1-4.... To increase the level of very weak signals from a microphone you would use:

1. an RF oscillator
2. an RF amplifier
3. an audio amplifier
4. an audio oscillator

B-004-1-5.... The range of frequencies to be amplified by a speech amplifier is typically:

1. 3 to 300 Hz
2. 300 to 1000 Hz
3. 40 to 40000 Hz
4. 300 to 3000 Hz

B-004-1-6.... Which of the following IS NOT amplified by an amplifier?

1. current
2. resistance
3. power
4. voltage

B-004-1-7.... The increase in signal level by an amplifier is called:

1. attenuation
2. amplitude
3. modulation
4. gain

B-004-1-8.... A device with gain has the property of:

1. attenuation
2. oscillation
3. modulation
4. amplification

B-004-1-9.... A device labelled "Gain = 10 dB" is likely to be an:

1. attenuator
2. oscillator
3. audio fader
4. amplifier

B-004-1-10.... Amplifiers can amplify:

1. current, power, or inductance
2. voltage, current, or power
3. voltage, power, or inductance
4. voltage, current, or inductance

B-004-1-11.... Which of the following is not a property of an amplifier?

1. gain
2. linearity
3. distortion
4. loss

RECEIVER FUNDAMENTALS

INTRODUCTION

SENSITIVITY - Sensitivity is the ability of a receiver to process weak signals. The more sensitive the receiver, the weaker the signal it can receive. Noise generated by internal active components limits receiver sensitivity. Natural background atmospheric noise level (cosmic noise) determines how sensitive a receiver is designed. A receiver's RF amplifier(s) design greatly affects sensitivity specifications. The receiver specification for sensitivity is the RF input signal needed to achieve a given signal plus noise to noise ratio.

SELECTIVITY - Selectivity describes the ability to select the desired transmission while excluding all others. Receiver selectivity needs to be tailored to the mode of transmission and this is usually done by selecting an appropriate filter. Filters are usually installed at the intermediate frequency stage but can be designed for other receiver stages.

STABILITY - Stability describes the ability to remain on the selected frequency. High frequency oscillators (HFO or local oscillators) designed for receivers must have excellent electrical, mechanical and thermal characteristics for stable performance.

INTRODUCTION continued

Of the following four modes of operation:
- CW occupies least bandwidth
- RTTY occupies more bandwidth than CW but less than SSB
- SSB voice transmissions occupies approximately 3 kHz
- FM voice transmissions occupies the most bandwidth

When receiving SSB, a notch filter can be used to attenuate narrow band types of interference on the received frequency. Filters used for receiving SSB are commonly designed for a 2.4 kHz passband. The notch filter is a stopband filter which operates within this passband.

Receiving CW when operating close to other stations may require the use of a passband filter with a very narrow bandwidth of 250 Hz. Audio CW filters would be operated with a narrow passband such as 750 to 850 Hz.

QUESTIONS

B-003-10-2.... The figure in a receiver's specifications which indicates its sensitivity is the:

1. *RF input signal needed to achieve a given signal plus noise to noise ratio*
2. audio output in watts
3. bandwidth of the IF in kilohertz
4. number of RF amplifiers

B-003-10-3..... If two receivers of different sensitivity are compared, the less sensitive receiver will produce:

1. a steady oscillator drift
2. more than one signal
3. *less signal or more noise*
4. more signal or less noise

B-003-10-1.... Which list of emission types is in order from the narrowest bandwidth to the widest bandwidth?

1. CW, SSB voice, RTTY, FM voice
2. CW, FM voice, RTTY, SSB voice
3. *CW, RTTY, SSB voice, FM voice*
4. RTTY, CW, SSB voice, FM voice

B-003-10-7.... What kind of filter would you use to attenuate an interfering carrier signal while receiving an SSB transmission?

1. *a notch filter*
2. a band-pass filter
3. an all-pass filter
4. a pi-network filter

B-003-10-9.... A communications receiver has four filters installed in it, respectively designated as 250 Hz, 500 Hz, 2.4 kHz, and 6 kHz. If you were listening to single sideband, which filter would you utilize?

1. 250 Hz
2. *2.4 kHz*
3. 6 kHz
4. 500 Hz

B-003-10-10.... A communications receiver has four filters installed in it, respectively designated as 250 Hz, 500 Hz, 2.4 kHz and 6 kHz. You are copying a CW transmission and there is a great deal of interference. Which one of the filters would you choose?

1. 500 Hz
2. 2.4 kHz
3. 6 kHz
4. *250 Hz*

B-003-10-11.... Selectivity can be placed in the audio stages of a receiver by the utilization of RC active or passive audio filters. If you were to copy CW which of the following bandpasses would you choose?

1. 2100 - 2300 Hz
2. 300 - 2700 Hz
3. *750 - 850 Hz*
4. 100 - 1100 Hz

B-003-10-8.... The three main parameters against which the quality of a receiver is measured are:

1. selectivity, stability and frequency range
2. sensitivity, stability and cross-modulation
3. sensitivity, selectivity and image rejection
4. *sensitivity, selectivity and stability*

RECEIVER FUNDAMENTALS continued

INTRODUCTION

PRODUCT DETECTOR - A product detector is used for single sideband reception. A signal from the beat frequency oscillator (BFO) is injected into the product detector to replace the carrier which was suppressed at the transmitter. The IF output and the BFO signal are mixed in the product detector. The difference frequencies are in the audio range and these are sent to the audio frequency amplifier.

MIXER - The amplified radio signal from the RF amplifier and the radio frequency output from the high frequency oscillator are fed to the mixer. The signals that appear in the output of the mixer are:

(a) the tuned radio frequency

(b) the high frequency oscillator frequency

(c) the frequency that is the sum of (a) plus (b)

(d) the frequency that is the difference between (a) and (b)

INTRODUCTION continued

All four mixer output frequencies will exhibit the characteristics of both input signals. Sum and difference frequencies are good choices for use in an IF amplifier. Most designs would use the difference frequency since the added advantage of a low frequency IF is improved selectivity.

QUESTIONS

B-003-10-4.... Which of the following modes of transmission is usually detected with a product detector?

1. double sideband full carrier
2. frequency modulation
3. pulse modulation
4. *single sideband suppressed carrier*

B-003-10-5.... A receiver designed for SSB reception must have a BFO (beat frequency oscillator) because:

1. it beats with the received carrier to produce the other sideband
2. it reduces the passband of the IF stages
3. *the suppressed carrier must be replaced for detection*
4. it phases out the unwanted sideband signal

B-003-10-6.... A receiver receives an incoming signal of 3.54 MHz. and the local oscillator produces a signal of 3.995 MHz. To which frequency should the IF be tuned?

1. 7.435 MHz.
2. 3.995 MHz.
3. *455 kHz.*
4. 3.54 MHz.

TRANSMITTER FUNDAMENTALS

INTRODUCTION

OSCILLATOR - Oscillators generate radio signals for transmission. Frequency conversion through mixing or frequency multiplication may occur before the radio signal is processed in a linear or power amplifier stage. Variable frequency oscillators are referred to as VFO's.

Oscillator mechanical and electrical stability is very important as small changes in transmitter frequency are especially noticeable in CW transmissions. Good mechanical design, electronic component choice and the use of regulated power sources can eliminate chirpy sounding CW transmissions. Frequency changes caused by thermal changes are called frequency drift.

MODULATION - FM modulators cause oscillators to vary frequency at the same rate as the applied audio. The center or carrier frequency is increased during one half of the modulating signal cycle and decreased during the other half cycle. The frequency deviation is proportional to the amplitude of the modulating signal. In phase modulation (PM), deviation is directly proportional to the instantaneous voltage and frequency of the modulating signal.

In AM, the instantaneous amplitude of the RF carrier envelope increases and decreases at the applied audio rate.

INTRODUCTION continued

POWER AMPLIFIER - Linear power amplifier stages are required for amplitude modulated (AM) modes of emission. Linearity is important as the information being conveyed is contained in the amplitude variations of the transmitted signal.

Linearity is not of great concern in power amplifiers stages for frequency modulated (FM, PM) modes of emission. In these modes, information is conveyed in frequency changes.

Constant continuous carriers without modulation contain no information. A carrier signal that is interrupted for periods equivalent to dashes and dots becomes a CW or Morse code transmission.

Amplifier stages draw or use more power than the power that is contained in the radio frequency signal. This difference in power is dissipated as heat.

Mismatched antenna or transmission lines may present an incorrect load to the power amplifier and may also cause excessive heating in addition to reduced antenna radiation.

QUESTIONS

B-003-11-1.... What does chirp mean?

1. a high-pitched tone which is received along with a CW signal
2. *a small change in a transmitter's frequency each time it is keyed*
3. a slow change in transmitter frequency as the circuit warms up
4. an overload in a receiver's audio circuit whenever CW is received

B-003-11-2..... What can be done to keep a CW transmitter from chirping?

1. add a key-click filter
2. *keep the power supply voltages very steady under transmit load*
3. keep the power supply current very steady under transmit load
4. add a low-pass filter

B-003-11-3.... What circuit has a variable frequency oscillator connected to a buffer/driver and a power amplifier?

1. a crystal controlled AM transmitter
2. *a VFO controlled CW transmitter*
3. a single sideband transmitter
4. a digital radio transmitter

B-003-11-9.... An RF oscillator should be electrically and mechanically stable. This is to ensure that the oscillator does not:

1. become over modulated
2. generate key clicks
3. *drift in frequency*
4. cause undue distortion

B-003-11-4.... What type of modulation system changes the amplitude of an RF wave for the purpose of conveying information?

1. phase modulation
2. *amplitude modulation*
3. amplitude-rectification modulation
4. frequency modulation

B-003-11-5.... In what emission type does the instantaneous amplitude (envelope) of the RF signal vary in accordance with the modulating audio?

1. frequency modulation
2. pulse modulation
3. *amplitude modulation*
4. frequency shift keying

B-003-11-6.... Morse code is usually transmitted by radio as:

1. a series of key clicks
2. a continuous carrier
3. *an interrupted carrier*
4. a voice modulated carrier

B-003-11-7.... A mismatched antenna or transmission line may present an incorrect load to the transmitter. The result may be:

1. loss of modulation in the transmitted signal
2. the driver stage will not deliver power to the final
3. *full power will not be transferred to the antenna*
4. the output tank circuit breaks down

B-003-11-8.... One result of a slight mismatch between the power amplifier of a transmitter and the antenna would be:

1. smaller DC current drain
2. lower modulation percentage
3. *reduced antenna radiation*
4. radiated key clicks

B-003-11-10.... The input power to the final stage of your transmitter is 200 watts and the output is 125 watts. What has happened to the remaining power?

1. *it has been dissipated as heat loss*
2. it has been used to provide greater efficiency
3. it has been used to provide negative feedback
4. it has been used to provide positive feedback

Finish question section on page 228

SINGLE SIDEBAND FUNDAMENTALS

INTRODUCTION

BALANCED MODULATOR & FILTER - In single-sideband transmissions, the carrier is usually suppressed and reinserted at the receiver. The carrier is suppressed in the balanced modulator of a transmitter. The balanced modulator produces a double-sideband signal which is fed to the filter stage. The filter passes the desired sideband (either USB or LSB). The unwanted sideband is attenuated and only the desired single-sideband signal is passed to the mixer stage.

Suppressing the unwanted sideband offers more transmitting efficiency and cuts the required occupied bandwidth in half. Suppressing the carrier also allows for more power to be concentrated into the desired sideband.

SPEECH PROCESSING - Adjusting the microphone gain control for too much sensitivity or using too much speech processing, can overdrive subsequent radio frequency stages in a transmitter. This could cause the transmitted signal to distort and occupy more bandwidth than is necessary. Other stations operating close to the transmitting frequency would likely receive splatter interference from such misadjusted transmitters. Automatic level control (ALC) circuitry is used for maintaining the output of a SSB transmitter at a relatively constant level. The ALC meter should make only slight movements on modulation peaks. ALC controls the peak audio input so that the power amplifier is not overdriven.

INTRODUCTION continued

PEAK ENVELOPE POWER - Peak envelope power is the term used to measure the power rating of a single sideband transmitter. The power of a signal measured at the maximum peak amplitude is the transmitter rating.

BANDWIDTH - The occupied bandwidth of the following radiotelephone emissions are:

- amplitude modulation (AM) - 6 kHz
- double side-band suppressed carrier (DSB) - 6 kHz
- single side-band suppressed carrier (SSB) - 3 kHz

QUESTIONS

B-003-12-5.... In a typical single-sideband phone transmitter, what circuit processes signals from the balanced modulator and sends signals to the mixer?

1. IF amplifier
2. *filter*
3. RF amplifier
4. carrier oscillator

B-003-12-6.... What is one advantage of carrier suppression in a double-sideband phone transmission?

1. *more power can be put into the sidebands for a given power amplifier capacity*
2. only half the bandwidth is required for the same information content
3. greater modulation percentage is obtainable with lower distortion
4. simpler equipment can be used to receive a double sideband suppressed-carrier signal

B-003-12-9.... The purpose of a balanced modulator in a SSB transmitter is to:

1. make sure that the carrier and both sidebands are 180 degrees out of phase
2. ensure that the percentage of modulation is kept constant
3. make sure that the carrier and both sidebands are in phase
4. *suppress the carrier and pass on the two sidebands*

B-003-12-10.... In a SSB transmission, the carrier is:

1. transmitted with one sideband
2. *reinserted at the receiver*
3. inserted at the transmitter
4. of no use at the receiver

B-003-12-11.... The automatic level control (ALC) in a SSB transmitter:

1. reduces the system noise
2. *controls the peak audio input so that the power amplifier is not overdriven*
3. increases the occupied bandwidth
4. reduces transmitter audio feedback

B-003-12-1.... What may happen if an SSB transmitter is operated with the microphone gain set too high?

1. it may cause interference to other stations operating on a higher frequency band
2. it may cause atmospheric interference in the air around the antenna
3. *it may cause splatter interference to other stations operating near its frequency*
4. it may cause digital interference to computer equipment

B-003-12-2.... What may happen if a SSB transmitter is operated with too much speech processing?

1. it may cause digital interference to computer equipment
2. it may cause atmospheric interference in the air around the antenna
3. it may cause interference to other stations operating on a higher frequency band
4. *it may cause audio distortion or splatter interference to other stations operating near its frequency*

B-003-12-7.... What happens to the signal of an overmodulated single-sideband or double-sideband phone transmitter?

1. it becomes stronger with no other effects
2. it occupies less bandwidth with poor high-frequency response
3. it has higher fidelity and improved signal-to-noise ratio
4. *it becomes distorted and occupies more bandwidth*

Finish question section on page 228

FM FUNDAMENTALS

INTRODUCTION

FREQUENCY MODULATION - Audio in an FM transmitter is controlled by the microphone gain and/or deviation control. The modulator causes the oscillator frequency to vary at the same rate as the applied audio.

Deviation control and the microphone gain settings determines how far the frequency will deviate from the center frequency. Transmissions that sound loud and distorted may be an indication that the transmitter frequency deviation is set too high.

If no audio is applied, the output from a FM transmitter will be an unmodulated carrier.

In frequency modulation (FM), the center or carrier frequency is increased during one half of the modulating signal cycle and decreased during the other half cycle. The frequency deviation is proportional to the amplitude of the modulating signal.

In phase modulation (PM), deviation is directly proportional to the instantaneous voltage and frequency of the modulating signal. A common phase modulator is the reactance modulator.

INTRODUCTION continued

Some advantages that FM has over AM are:

- modulation occurs in the low power level stages in both high & low power transmitters
- the final transmitter stages do not need to be linear
- fidelity is superior even when signals are somewhat weak
- capture effect - a signal only has to be 6 dB stronger for the receiver to only hear the strongest signal

Most amateur FM transmitters are designed and adjusted to operate with a deviation of +/- 5 kHz resulting in an occupied bandwidth between 10 and 20 kHz.

FM is generally not used in amateur bands below 28 MHz since the occupied bandwidth would exceed limits specified in Regulations.

QUESTIONS

B-003-13-1.... What may happen if an FM transmitter is operated with the microphone gain or deviation control set too high?

1. it may cause digital interference to computer equipment
2. it may cause atmospheric interference in the air around the antenna
3. it may cause interference to other stations operating on a higher frequency band
4. *it may cause interference to other stations operating near its frequency*

B-003-13-2.... What may your FM hand-held or mobile transceiver do if you shout into its microphone and the deviation adjustment is set too high?

1. *it may cause interference to other stations operating near its frequency*
2. it may cause digital interference to computer equipment
3. it may cause atmospheric interference in the air around the antenna.
4. it may cause interference to other stations operating on a higher frequency band

B-003-13-3.... What can you do if you are told your FM hand-held or mobile transceiver is over deviating?

1. talk louder into the microphone
2. let the transceiver cool off
3. change to a higher power level
4. *talk farther away from the microphone*

B-003-13-4.... What kind of emission would your FM transmitter produce if its microphone failed to work?

1. a frequency-modulated carrier
2. an amplitude-modulated carrier
3. *an unmodulated carrier*
4. a phase-modulated carrier

B-003-13-7.... What is the result of overdeviation in an FM transmitter?

1. *out-of-channel emissions*
2. increased transmitter power
3. increased transmitter range
4. poor carrier suppression

B-003-13-8.... What emission is produced by a reactance modulator connected to an RF power amplifier?

1. multiplex modulation
2. amplitude modulation
3. pulse modulation
4. *phase modulation*

B-003-13-10.... You are transmitting FM on the 2 meter band. Several stations advise you that your transmission is loud and distorted. A quick check with a frequency counter tells you that the transmitter is on the proper frequency. Which of the following is the most probable cause of the distortion?

1. *the frequency deviation of your transmitter is set too high*
2. the power supply output voltage is low
3. the repeater is reversing your sidebands
4. the frequency counter is giving an incorrect reading and you are indeed off frequency

B-003-13-5.... Why is FM voice best for local VHF/UHF radio communications?

1. *it provides good signal plus noise to noise ratio at low RF signal levels*
2. the carrier is not detectable
3. it is more resistant to distortion caused by reflected signals
4. its RF carrier stays on frequency better than the AM modes

Finish question section on page 228

122

DIGITAL FUNDAMENTALS

INTRODUCTION

PACKET RADIO - Amateur voice communications are mainly done with analog transmissions. Digital transmissions are popular for non-voice communications. Digital signal processing in transceivers is also becoming common. Most digital systems convert analog information into a digital format, process the information and then convert it back to an analog format.

Information using two states, on/off, mark/space, 0/1 are digital values. Morse code (CW) was the earliest form of digital radio communication.

Packet radio involves gathering data, processing information into batches of predetermined sizes and sending these pieces of data within a bundle of control information. This bundled information is referred to as a packet. The format is determined by a protocol and currently most amateur stations use a protocol named AX.25. A special purpose device known as a TNC or terminal node controller, processes information in accordance with the protocol. Computer software designed to perform TNC functions is also available.

Most amateurs use a computer as an input/output device in a packet radio system. The use of FM transceivers with the TNC output data channelled through to the microphone input is popular.

INTRODUCTION continued

When a connection is made to a specific station, the computer monitor will indicate connected at both stations. Any communications between the two stations will be error free while the connection is maintained. It is also possible to operate a packet radio station in monitoring mode which will display all messages heard by the receiver and processed by the TNC.

A repeater station that is a digipeater, retransmits data that it receives. Digipeaters are frequently strategically situated to form part of a network of packet radio stations. This permits messaging over long distances.

VHF packet communication systems commonly use a data rate of 1200 baud.

QUESTIONS

B-003-15-1.... What does "connected" mean in an AX.25 packet-radio link?

1. a telephone link is working between two stations
2. a message has reached an amateur station for local delivery
3. a transmitting and receiving station are using a digipeater, so no other contacts can take place until they are finished
4. *a transmitting station is sending data to only one receiving station, it replies that the data is being received correctly*

B-003-15-2.... What does "monitoring" mean on a packet-radio frequency?

1. a member of the Amateur Auxiliary is copying all messages
2. *a receiving station is displaying messages that may not be sent to it, and is not replying to any message*
3. a receiving station is displaying all messages sent to it, and replying that the messages are being received correctly
4. Industry Canada is monitoring all messages

B-003-15-3.... What is a digipeater?

1. a repeater built using only digital electronics parts
2. a repeater that changes audio signals to digital data
3. *a station that retransmits only data that is marked to be retransmitted*
4. a station that retransmits any data that it receives

B-003-15-4.... What does "network" mean in packet radio?

1. *a way of connecting packet radio stations so data can be sent over long distances*
2. a way of connecting terminal-node controllers by telephone so data can be sent over long distances
3. the connections on terminal-node controllers
4. the programming in a terminal-node controller that rejects other callers if a station is already connected

B-003-15-5.... In AX.25 packet-radio operation, what equipment connects to a terminal-node controller?

1. a transceiver and a modem
2. a DTMF keypad, a monitor and a transceiver
3. a DTMF microphone, a monitor and a transceiver
4. *a transceiver, a computer and possibly a GPS receiver*

B-003-15-6.... How would you modulate a 2 meter FM transceiver to produce packet-radio emissions?

1. *connect a terminal-node controller to the transceiver's microphone input*
2. connect a terminal-node controller to interrupt the transceiver's carrier wave
3. connect a keyboard to the transceiver's microphone input
4. connect a DTMF key pad to the transceiver's microphone input

B-003-15-9.... Which of the following terms does not apply to packet radio?

1. ASCII
2. *Baudot*
3. automatic packet reporting system (APRS)
4. AX.25

B-003-15-11.... With a digital communication mode based on a computer sound card, what is the result of feeding too much audio in the transceiver?

1. higher signal-to-noise ratio
2. lower error rate
3. power amplifier overheating
4. *splatter or out-of-channel emissions*

DIGITAL FUNDAMENTALS continued

INTRODUCTION

RTTY or radio-teletype refers to a technique where two states of information are encoded on two separate frequencies referred to as the mark and space.

The difference between the mark and space frequency is the shift. Most amateurs use a 170 Hz. shift. A signalling rate of 45 bauds is common.

The baud is a unit which describes the number of pulses or events per second.

To minimize interference when using RTTY, it is recommended that the minimum frequency separation from other stations should be in the order of 250 to 500 Hz.

INTRODUCTION continued

AMTOR has been coined from Amateur Teleprinting Over Radio. There are two modes of operating. Mode A (ARQ or Automatic Repeat Request) is used for communicating with one other station after contact has been established. Mode B (FEC or Forward Error Correction) is used for making general calls (CQ) or transmitting to multiple stations.

QUESTIONS

B-003-15-7.... When selecting an RTTY transmitting frequency, what minimum frequency separation from a contact in progress should you allow (center to center) to minimize interference?

1. approximately 6 kHz.
2. approximately 3 kHz.
3. *250 to 500 Hz.*
4. 60 Hz.

B-003-15-8.... Digital transmissions use signals called _____ to transmit the states 1 and 0.

1. packet and AMTOR
2. Baudot and ASCII
3. *mark and space*
4. dot and dash

B-003-15-10.... When using AMTOR transmissions, there are two modes that may be utilized. Mode A uses Automatic Repeat Request (ARQ) protocol and is normally used:

1. at all times. Mode B is for test purposes only
2. only when communications have been completed
3. *for communications after contact has been established*
4. when making a general call

POWER SUPPLIES

INTRODUCTION

Radio equipment and accessories need a power source for operation. Power supplies may use transformers or switching technology to change 120/240 volts AC to the desired secondary voltage. Rectifier diodes are used to convert AC into pulsating DC. Diodes allow current to flow in one direction only, namely from cathode to anode. The pulsating DC is made smooth by the filters and regulators control the output voltage and current.

If AC hum is detected in your receiver or your transmitter, it is prudent to troubleshoot the power supply first. It may be possible that a diode has failed or a filter capacitors no longer has the capacity to smooth out DC ripple.

Power supplies are rated by current & voltage. Power ratings can be calculated by using P = E I. For example, a 12 volt, 5 amp power supply operating at full capacity will consume at least 60 watts of power.

Fuse conductors supplying power to your mobile transceivers as close as possible to the battery to prevent overcurrent situations from starting fires. Voltage drops of 0.5 volts or less along this conductor is usually acceptable. Three metres of No. 12 wire, conducting 22 amperes on transmit, will result in a 0.33 voltage drop. (Based on wire specifications of 0.11V drop per metre). No.12 wire will work well.

INTRODUCTION continued

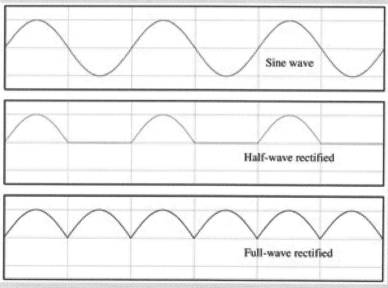

AC power sources are usually 60 Hz. The voltage and current are sine waves.

If the power supply uses a single diode to rectify the sine wave, the circuit is called a half wave rectifier and 60 Hz. pulsating DC is created. A full wave rectifier circuit uses two or four diodes to rectify the sine wave and creates 120 Hz. pulsating DC.

It is easier to filter the direct current from a full wave rectifier because there are twice as many DC pulses.

Credit for diagram - Omegatron - Wikipedia.

127

QUESTIONS

B-003-17-1.... If your mobile transceiver works in your car but not in your home, what should you check first?

1. the power supply
2. the speaker
3. the microphone
4. the SWR meter

B-003-17-2.... What device converts household current to 12 volts DC?

1. a low-pass filter
2. a power supply
3. an RS-232 interface
4. a catalytic converter

B-003-17-3.... Which of these usually needs a high current capacity power supply?

1. an antenna switch
2. a receiver
3. a transceiver
4. an SWR meter

B-003-17-4.... What may cause a buzzing or hum in the signal of an AC-powered transmitter?

1. a bad filter capacitor in the transmitter's power supply
2. using an antenna which is the wrong length
3. energy from another transmitter
4. bad design of the transmitters RF power output circuit

B-003-17-6.... The diode is an important part of a simple power supply. It converts AC to DC, since it:

1. has a high resistance to AC but not to DC
2. allows electrons to flow in only one direction from cathode to anode.
3. has a high resistance to DC but not to AC
4. allows electrons to flow in only one direction from anode to cathode

Finish question section on page 229

B-003-17-5.... A power supply is to supply DC at 12 volts at 5 amperes. The power transformer should be rated higher than:

1. 17 watts
2. 2.4 watts
3. 6 watts
4. 60 watts

B-003-17-7.... To convert AC to pulsating DC, you could use a:

1. transformer
2. capacitor
3. diode
4. resistor

B-003-17-8.... Power-line voltages have been made standard over the years and the voltages generally supplied to homes are approximately:

1. 120 and 240 volts
2. 110 and 220 volts
3. 100 and 200 volts
4. 130 and 260 volts

B-003-17-9.... Your mobile HF transceiver draws 22 amperes on transmit. The manufacturer suggests limiting voltage drop to 0.5 volt and the vehicle battery is 3 metres (10 feet) away. Given the losses below at the current, which minimum wire gauge must you use?

1. number 8, 0.05 V per metre (0.01 V per foot)
2. number 10, 0.07 V per metre (0.02 V per foot)
3. number 14, 0.19 V per metre (0.06 V per foot)
4. number 12, 0.11 V per metre (0.03 V per foot)

B-003-17-10.... Why are fuses needed as close as possible to the vehicle battery when wiring a transceiver directly to the battery?

1. to prevent interference to the vehicle's electronic systems
2. to prevent an overcurrent situation from starting a fire
3. to reduce the voltage drop in the radio's DC supply
4. to protect the radio from transient voltages

REGULATED POWER SUPPLY

INTRODUCTION

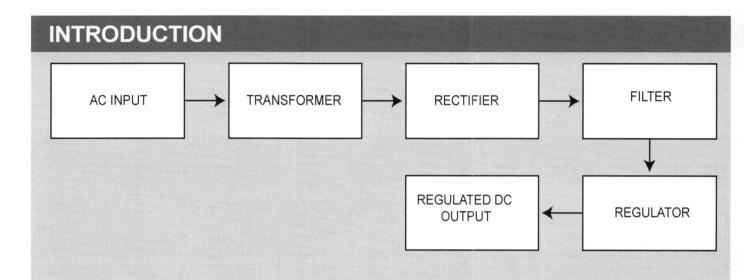

INPUT - The input to a transformer operated regulated power supply is usually a 110 or 220 volts AC power source.

INTRODUCTION continued

TRANSFORMER - The transformer's primary voltage rating matches the input voltage. The secondary winding voltage is chosen to be compatible with the input voltage of the regulator stage. The current and power ratings of the transformer should not be exceeded.

RECTIFIER - The rectifier changes alternating current (AC) to direct current (DC).

FILTER - The filter smooths out the pulsating direct current output from the rectifier. The filter can be comprised of a large capacitor, or a combination of capacitors and inductors (chokes).

REGULATOR - The regulator keeps the desired output voltage constant. Circuitry may also include over-voltage and over-current protection.

OUTPUT - The output of the regulated power supply is connected to devices designed to operate at the power supply rated output voltage. The total current demand of the connected devices should not exceed the current rating of the power supply. Duty cycle may also be a factor.

QUESTIONS

B-003-8-1.... In a regulated power supply, the transformer connects to an external source which is referred to as a _____.

1. regulator
2. *input*
3. filter
4. rectifier

B-003-8-2.... In a regulated power supply, the _____ is between the input and the rectifier.

1. *transformer*
2. output
3. regulator
4. filter

B-003-8-3.... In a regulated power supply, the _____ is between the transformer and the filter.

1. *rectifier*
2. input
3. output
4. regulator

B-003-8-4.... In a regulated power supply, the output of the rectifier is connected to the _____ .

1. *filter*
2. output
3. transformer
4. regulator

B-003-8-5.... In a regulated power supply, the output of the filter connects to the _____.

1. *regulator*
2. transformer
3. rectifier
4. output

B-003-8-6.... In a regulated power supply, the _____ is connected to the regulator.

1. *output*
2. rectifier
3. input
4. transformer

CW TRANSMITTER

INTRODUCTION

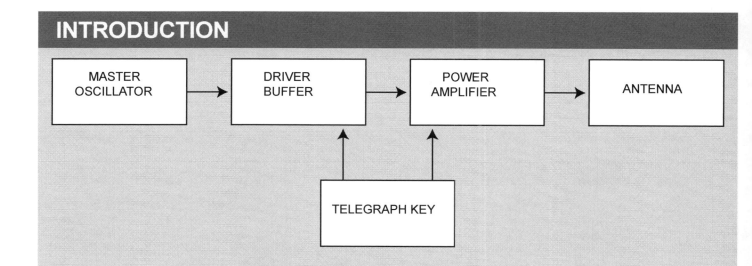

MASTER OSCILLATOR - The master oscillator is the circuit that produces a radio frequency signal on the desired operating frequency. To improve frequency stability, the master oscillator is sometimes operated on a lower but harmonically related frequency.

INTRODUCTION continued

DRIVER BUFFER - The driver buffer stage provides isolation between the master oscillator and the power amplifier resulting in improved frequency stability. This stage also amplifies the desired radio frequency signal to a power level that is adequate to operate the power amplifier.

POWER AMPLIFIER - The power amplifier (PA) uses the output of the driver/buffer. Through amplification, this stage increases the amount of radio frequency power that will be available for transmission to the antenna.

ANTENNA - The antenna radiates the radio frequency signals transmitted by the power amplifier.

TELEGRAPH KEY - The driver/buffer and power amplifier stages are turned off and on by the telegraph key. The master oscillator is operated continuously to maintain a stable frequency output. With this design, the master oscillator would have to be turned off during periods of reception.

POWER SUPPLY (not shown) - Provides the direct current (DC) to operate the first three stages shown.

NOTES

B-003-4-1.... In a CW transmitter, the output from the_____ is connected to the driver/buffer.

1. power amplifier
2. telegraph key
3. *master oscillator*
4. power supply

B-003-4-3.... In a CW transmitter, the _____ is between the master oscillator and the power amplifier.

1. audio amplifier
2. *driver/buffer*
3. power supply
4. telegraph key

B-003-4-5.... In a CW transmitter, the _____ is in between the driver/buffer stage and the antenna.

1. power supply
2. *power amplifier*
3. telegraph key
4. master oscillator

B-003-4-6.... In a CW transmitter, the output of the _____ is transferred to the antenna.

1. *power amplifier*
2. driver/buffer
3. power supply
4. master oscillator

B-003-4-4.... In a CW transmitter, the _____ controls when RF energy is applied to the antenna.

1. master oscillator
2. driver/buffer
3. *telegraph key*
4. power amplifier

B-003-4-2.... In a typical CW transmitter, the _____ is the primary source of direct current.

1. driver buffer
2. *power supply*
3. power amplifier
4. master oscillator

SSB TRANSMITTER

INTRODUCTION

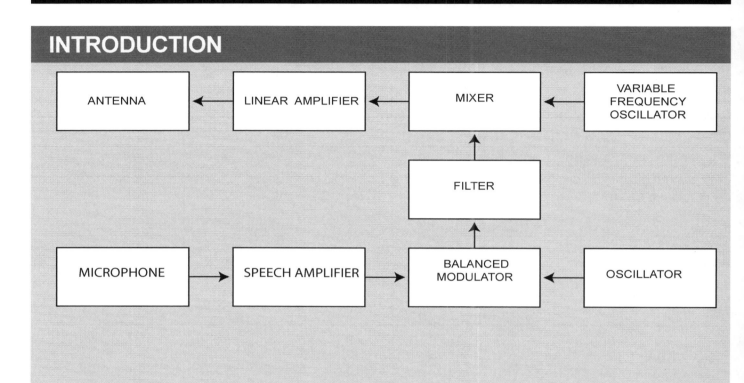

INTRODUCTION Continued

MICROPHONE - The microphone produces small electrical signals in response to sound waves. The design and type of microphone determines the frequency ranges that are converted from sound to electrical signals. The impedance of the microphone should match the input impedance of the speech amplifier.

SPEECH AMPLIFIER - The speech amplifier amplifies the weak audio frequency signals from the microphone to a level sufficient for the modulator.

BALANCED MODULATOR - The balanced modulator is driven by the speech amplifier and radio frequency oscillator. In the output, there will be the sum (USB) & difference (LSB) frequencies while the original radio frequency oscillator signal is greatly attenuated.

RADIO FREQUENCY OSCILLATOR - The radio frequency oscillator produces the radio frequency signal for the balanced modulator.

Continued

QUESTIONS

B-003-6-4.... In a single sideband transmitter, the _____ is connected to the speech amplifier.

1. radio frequency oscillator
2. filter
3. mixer
4. *microphone*

B-003-6-5.... In a single sideband transmitter, the output of the _____ is connected to the balanced modulator.

1. filter
2. variable frequency oscillator
3. *speech amplifier*
4. linear amplifier

B-003-6-2.... In a single sideband transmitter, the output of the _____ is connected to the filter.

1. microphone
2. *balanced modulator*
3. mixer
4. radio frequency oscillator

B-003-6-1.... In a single sideband transmitter, the output of the _____ is connected to the balanced modulator.

1. *radio frequency oscillator*
2. variable frequency oscillator
3. linear amplifier
4. mixer

SSB TRANSMITTER continued

INTRODUCTION continued

FILTER - The filter (or sideband filter) design determines which sideband (USB or LSB) is passed on to the mixer. The desired sideband is passed with little attenuation while rejecting the unwanted sideband.

MIXER - The single sideband signal passed through the filter is mixed with the output of the variable frequency oscillator in the mixer stage to arrive at the final operating frequency.

VARIABLE FREQUENCY OSCILLATOR - The signal from the variable frequency oscillator mixes with the single sideband signal from the filter to produce the final desired range of operating frequencies.

LINEAR AMPLIFIER - The linear amplifier produces the required amount of radio frequency (RF) power intended to be radiated by the antenna.

ANTENNA - The antenna radiates the radio frequency signals transmitted by the linear amplifier.

NOTES

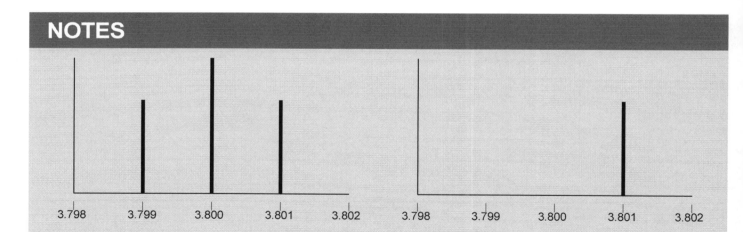

AM transmission showing the carrier, lower sideband (LSB) and the upper sideband (USB). In this case, a 1 kHz tone is transmitted. Note the difference in frequency between the carrier and USB and/or LSB.

SSB transmission of a 1 kHz tone. In this case only the USB is transmitted. To recapture the intelligence contained in the sideband, the receiver's BFO signal replaces the carrier.

QUESTIONS

**B-003-6-3.... In a single sideband transmitter, the
_____ is in between the balanced modulator
and the mixer.**

1. radio frequency oscillator
2. speech amplifier
3. *filter*
4. microphone

**B-003-6-6.... In a single sideband transmitter, the
output of the variable frequency oscillator is
connected to the _____.**

1. antenna
2. balanced modulator
3. linear amplifier
4. *mixer*

**B-003-6-7.... In a single sideband transmitter, the
output of the _____ is connected to the
mixer.**

1. *variable frequency oscillator*
2. radio frequency oscillator
3. linear amplifier
4. antenna

**B-003-6-8.... In a single sideband transmitter, the _____
_____ is in between the mixer and the antenna.**

1. variable frequency oscillator
2. *linear amplifier*
3. balanced modulator
4. radio frequency oscillator

**B-003-6-9.... In a single sideband transmitter, the
output of the linear amplifier is connected to the
_____.**

1. *antenna*
2. filter
3. variable frequency oscillator
4. speech amplifier

SSB/CW RECEIVER

INTRODUCTION

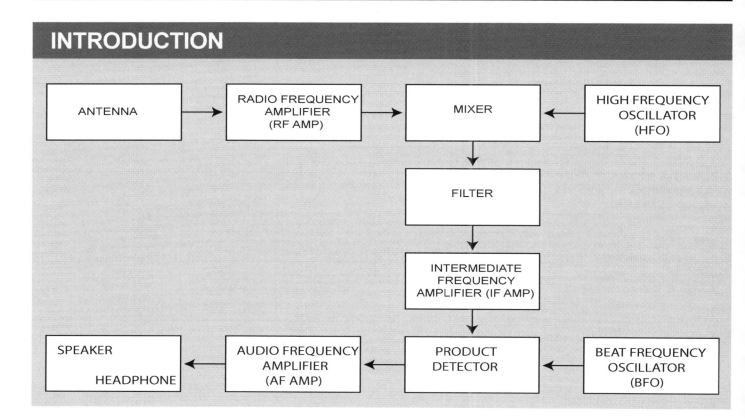

INTRODUCTION Continued

ANTENNA - Radio waves induce small voltages on the antenna. These tiny voltages are conducted to the receiver by a transmission line (eg. coaxial cable). Using antennas which are designed to operate in the desired frequency range improves the ability to capture weak radio waves.

RADIO FREQUENCY AMPLIFIER - This stage amplifies the signals received from the antenna and determines receiver sensitivity, the ability to receive weak signals. Tuned circuits in this stage also contribute to receiver selectivity, the ability to discriminate between signals of different frequencies. RF amplifier stages also improves a receiver ability to reject images.

MIXER - The amplified radio signal from the RF amplifier and the radio frequency output from the high frequency oscillator are fed to the mixer. The characteristics of the two input signals are reflected in all four output signals. The signals that appear in the output of the mixer are:

    (a) the tuned radio frequency   (b) the high frequency oscillator frequency
    (c) the frequency that is the sum of (a) plus (b)
    (d) the frequency that is the difference between (a) and (b)

Continued

QUESTIONS

B-003-5-1.... In a single sideband and CW receiver, the antenna is connected to the _____.

1. product detector
2. local oscillator
3. intermediate frequency amplifier
4. *radio frequency amplifier*

B-003-5-2.... In a single sideband and CW receiver, the output of the _____ is connected to the mixer.

1. filter
2. intermediate frequency amplifier
3. audio frequency amplifier
4. *radio frequency amplifier*

B-003-5-3.... In a single sideband and CW receiver, the _____ is connected to the radio frequency amplifier and the local oscillator.

1. beat frequency oscillator
2. product detector
3. *mixer*
4. filter

B-003-5-4.... In a single sideband and CW receiver, the output of the _____ is connected to the mixer.

1. intermediate frequency amplifier
2. *local oscillator*
3. beat frequency oscillator
4. product detector

SSB/CW RECEIVER continued

INTRODUCTION continued

HIGH FREQUENCY OSCILLATOR - The high frequency oscillator (HFO or local oscillator) generates a radio frequency signal that is used in the mixer. This is normally a variable frequency oscillator in order to receive a range of frequencies. The design and quality of this stage will greatly determine receiver stability.

FILTER - The filter contributes greatly to receiver selectivity. Filters are usually designed to pass the difference frequency from the mixer stage while greatly attenuating the other three signals present in the mixer output.

INTERMEDIATE FREQUENCY AMPLIFIER - The intermediate frequency (IF) amplifier in one or more stages, provides amplification and contributes towards receiver selectivity.

PRODUCT DETECTOR - To receive SSB signals where the carrier has been suppressed, it is necessary to re-insert a carrier to recover the original modulation. The product detector is the stage which accepts the outputs of the intermediate frequency amplifier and the beat frequency oscillator to complete the recovery of transmitted information.

INTRODUCTION Continued

For CW, the beat frequency oscillator is adjusted to create a difference frequency which results in a tone pleasing to the operator. For example, to listen to morse code with a tone of 1000 Hz., the frequency of the beat frequency oscillator needs to be adjusted 1000 Hz. above or below the intermediate frequency. If the receiver IF operates at 455 kHz, then the BFO frequency should be either 456 or 454 kHz.

BEAT FREQUENCY OSCILLATOR - The beat frequency oscillator (BFO) signal replaces the carrier that was suppressed in a SSB transmission. The difference frequency between the IF and the BFO makes it possible to hear morse code signals as a tone.

AUDIO FREQUENCY AMPLIFIER - The audio frequency amplifier produces the required audio frequency power output to operate speakers and headphones.

SPEAKER & HEADPHONES - Speakers and headphones convert electrical energy to sound.

QUESTIONS

B-003-5-5.... In a single sideband and CW receiver, the _____ is in between the mixer and the intermediate frequency amplifier.

1. *filter*
2. radio frequency amplifier
3. beat frequency oscillator
4. product detector

B-003-5-6.... In a single sideband and CW receiver, the_____ is in between the filter and product detector.

1. *intermediate frequency amplifier*
2. audio frequency amplifier
3. beat frequency oscillator
4. radio frequency amplifier

B-003-5-7.... In a single sideband and CW receiver, the _____ output is connected to the audio frequency amplifier.

1. *product detector*
2. local oscillator
3. beat frequency oscillator
4. intermediate frequency amplifier

B-003-5-8.... In a single sideband and CW receiver, the output of the _____ is connected to the product detector.

1. mixer
2. *beat frequency oscillator*
3. radio frequency amplifier
4. audio frequency amplifier

B-003-5-9.... In a single sideband and CW receiver, the _____ is connected to the output of the product detector.

1. intermediate frequency amplifier
2. *audio frequency amplifier*
3. local oscillator
4. radio frequency amplifier

B-003-5-10.... In a single sideband and CW receiver, the _____ is connected to the output of the audio frequency amplifier.

1. *speaker or headphones*
2. mixer
3. radio frequency amplifier
4. beat frequency oscillator

HF STATION COMPONENTS

INTRODUCTION

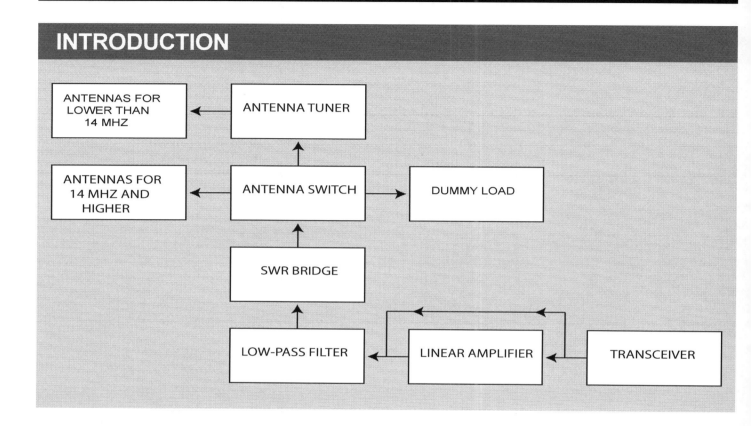

INTRODUCTION Continued

TRANSCEIVER - A combination HF transmitter and receiver. Numerous models are available.

LINEAR AMPLIFIER - The amplifier is used to increase the power output of the transceiver to the desired power level. Most amplifiers have a built in by-pass switch.

LOW-PASS FILTER - Low pass filters are designed to pass frequencies below the design cut-off frequency and attenuate frequencies higher than the cut-off frequency.

HF stations commonly use low pass filters with a design cut-off frequency just above 30 MHz. These are ideal for reducing or eliminating harmonic energy from the transmitter or amplifier.

Antenna transmission lines exhibit leakage. Therefore, it is important to connect the low-pass filter as close to the linear amplifier or transceiver as possible. This will reduce the likelihood of the higher unwanted frequencies being radiated from the transmission line.

Continued

QUESTIONS

B-003-1-1.... A low-pass filter in an HF station is most effective when connected:

1. as close as possible to the transceiver output
2. as close as possible to the antenna tuner output
3. as close as possible to the antenna
4. midway between the transceiver and antenna

B-003-1-2.... A low-pass filter in an HF station is most effective when connected:

1. as close as possible to the antenna
2. as close as possible to the antenna tuner output
3. as close as possible to the linear amplifier input
4. as close as possible to the linear amplifier output

B-003-1-3 .... In designing an HF station, which component would you use to reduce the effects of harmonic radiation?

1. dummy load
2. low-pass filter
3. antenna switch
4. SWR bridge

HF STATION COMPONENTS continued

INTRODUCTION

SWR BRIDGE - The Standing Wave Ratio bridge provides an indication of reflected power expressed as a ratio compared to the forward power. This meter is very useful for determining the effectiveness of antenna impedance matching.

Most modern transceivers need the SWR ratio to be 2.0:1 or less for normal operation. If the SWR reads high, it may be that the wrong antenna has been selected or that the antenna system is defective.

ANTENNA SWITCH - The antenna switch is a handy device that connects after the low-pass filter. It can be used to select the dummy load, a particular antenna such as a Yagi or tuned dipoles and also the antenna tuner. The better quality antenna switches ground the unselected antennas and devices.

ANTENNA TUNER - These are also referred to as a tuner, match box or transmatch. Antenna tuners are used to match impedances between transmitters and antennas to maximize the power transfer.

INTRODUCTION continued

DUMMY LOAD - These are resistive devices (normally 50 ohms) used instead of antennas during periods of tuning and testing to minimize the possibility of causing interference to other amateur stations. The RF power is dissipated in the dummy load and converted to heat. The power dissipation and duty cycle rating of dummy loads should not be exceeded to prevent overheating and/or permanent damage.

ANTENNAS FOR 14 MHZ & HIGHER - The mono-band and tri-band yagi is commonly used for bands between 10 and 20 meters. Most transceivers are able to operate on any amateur frequency within these bands with low SWR.

ANTENNAS FOR LOWER THAN 14 MHZ - Dipole, inverted V and long wire antennas are popular for amateur bands between 30 and 160 meters. The bandwidths of these antennas are narrow and therefore are frequently used in conjunction with an antenna tuner.

NOTE - Higher quality modern transceivers may already have built in band-pass filtering, SWR metering and antenna switching. The configuration shown in the block diagram is one of many options.

B-003-1-4.... Which component in an HF station is the most useful for determining the effectiveness of the antenna system?

1. *SWR bridge*
2. antenna switch
3. linear amplifier
4. dummy load

B-003-1-5.... Of the components in an HF station, which component would normally be connected closest to the antenna, antenna tuner and dummy load?

1. transceiver
2. low-pass filter
3. *antenna switch*
4. SWR bridge

B-003-1-6.... Of the components in an HF station, which component would be used to match impedances between the transceiver and antenna?

1. *antenna tuner*
2. antenna switch
3. dummy load
4. SWR bridge

B-003-1-8.... In an HF station, the antenna tuner is usually used for matching the transceiver with:

1. *most antennas when operating below 14 MHz.*
2. most antennas when operating above 14 MHz.
3. mono-band Yagi type antennas
4. tri-band Yagi antennas

B-003-1-9.... In an HF station, the antenna tuner is commonly used:

1. with most antennas when operating above 14 MHz
2. to tune into dummy loads
3. to tune low pass filters
4. *with most antennas when operating below 14 MHz*

B-003-1-7.... In an HF station, which component is temporarily connected in the tuning process or for adjustments to the transmitter?

1. SWR bridge
2. low pass filter
3. antenna tuner
4. *dummy load*

FM TRANSMITTER

INTRODUCTION

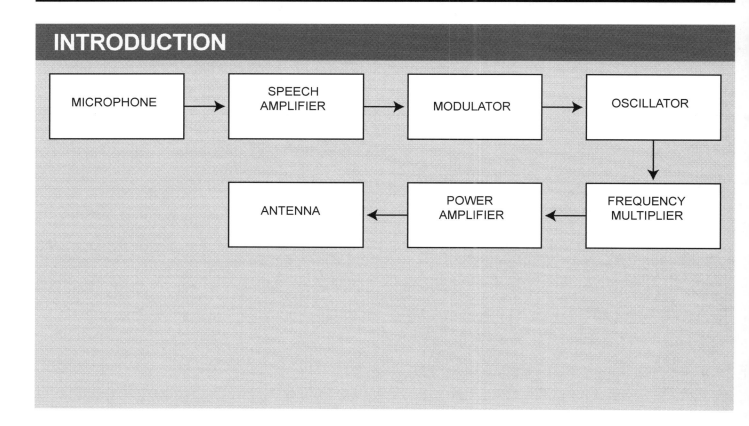

INTRODUCTION Continued

MICROPHONE - The microphone produces small electrical signals in response to sound waves. The design and type of microphone determines the frequency ranges that are converted from sound to electrical signals. The impedance of the microphone should match the input impedance of the speech amplifier.

SPEECH AMPLIFIER - The speech amplifier amplifies the weak audio frequency signals from the microphone to a level sufficient for the modulator.

MODULATOR - The modulator causes the oscillator to vary its radio frequency output at audio frequency rates. The result is that the audio frequencies from the microphone are super-imposed on the radio frequency signal produced by the oscillator.

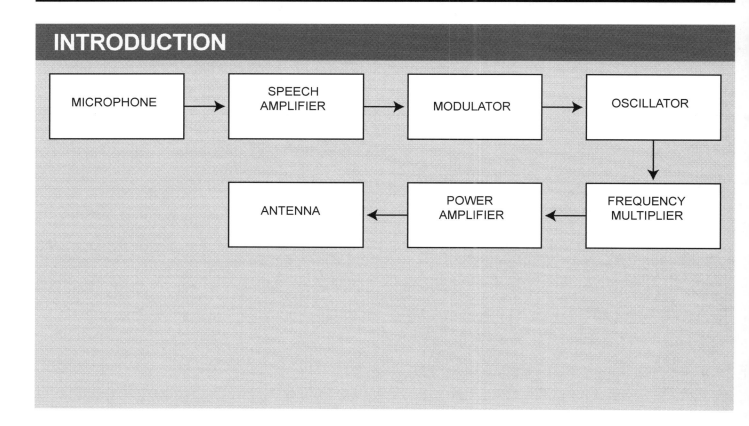Continued

QUESTIONS

B-003-2-2.... In a frequency modulation transmitter, the microphone is connected to the:

1. modulator
2. power amplifier
3. *speech amplifier*
4. oscillator

B-003-2-1.... In a frequency modulation transmitter, the input to the speech amplifier is connected to the:

1. *microphone*
2. modulator
3. power amplifier
4. frequency multiplier

B-003-2-3.... In a frequency modulation transmitter, the _____ is in between the speech amplifier and the oscillator.

1. *modulator*
2. power amplifier
3. microphone
4. frequency multiplier

B-003-2-4.... In a frequency modulation transmitter, the _____ is located between the modulator and the frequency multiplier.

1. speech amplifier
2. *oscillator*
3. power amplifier
4. microphone

FM TRANSMITTER continued

INTRODUCTION continued

OSCILLATOR - The oscillator produces a radio frequency signal. In FM transmitters, the oscillator frequency is usually much lower than the final operating frequency but is harmonically related.

FREQUENCY MULTIPLIER - The frequency multiplier circuit converts the oscillator frequency to a harmonically related final operating frequency. For example: If the oscillator operates at 12.21 MHz and the multiplier circuit is designed so that the output frequency is 12 times greater than the input frequency, the output frequency will be (12.21 X 12) 146.52 MHz.

POWER AMPLIFIER - The power amplifier amplifies the radio frequency signals produced to the desired power level.

ANTENNA - The antenna radiates the radio frequency signals transmitted by the power amplifier.

The diagram below shows an audio frequency signal modulating a radio frequency carrier. The carrier frequency varies but amplitude is constant. Only the frequency modulated signal is transmitted and the audio signal is recovered by receiver circuitry. Diagram is public domain.

SUPPLEMENT

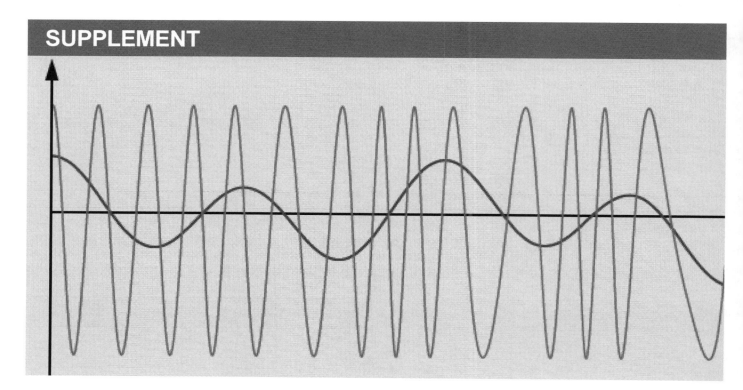

QUESTIONS

B-003-2-5.... In a frequency modulation transmitter, the _____ is located between the oscillator and the power amplifier.

1. frequency multiplier
2. microphone
3. speech amplifier
4. modulator

B-003-2-6.... In a frequency modulation transmitter, the _____ is located between the frequency multiplier and the antenna.

1. modulator
2. power amplifier
3. speech amplifier
4. oscillator

B-003-2-7.... In a frequency modulation transmitter, the power amplifier output is connected to the:

1. frequency multiplier
2. microphone
3. antenna
4. modulator

FM RECEIVER

INTRODUCTION

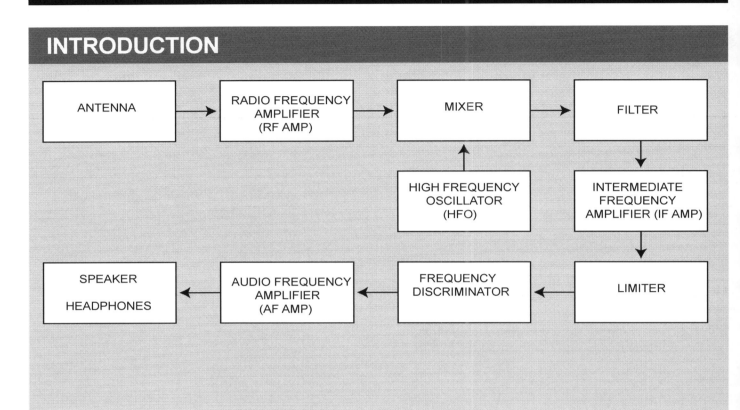

INTRODUCTION Continued

ANTENNA - Radio waves induce small voltages on the antenna. These tiny voltages are conducted to the receiver by a transmission line (eg. coaxial cable). Antennas designed for the correct purpose and frequency range make it possible to capture the weakest radio waves.

RADIO FREQUENCY AMPLIFIER - The RF amplifier amplifies the signals received from the antenna and increases receiver sensitivity, the ability to receive weak signals. Tuned circuits in this stage also contribute to a receivers selectivity, the ability to discriminate between signals of different frequencies. RF amplifier stages also improves a receivers ability to reject images.

HIGH FREQUENCY OSCILLATOR - The high frequency oscillator (HFO and also known as the local oscillator) generates a radio frequency signal that is used in the mixer. If this is a fixed frequency oscillator, the receiver will only be capable of reception on one frequency. If a variable frequency oscillator is used, it will be possible to receive a range of frequencies. The design and quality of this stage will greatly determine a receivers stability.

Continued

QUESTIONS

**B-003-3-1.... In a frequency modulation receiver, the
_____ is connected to the input of the radio
frequency amplifier.**

1. mixer
2. frequency discriminator
3. *antenna*
4. limiter

**B-003-3-2.... In a frequency modulation receiver,
the_____ is in between the antenna and
the mixer.**

1. audio frequency amplifier
2. local oscillator
3. intermediate frequency amplifier
4. *radio frequency amplifier*

**B-003-3-3.... In a frequency modulation receiver, the
output of the local oscillator is fed to the:**

1. radio frequency amplifier
2. limiter
3. antenna
4. *mixer*

**B-003-3-4.... In a frequency modulation receiver, the
output of the _____ is connected to the
mixer.**

1. frequency discriminator
2. intermediate frequency amplifier
3. speaker or headphones
4. *local oscillator*

FM RECEIVER continued

INTRODUCTION continued

MIXER - The amplified radio signal from the RF amplifier and the radio frequency output from the high frequency oscillator are fed to the mixer. The 4 signals that appear in the output of the mixer are:

      (a) the tuned radio frequency
      (b) the high frequency oscillator (local oscillator) frequency
      (c) the frequency that is the sum of (a) plus (b)
      d) the frequency that is the difference between (a) and (b)

The characteristics of the two input signals will be exhibited on all four mixer output signals.

FILTER - The filter contributes greatly to receiver selectivity. These filters pass the difference frequency from the mixer stage while greatly attenuating the other three signals present in the mixer output.

INTERMEDIATE FREQUENCY AMPLIFIER - The intermediate frequency (IF) amplifier in one or more stages provides amplification and also contributes towards receiver selectivity.

INTRODUCTION Continued

LIMITER - The limiter removes amplitude variations from the signal that may have been produced by noise or other interference.

FREQUENCY DISCRIMINATOR - Discriminator circuits demodulate FM signals. Frequency variations at audio rates are separated from the radio signal and are converted into audio frequencies (AF).

AUDIO FREQUENCY AMPLIFIER - The audio frequency amplifier produces the required audio frequency power output to operate speakers or headphones.

SPEAKER & HEADPHONES - Speakers and headphones convert electrical energy to sound.

QUESTIONS

B-003-3-5.... In a frequency modulation receiver, the _____ is in between the mixer and the intermediate frequency amplifier.

1. *filter*
2. limiter
3. frequency discriminator
4. radio frequency amplifier

B-003-3-6.... In a frequency modulation receiver, the _____ is located between the filter and the limiter.

1. local oscillator
2. *intermediate frequency amplifier*
3. mixer
4. radio frequency amplifier

B-003-3-7.... In a frequency modulation receiver, the _____ is in between the intermediate frequency amplifier and the frequency discriminator.

1. filter
2. local oscillator
3. *limiter*
4. radio frequency amplifier

B-003-3-8.... In a frequency modulation receiver, the _____ is located between the limiter and the audio frequency amplifier.

1. intermediate frequency amplifier
2. speaker or headphones
3. local oscillator
4. *frequency discriminator*

B-003-3-9.... In a frequency modulation receiver, the _____ is located between the speaker or headphones and the frequency discriminator.

1. limiter
2. intermediate frequency amplifier
3. radio frequency amplifier
4. *audio frequency amplifier*

B-003-3-10.... In a frequency modulation receiver, the _____ connects to the audio frequency amplifier output.

1. intermediate frequency amplifier
2. frequency discriminator
3. *speaker or headphones*
4. limiter

DIGITAL SYSTEM

INTRODUCTION

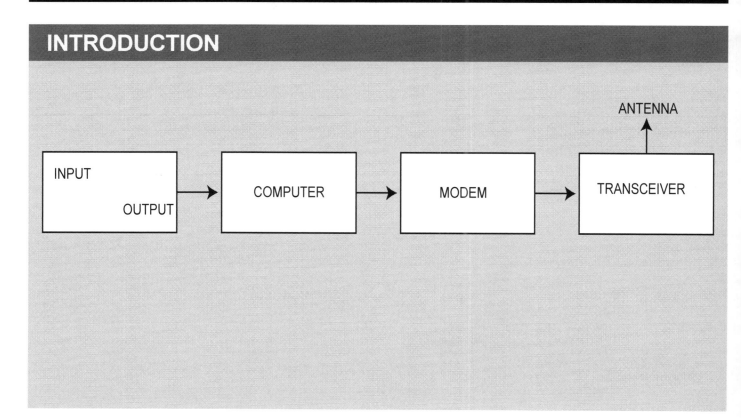

BLOCK DIAGRAM

INPUT/OUTPUT - An input device could be the keyboard and the output device could be the monitor or printer. Input can also be considered as the information sent and the output could be considered as the processed information received.

COMPUTER - The computer is the device which manages input, output and instructions. For example, the input could be typing, the output could be received information displayed on a monitor and the instructions could be software.

MODEM - The modem accepts instructions from the computer and processes incoming and outgoing data from the transceiver or computer.

TRANSCEIVER - The transceiver creates the data path between two digital communication systems.

QUESTIONS

B-003-7-1.... In an amateur digital radio system, the _____ interfaces with the computer.
1. antenna
2. power supply
3. transceiver
4. *input/output*

B-003-7-2.... In an amateur digital radio system, the modem is connected to the _____.

1. amplifier
2. *computer*
3. antenna
4. input/output

B-003-7-3.... In an amateur digital radio system, the transceiver is connected to the _____.

1. *modem*
2. computer
3. scanner
4. input/output

B-003-7-4.... In an amateur digital radio digital system, the audio connections of the modem/sound card are connected to the _____.

1. input/output
2. *transceiver*
3. scanner
4. antenna

B-003-7-5.... In an amateur digital radio system, the modem function is often performed by the computer _____.

1. serial port
2. *sound card*
3. keyboard
4. scanner

SPURIOUS EMISSIONS & KEY-CLICKS

INTRODUCTION

Spurious emissions or spurs are usually caused by mixing processes inside radio apparatus. These can occur above and below the transmitting frequency. Correct transmitter alignment and adjustment minimizes harmful spurious emissions. In some situations, it may be necessary to install additional filters at the transmitter.

Parasitic oscillations are unwanted emissions from a transmitter that may occur on any frequency. Correct transmitter alignment and adjustment is necessary to avoid parasitic emissions.

Key-clicks are a product of fast rise and decay times of the transmitter carrier when the Morse code key is operated. This can create interference for other stations operating on nearby frequencies.

Key-click filters can be made with a capacitor and choke at the Morse key. These components change the rise and decay times of the transmitted carrier. Most new modern transceivers incorporate this type of filtering in their design and external filters seldom need to be used.

If your transmitter is producing key-clicks, troubleshoot the keying filter and the functioning of later stages.

SUPPLEMENT

The three dots and dash represents the letter "V" in morse code. The top row represents the radio frequency output from a transmitter exhibiting very fast rise and decay times.

The bottom row represents the output of a transmitter with key-click filtering incorporated in the circuitry. The transmitter output signal is wave-shaped which results in the reduction or elimination of key-clicks.

B-008-3-2.... If someone tells you that signals from your hand-held transceiver are interfering with other signals on a frequency near yours, what could be the cause?

1. your hand-held is transmitting spurious emissions
2. you need a power amplifier for your hand-held
3. your hand-held has a chirp from weak batteries
4. you need to turn the volume up on your hand-held

B-008-3-3.... If your transmitter sends signals outside the band where it is transmitting, what is this called?

1. side tones
2. transmitter chirping
3. spurious emissions
4. off-frequency emissions

B-008-3-4.... What problem may occur if your transmitter is operated without the cover and other shielding in place?

1. it may transmit a weak signal
2. it may radiate spurious emissions
3. it may interfere with other stations operating near its frequency
4. it may transmit a chirpy signal

B-008-3-5.... In Morse code transmission, local RF interference (key-clicks) is produced by:

1. the making and breaking of the circuit at the Morse key
2. frequency shifting caused by poor voltage regulation
3. the power amplifier, and is caused by high frequency parasitic oscillations
4. poor waveshaping caused by a poor voltage regulator

B-008-3-8.... What should you do if you learn your transmitter is producing key-clicks?

1. check the keying filter and the functioning of later stages
2. turn the receiver down
3. regulate the oscillator supply voltage
4. use a choke in the RF power output

B-008-3-1.... How can you prevent key-clicks?

1. by increasing power
2. by using a key-click filter
3. by using a better power supply
4. by sending CW more slowly

B-008-3-6.... Key-clicks, heard from a Morse code transmitter at a distant receiver, are the result of:

1. power supply hum modulating the carrier
2. too sharp rise and decay times of the keyed carrier
3. sparks emitting RF from the key contacts
4. changes in oscillator frequency on keying

B-008-3-7.... In a Morse code transmission, broad bandwidth RF interference (key-clicks) heard at a distance is produced by:

1. shift in frequency when keying the transmitter
2. sparking at the key contacts
3. sudden movement in the receiver loudspeaker
4. poor shaping of the waveform

B-008-3-9.... A parasitic oscillation:

1. is generated by parasitic elements of a Yagi beam
2. does not cause any radio interference
3. is produced in a transmitter oscillator stage
4. is an unwanted signal developed in a transmitter

B-008-3-10.... Parasitic oscillations in the RF power amplifier stage of a transmitter may be found:

1. at high or low frequencies
2. on harmonic frequencies
3. at high frequencies only
4. at low frequencies only

B-008-3-11.... Transmitter RF amplifiers can generate parasitic oscillations:

1. on VHF frequencies only
2. on the transmitter fundamental frequency
3. above or below the transmitter frequency
4. on harmonics of the transmitter frequency

HARMONICS & SPLATTER

INTRODUCTION

Harmonic emissions are spurious emissions that are exact multiples of fundamental frequencies.

Transmitters with over driven stages can have the strongest harmonics. The proper adjustment and alignment of transmitters is the first step in minimizing harmonics. Low-pass filters can also be installed as close to the transmitter as practical to reduce or eliminate harmonic radiation.

Some examples of how harmonics can create interference are:

- Transmitter operates on 7.125 MHz and has a third harmonic on 21.375 MHz. If a multi-band antenna is being used, the third harmonic could be efficiently radiated and cause interference to users of the 15 meter band.

- Transmitter operates 28.500 MHz and has a second harmonic on 57.000 MHz. A TV in the area could be receiving channel 2 (54-60 MHz). The harmonic signal could cause strong interference.

- Transmitter operates 21.200 MHz and has a third harmonic on 63.600 MHz. A TV in the area could be receiving channel 3 (60-66 MHz). The harmonic signal could cause strong interference.

INTRODUCTION continued

- Operating a SSB transmitter that is flat topping (driving the final amplifier into non-linear operation) can cause strong harmonics to be generated. The most appropriate remedy for this is to reduce excessive drive, which may include reduction of microphone gain.

Splatter is comprised of radio frequency emissions outside of the necessary bandwidth. The prime cause of splatter is overly-processed voice signals. Monitoring the modulation levels of transmitters is important to prevent overmodulation of a transmitter.

Low pass filters are used with HF transmitters. The power rating of the filter should be greater than that of the transmitter output. The antenna, transmission line and transmitter should also be properly impedance matched. Many new transmitter designs have good harmonic rejection in which case external filtering may not be required.

QUESTIONS

B-008-4-1.... If a neighbour reports television interference on one or two channels only when you transmit on 15 metres, what is probably the cause of the interference?

1. deionization of the ionosphere near your neighbour's TV antenna
2. *harmonic radiation from your transmitter*
3. TV receiver front-end overload
4. too much low-pass filtering on the transmitter

B-008-4-2.... What is meant by harmonic radiation?

1. *unwanted signals at frequencies which are multiples of the fundamental (chosen) frequency*
2. unwanted signals that are combined with a 60 Hz hum
3. unwanted signals caused by sympathetic vibrations from a nearby transmitter
4. signals which cause skip propagation to occur

B-008-4-10.... An interfering signal from a transmitter is found to have a frequency of 57 MHz (TV channel 2 is 54 - 60 MHz). This signal could be the:

1. crystal oscillator operating on its fundamental
2. seventh harmonic of an 80 metre transmission
3. *second harmonic of a 10 metre transmission*
4. third harmonic of a 15 metre transmission

B-008-4-5.... If you are told your station was heard on 21375 kHz, but at the time you were operating on 7125 kHz, what is one reason this could happen?

1. your transmitter's power-supply filter choke was bad
2. you were sending CW too fast
3. *your transmitter was radiating harmonic signals*
4. your transmitter's power-supply filter capacitor was bad

B-008-4-9.... In a transmitter, excessive harmonics are produced by:

1. low SWR
2. resonant circuits
3. a linear amplifier
4. *overdriven stages*

B-008-4-7.... Your amateur radio transmitter appears to be creating interference to the television on channel 3 (60-66 MHz) when you are transmitting on the 15 metre band. Other channels are not affected. The most likely cause is:

1. no high-pass filter on the TV
2. a bad ground at the transmitter
3. *harmonic radiation from the transmitter*
4. front-end overload of the TV

B-008-4-3.... Why is harmonic radiation from an amateur station not wanted?

1. it uses large amounts of electric power
2. it may cause sympathetic vibrations in nearby transmitters
3. it may cause auroras in the air
4. *it may cause interference to other stations and may result in out-of-band signals*

B-008-4-4.... What type of interference may come from a multi-band antenna connected to a poorly tuned transmitter?

1. parasitic excitation
2. *harmonic radiation*
3. intermodulation
4. auroral distortion

B-008-4-6.... What causes splatter interference?

1. keying a transmitter too fast
2. signals from a transmitter's output circuit are being sent back to its input circuit
3. the transmitting antenna is the wrong length
4. *overmodulating a transmitter*

B-008-4-8.... One possible cause of TV interference by harmonics from an SSB transmitter is from "flat topping" - driving the power amplifier into non-linear operation. The most appropriate remedy for this is:

1. retune transmitter output
2. use another antenna
3. *reduce microphone gain*
4. reduce oscillator output

Finish question section on page 235

FILTERS

INTRODUCTION

LOW-PASS filters allow lower frequencies to pass while attenuating higher frequencies. These are commonly used with HF transmitters to pass frequencies under 30 MHz and to attenuate the higher harmonic frequencies. Most are designed for an input/output impedance of 50 ohms and are connected as close to the transmitter as practical.

HIGH-PASS filters allow higher frequencies to pass while attenuating lower frequencies. This type of filter is installed as close to TV tuners as practical to overcome front-end-overload interference from nearby HF transmitters. It is important to use filters with input/output impedances that match the impedance of the TV tuner and antenna or cable.

BAND-PASS filters allow the design frequencies to pass with very little attenuation while the RF energy above and below are blocked.

BAND-REJECT filters attenuate a range of frequencies while allowing higher and lower frequencies to to pass with very little attenuation..

INTRODUCTION continued

Antenna systems for television reception and antenna systems for the amateur station should be correctly impedance matched for best performance. It is also good practice to provide as much distance separation as practical between the two antenna systems.

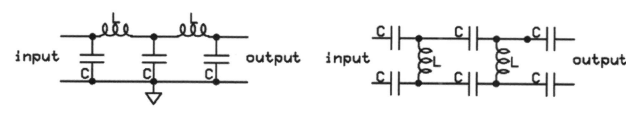

A design for a low-pass filter is shown directly above. The input connects to the amateur's transmitter and the output to the antenna feed line.

This is a circuit diagram for a high-pass filter. The input connects to the television antenna cable and the output to the television antenna terminals.

QUESTIONS

B-008-5-1.... What type of filter might be connected to an amateur HF transmitter to cut down on harmonic radiation?

1. a low-pass filter
2. a key-click filter
3. a high-pass filter
4. a CW filter

B-008-5-2.... Why do modern HF transmitters have a built-in low-pass filter in their RF output circuits?

1. to reduce fundamental radiation
2. to reduce low frequency interference to other amateurs
3. to reduce harmonic radiation
4. to reduce RF energy below a cut off point

B-008-5-4.... What should be the impedance of a low-pass filter as compared to the impedance of the transmission line into which it is inserted?

1. substantially lower
2. twice the transmission line impedance
3. about the same
4. substantially higher

B-008-5-5.... In order to reduce the harmonic output of a high frequency (HF) transmitter, which of the following filters should be installed at the transmitter?

1. key-click
2. high-pass
3. rejection
4. low-pass

B-008-5-6.... To reduce harmonic output from a high frequency transmitter, you would put a _____ in the transmission line as close to the transmitter as possible:

1. high-pass filter
2. low-pass filter
3. band-reject filter
4. wave trap

B-008-5-3.... What circuit blocks RF energy above and below a certain limit?

1. a high-pass filter
2. an input filter
3. a low-pass filter
4. a band-pass filter

B-008-5-7.... To reduce energy from an HF transmitter getting into a television set, you would place a _____ as close to the TV as possible:

1. low-pass filter
2. wave trap
3. band reject filter
4. high-pass filter

B-008-5-8.... A band-pass filter will:

1. attenuate high frequencies but not low
2. pass frequencies each side of a band
3. allow only certain frequencies through
4. stop frequencies in a certain band

B-008-5-9.... A band-reject filter will:

1. allow only two frequencies through
2. pass frequencies each side of a band
3. pass frequencies below 100 MHz
4. stop frequencies each side of a band

B-008-5-10.... A high-pass filter would normally be fitted:

1. between microphone and speech amplifier
2. at the Morse key or keying relay in a transmitter
3. at the antenna terminals of the TV receiver
4. between transmitter output and transmission line

B-008-5-11.... A low-pass filter suitable for a high frequency transmitter would:

1. pass audio frequencies above 3 kHz
2. attenuate frequencies below 30 MHz
3. attenuate frequencies above 30 MHz
4. pass audio frequencies below 3 kHz

STATION ACCESSORIES

INTRODUCTION

AUDIO DEVICES - The microphone used for voice communication should be chosen for characteristics such as:

> impedance
> output voltage
> frequency response
> noise cancelling properties

Some small portable transceivers use speakers for dual purposes. Firstly to change audio signals into sound and secondly to change sound into electrical signals.

The VOX (voice operated switch) is an electronic switch which automatically switches a transceiver from receive to transmit by merely speaking into the microphone.

Speech processing is used to increase the level of audio power for transmission. Most HF transceivers have speech processors to accomplish this. When these are properly adjusted, signal intelligibility improves.

INTRODUCTION continued

MORSE CODE KEYER - Electronic keyers are designed to automatically form dots and dashes from the operation of manually operated keyer paddles. Many newer high end HF transceivers have electronic keyer circuitry built in.

ANTENNA SWITCH - Antenna switches provide easy selection of antennas, tuners and dummy loads. Most are manually controlled but fully automated switching systems controlled by transceivers are becoming more common. Transceivers use electronic antenna switching to provide isolation between the transmitter and receiver. Normally the unused unit is disabled by the same switching system. This type of switching allows a single antenna to be used for transmitting and receiving.

DUMMY LOAD - A dummy load is a resistive device (normally 50 ohms) used in place of antennas for tuning and testing. Using dummy loads for this purpose helps to minimize the possibility of causing interference to other amateur stations. The RF signal is dissipated and converted to heat. The power dissipation and duty cycle rating of dummy loads should not be exceeded. Overheating can cause permanent damage.

QUESTIONS

B-003-14-2.... Where would you connect a microphone for voice operation?

1. to a transceiver
2. to a power supply
3. to an antenna switch
4. to an antenna

B-003-14-3.... What would you connect to a transceiver for voice operation?

1. a receiver audio filter
2. a terminal-voice controller
3. a microphone
4. a splatter filter

B-003-14-5.... What is the circuit called which causes a transmitter to automatically transmit when an operator speaks into its microphone?

1. VXO
2. VCO
3. VFO
4. VOX

B-003-14-6.... What is the reason for using a properly adjusted speech processor with a single-sideband phone transmitter?

1. it improves signal intelligibility at the receiver
2. it reduces average transmitter power requirements
3. it reduces unwanted noise pickup from the microphone
4. it improves voice frequency fidelity

B-003-14-7.... If a single-sideband phone transmitter is 100% modulated, what will a speech processor do to the transmitter's power?

1. it will add nothing to the output Peak Envelope Power (PEP)
2. it will increase the output PEP
3. it will decrease the peak power output
4. it will decrease the average power output

B-003-14-8.... When switching from receive to transmit:

1. the receiver should be muted
2. the transmit oscillator should be turned off
3. the receiving antenna should be connected
4. the power supply should be off

B-003-14-11.... Which of the following components could be used as a dynamic microphone?

1. crystal earpiece
2. resistor
3. loudspeaker
4. capacitor

B-003-14-1.... What do many amateurs use to help form good Morse code characters?

1. an electronic keyer
2. a key-operated on/off switch
3. a notch filter
4. a DTMF keypad

B-003-14-9.... A switching system to enable the use of one antenna for a transmitter and receiver should also:

1. ground the antenna on receive
2. disable the unit not being used
3. switch between meters
4. disconnect the antenna tuner

B-003-14-10.... An antenna changeover switch in a transmitter-receiver combination is necessary:

1. so that one antenna can be used for transmitter and receiver
2. to change antennas for operation on other frequencies
3. to prevent RF currents entering the receiver circuits
4. to allow more than one transmitter to be used

Finish question section on page 229.

ELECTROMAGNETIC WAVES

INTRODUCTION

A ground-wave, also known as a surface wave, is that part of the signal that is affected by the earth's surface. Ground-wave coverage decreases as operating frequencies increase.

A direct wave is a line-of-sight wave which travels directly from the transmitting antenna to the receiving antenna.

A tropospheric wave is a wave that is redirected by the troposphere.

A sky-wave, also known as ionospheric wave, is a wave that is refracted by the ionosphere. Very long distance communications are possible with this type of propagation.

Below is a diagram of an electromagnetic wave radiated from a vertical antenna. The wave consists of an electric field and a magnetic field. In the diagram the electric field is vertically polarized. The magnetic field is horizontally polarized.

SUPPLEMENT

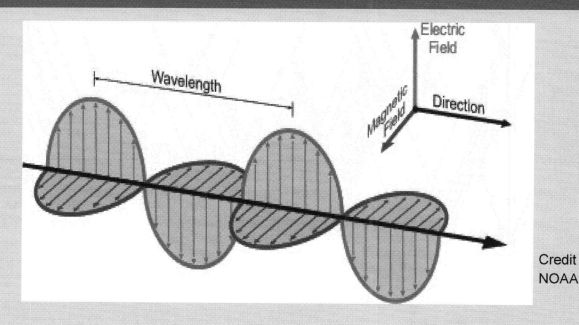

Credit
NOAA

QUESTIONS

B-007-1-1.... What type of propagation usually occurs from one hand-held VHF transceiver to another nearby?

1. tunnel propagation
2. sky-wave propagation
3. auroral propagation
4. *line-of-sight propagation*

B-007-1-2.... How does the range of sky-wave propagation compare to ground-wave propagation?

1. it is much shorter
2. it is about the same
3. it depends on the weather
4. *it is much longer*

B-007-1-3.... When a signal is returned to earth by the ionosphere, what is this called?

1. tropospheric propagation
2. ground-wave propagation
3. *sky-wave propagation*
4. earth-moon-earth propagation

B-007-1-4.... How are VHF signals propagated within the range of the visible horizon?

1. *by direct wave*
2. by sky-wave
3. by plane wave
4. by geometric wave

B-007-1-5.... Sky-wave is another name for:

1. *ionospheric wave*
2. tropospheric wave
3. ground-wave
4. inverted wave

B-007-1-6.... That portion of the radiation which is directly affected by the surface of the earth is called:

1. tropospheric wave
2. ionospheric wave
3. inverted wave
4. *ground-wave*

B-007-1-7.... At lower HF frequencies, radiocommunication out to 200 km is made possible by:

1. troposphere
2. skip wave
3. ionosphere
4. *ground wave*

B-007-1-8.... The distance travelled by ground waves:

1. depends on the maximum usable frequency
2. is more at higher frequencies
3. *is less at higher frequencies*
4. is the same for all frequencies

B-007-1-9.... The radio wave which follows a path from the transmitter to the ionosphere and back to earth is known correctly as the:

1. F layer
2. surface wave
3. *ionospheric wave*
4. skip wave

B-007-1-10.... Reception of high frequency (HF) radio waves beyond 4000 km is generally made possible by:

1. ground-wave
2. *ionospheric wave*
3. skip wave
4. surface wave

IONOSPHERE

INTRODUCTION

Solar radiation causes some electrons from air molecules to be dislodged. This process, which creates ions and free electrons, is called ionization. Maximum ionization occurs at midday. Minimum ionization occurs shortly before dawn. The region where ionization occurs is called the ionosphere. The ionosphere extends from approximately 50 to 600 Km above earth. The ionosphere has distinct layers. These are D, E and F.

The D layer exists during daylight hours and rapidly disappears after sunset. This layer is closest to the earth, typically between 75 and 95 Km. Transmissions below 5 MHz are effectively absorbed by this layer.

The E layer, generally between 95 and 150 Km above earth, also diminishes greatly during the night. Absorption of signals is less than that of the D layer. Normally this layer reflects frequencies lower than 10 MHz. During sporadic E events, this layer can reflect frequencies up to 50 MHz and higher.

The F layer, above 150 km, is the most important layer for HF communications. During the night this is one broad layer. In the daytime the F layer forms two distinct F1 and F2 layers. The F2 layer is the highest and is responsible for the longest distance radio wave propagation.

SUPPLEMENT

GREY-LINE - The region between daylight and darkness can be very efficient for north/south propagation of HF radio signals. The best time to experience this effect is near the local sunrise or sunset.

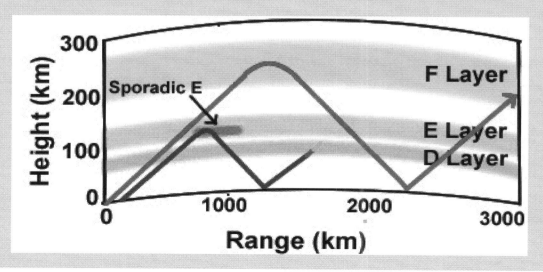

Credit NPS

QUESTIONS

B-007-2-1.... What causes the ionosphere to form?

1. lightening ionizing the outer atmosphere
2. *solar radiation ionizing the outer atmosphere*
3. release of fluorocarbons into the atmosphere
4. temperature changes ionizing the outer atmosphere

B-007-2-2....What type of solar radiation is most responsible for ionization in the outer atmosphere?

1. microwave
2. ionized particles
3. *ultraviolet*
4. thermal

B-007-2-3.... Which ionospheric region is closest to the earth?

1. the E region
2. *the D region*
3. the F region
4. the A region

B-007-2-4.... Which region of the ionosphere is the least useful for long distance radio-wave propagation?

1. the F2 region
2. the F1 region
3. *the D region*
4. the E region

B-007-2-5.... What two sub-regions of the ionosphere exist only in the daytime?

1. troposphere and stratosphere
2. electrostatic and electromagnetic
3. *F1 and F2*
4. D and E

B-007-2-6.... When is the ionosphere most ionized?

1. dawn
2. midnight
3. *midday*
4. dusk

B-007-2-7.... When is the ionosphere least ionized?

1. *shortly before dawn*
2. just after noon
3. just after dusk
4. shortly before midnight

B-007-2-8.... Why is the F2 region mainly responsible for the longest distance radio-wave propagation?

1. because it exists only at night
2. because it is the lowest ionospheric region
3. because it does not absorb radio waves as much as other ionospheric regions
4. *because it is the highest ionospheric region*

B-007-2-9.... What is the main reason the 160, 80 and 40 metre amateur bands tend to be useful only for short-distance communications during daylight hours?

1. because of auroral propagation
2. *because of D region absorption*
3. because of magnetic flux
4. because of a lack of activity

B-007-2-10.... During the day, one of the ionospheric layers splits into two parts called:

1. D1 & D2
2. E1 & E2
3. A & B
4. *F1 & F2*

B-007-2-11.... The position of the E layer in the ionosphere is:

1. below the D layer
2. *below the F layer*
3. sporadic
4. above the F layer

SKIP

INTRODUCTION

Skip occurs when a signal enters the ionosphere at an angle and refracts back towards earth.

Skip zone is an area which is too far away for ground-wave propagation, but too close for sky-wave propagation.

Skip distance is the distance from the transmitter to the nearest point where the sky wave returns to the earth. The higher the refracting layer, the further the skip distance. The lower the angle of radiation from an antenna, the greater the skip distance. Multiple hops are not uncommon. A single hop can be as far as:

- F2 layer - 4000 Km (2500 miles)
- E layer - 2000 Km (1250 miles)

When designing your HF station, consider using antennas that have the lowest angle of radiation. This will enhance your ability to communicate with far away stations (DX).

SUPPLEMENT

The diagram shows signals penetrating the ionosphere to travel into space. Also shown are radio signals reflected back to the ground. The area where no signals are being returned to ground is the skip zone.

Credit - C. Oler

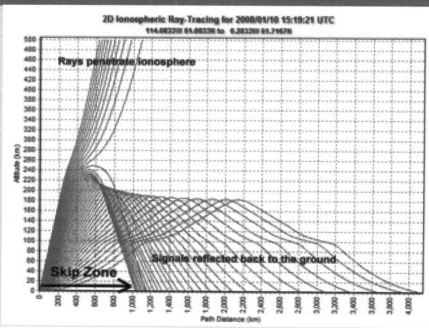

QUESTIONS

B-007-3-1.... What is a skip zone?

1. an area which is too far away for ground-wave or sky-wave propagation
2. an area covered by sky-wave propagation
3. *an area which is too far away for ground-wave propagation, but too close for sky-wave propagation*
4. an area covered by ground-wave propagation

B-007-3-2.... What is the maximum distance along the earth's surface that is normally covered in one hop using the F2 region?

1. none, the F2 region does not support radio-wave propagation
2. 2000 km (1250 miles)
3. *4000 km (2500 miles)*
4. 300 km (190 miles)

B-007-3-3.... What is the maximum distance along the earth's surface that is normally covered in one hop using the E region?

1. *2000 km (1250 miles)*
2. 300 km (190 miles)
3. 4000 km (2500 miles)
4. none, the E region does not support radio-wave propagation

B-007-3-4.... Skip zone is:

1. a zone of silence caused by lost sky waves
2. a zone between any two refracted waves
3. *a zone between the end of the ground wave and the point where the first refracted wave returns to earth*
4. a zone between the antenna and the return of the first refracted wave

B-007-3-5.... The distance to Europe from your location is approximately 5000 km. What sort of propagation is most likely to be involved?

1. sporadic "E"
2. back scatter
3. *multihop*
4. tropospheric scatter

B-007-3-6.... For radio signals, the skip distance is determined by the:

1. power fed to the power amplifier
2. angle of radiation
3. type of transmitting antenna used
4. *height of the ionosphere and the angle of radiation*

B-007-3-7.... The distance from the transmitter to the nearest point where the sky wave returns to the earth is called the:

1. skip zone
2. angle of radiation
3. *skip distance*
4. maximum usable frequency

B-007-3-8.... Skip distance is:

1. *the minimum distance reached by a signal after one reflection by the ionosphere*
2. the maximum distance reached by a signal after one reflection by the ionosphere
3. the minimum distance reached by a ground-wave signal
4. the maximum distance a signal will travel by both a ground-wave and reflected wave

B-007-3-9.... Skip distance is a term associated with signals from the ionosphere. Skip effects are due to:

1. *reflection and refraction from the ionosphere*
2. selective fading of local signals
3. high gain antennas being used
4. local cloud cover

B-007-3-10.... The skip distance of a sky wave will be greatest when the:

1. polarization is vertical
2. ionosphere is most densely ionized
3. *angle between the ground and the radiation is smallest*
4. signal given out is strongest

Finish question section on page 234.

CRITICAL & MAXIMUM USABLE FREQUENCY

INTRODUCTION

Critical frequency - the highest frequency directed upward vertically that will be reflected back to earth.

Maximum usable frequency (MUF) - the highest frequency that will be reflected by the ionosphere.

Optimum working frequency (OWF) - the strongest frequency reflected by the ionosphere and is usually slightly lower than the MUF.

The amount of radiation received from the sun causes the MUF to vary. On HF, if sudden ionospheric disturbances make communications difficult, continued operation on a higher band may be possible.

Each HF amateur band offers different propagation characteristics. For example, the 20 metre band supports worldwide communications during daylight hours at any point in the solar cycle. On the other hand, communications on the 160 and 80 metre bands are generally the most difficult during summer daytime hours.

INTRODUCTION continued

On the higher HF bands, it is also possible to listen for beacons from all parts of the world. Beacon reception will give a good indication as to whether or not communications to that particular part of the world is probable. Check these frequencies - 14.100, 18.110, 21.150, 24.930, & 28.200 MHz.

Radio coverage for some HF bands :

        160 meters - nighttime - regional
        80 meters - daytime - provincial
        80 meters - nighttime - regional
        40 meters - daytime - regional
        40 meters - nighttime - continental
        20 meters - daytime/nighttime - continental & world wide
        15 meters - daytime/nighttime - continental & world wide
        10 meters - daytime - continental & world wide
        10 meters - nighttime - local

QUESTIONS

B-007-6-1....What happens to signals higher in frequency than the critical frequency?

1. they pass through the ionosphere
2. they are absorbed by the ionosphere
3. their frequency is changed by the ionosphere to be below the maximum usable frequency
4. they are reflected back to their source

B-007-6-2.... What causes the maximum usable frequency to vary?

1. the amount of radiation received from the sun, mainly ultraviolet
2. the temperature of the ionosphere
3. the speed of the winds in the upper atmosphere
4. the type of weather just below the ionosphere

B-007-6-3....What does maximum usable frequency mean?

1. the lowest frequency signal that will reach its intended destination
2. the highest frequency signal that is most absorbed by the ionosphere
3. the lowest frequency signal that is most absorbed by the ionosphere
4. the highest frequency signal that will reach its intended destination

B-007-6-4.... What can be done at an amateur station to continue HF communications during a sudden ionospheric disturbance?

1. try a higher frequency band
2. try the other sideband
3. try a different antenna polarization
4. try a different frequency shift

B-007-6-9....Communication on the 80 metre band is generally most difficult during:

1. daytime in summer
2. evening in winter
3. evening in summer
4. daytime in winter

Finish question section on page 234.

B-007-6-5.... What is one way to determine if the maximum usable frequency (MUF) is high enough to support 28 MHz propagation between your station and western Europe?

1. listen for signals from 10 metre beacon frequency
2. listen for signals from 20 metre beacon stations
3. listen for signals from 39 metre broadcast stations
4. listen for WWVH time signals on 20 MHz

B-007-6-6.... What usually happens to radio waves with frequencies below the maximum usable frequency (MUF) when they are sent into the ionosphere?

1. they are changed to a frequency above the MUF
2. they are completely absorbed by the ionosphere
3. they are bent back to the earth
4. they pass through the ionosphere

B-007-6-7....At what point in the solar cycle does the 20 metre band usually support worldwide propagation during daylight hours?

1. only at the minimum point of the solar cycle
2. only at the maximum point of the solar cycle
3. at any point in the solar cycle
4. at the summer solstice

B-007-6-8....If we transmit a signal, the frequency of which is so high we no longer receive a reflection from the ionosphere, the signal frequency is above the:

1. skip distance
2. maximum usable frequency
3. speed of light
4. sun spot frequency

B-007-6-11....During summer daytime, which bands are the most difficult for communications beyond ground wave?

1. 160 and 80 metres
2. 40 metres
3. 30 metres
4. 20 metres

HAMSTUDY Basic 2017/2018

FADING

INTRODUCTION

Frequencies lower than 4.5 MHz are usually absorbed by the ionization of the D region during the daytime.

The polarization of transmitted signals can change when they pass through magnetic fields (Faraday rotation) or when they are reflected or refracted from the ionosphere. This makes antenna polarization on HF bands relatively unimportant.

When parts of the radio wave follow different paths during propagation, it can cause phase differences at the receiver. This effect is called selective fading. It is more pronounced for signals with wide bandwidths. SSB & CW signals are relatively unaffected because the occupied bandwidth is narrow.

Small changes in the ionosphere cause variations of signal strength. Ionospheric storms can cause complete fade out of sky-wave signals.

SUPPLEMENT

Listen to short wave broadcasting to experience the effects of fading. Distant AM broadcast stations will fade and peak throughout late evenings and during the night.

171

QUESTIONS

B-007-4-1.... What effect does the D region of the ionosphere have on lower frequency HF signals in the daytime?

1. it absorbs the signals
2. it bends the radio waves out into space
3. it refracts the radio waves back to earth
4. it has little or no effect on 80 metre radio waves

B-007-4-2.... What causes distant AM broadcast and 160 metre ham band stations not to be heard during daytime hours?

1. the presence of ionized clouds in the E region
2. the ionization of the D region
3. the splitting of the F region
4. the weather below the ionosphere

B-007-4-3.... Two or more parts of the radio wave follow different paths during propagation and this may result in phase differences at the receiver. This "change" at the receiver is called:

1. fading
2. baffling
3. absorption
4. skip

B-007-4-4.... A change or variation in signal strength at the antenna, caused by differences in path lengths, is called:

1. absorption
2. fluctuation
3. path loss
4. fading

B-007-4-5.... When a transmitted radio signal reaches a station by a one-hop and two-hop skip path, small changes in the ionosphere can cause:

1. consistent fading of received signal
2. consistently stronger signals
3. variations in signal strength
4. a change in the ground-wave signal

B-007-4-6.... The usual effect of ionospheric storms is to:

1. produce extreme weather changes
2. cause a fade-out of sky-wave signals
3. prevent communications by ground-wave
4. increase the maximum usable frequency

B-007-4-7.... On the VHF and UHF bands, polarization of the receiving antenna is very important in relation to the transmitting antenna, yet on HF bands it is relatively unimportant . Why is that so?

1. the ionosphere can change the polarization of the signal from moment to moment
2. the ground-wave and the sky-wave continually shift the polarization
3. anomalies in the earth's magnetic field produce a profound effect on HF polarization but not on VHF & UHF frequencies
4. greater selectivity is possible with HF receivers making changes in polarization redundant

B-007-4-8.... What causes selective fading?

1. phase differences between radio wave components of the same transmission, as experienced at the receiving station
2. small changes in beam heading at the receiving station
3. time differences between the receiving and transmitting stations
4. large changes in the height of the ionosphere at the receiving station ordinarily occurring shortly before sunrise and sunset

B-007-4-9.... How does the bandwidth of a transmitted signal affect selective fading?

1. it is the same for both wide and narrow bandwidths
2. it is more pronounced at wide bandwidths
3. only the receiver bandwidth determines the selective fading effect
4. it is more pronounced at narrow bandwidths

Finish question section on page 234.

SOLAR ACTIVITY

INTRODUCTION

Solar radiation determines the density of ionospheric layers which affects long range radio communications. Solar radiation varies daily, seasonally and with the 11 year cycle of solar activity.

Appearances of dark spots or sunspots on the sun have been observed for many decades. When sunspot numbers are high, frequencies in HF bands and those up to 40 MHz or higher can be usable for long-distance communications.

Solar flares on the surface of the sun can releases huge amounts of electromagnetic radiation as well as ejecting particles. These can have dramatic effects on the ionosphere and can distort the earth's geomagnetic field, causing a geomagnetic storm.

Another method of gauging solar activity is the solar flux index. This is an intensity measurement of radio noise or energy coming from the sun. Canadian radio telescopes at Ottawa & Penticton measure the solar flux intensity daily using the frequency 2800 MHz. (10.7 cm).

Solar flux units are shown on the graph below. Solar flux measurements and observed sunspot numbers have trend lines that are correlated.

SUPPLEMENT

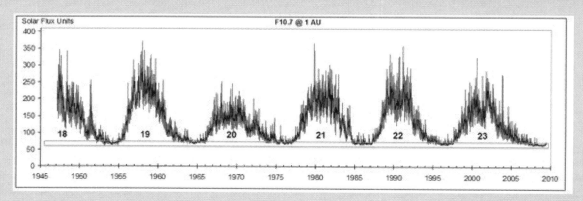

Credit - Svalgaard

QUESTIONS

B-007-5-1.... How do sunspots change the ionization of the atmosphere?

1. the more sunspots there are, the greater the ionization
2. the more sunspots there are, the less the ionization
3. unless there are sunspots, the ionization is zero
4. they have no effect

B-007-5-2.... How long is an average sunspot cycle?

1. 17 years
2. 5 years
3. 11 years
4. 7 years

B-007-5-3.... What is solar flux?

1. a measure of the tilt of the earth's ionosphere on the side toward the sun
2. the number of sunspots on the side of the sun facing the earth
3. the radio energy emitted by the sun
4. the density of the sun's magnetic field

B-007-5-4.... What is the solar flux index?

1. another name for the American sunspot number
2. a measure of solar activity that compares daily readings with results from the last six months
3. a measure of solar activity that is taken at a specific frequency
4. a measure of solar activity that is taken annually

B-007-5-7.... When sunspot numbers are high, how is propagation affected?

1. frequencies up to 40 MHz or even higher become usable for long distance communication
2. high frequency radio signals are absorbed
3. frequencies up to 100 MHz or higher are normally usable for long distance communication
4. high frequency radio signals become weak and distorted

B-007-5-5.... What influences all radio communication beyond ground-wave or line-of-sight ranges?

1. the F2 region of the ionosphere
2. the F1 region of the ionosphere
3. solar radiation
4. lunar tidal effects

B-007-5-6.... Which two types of radiation from the sun influence propagation?

1. subaudible and audio frequency emissions
2. polar region and equatorial emissions
3. infrared and gamma-ray emissions
4. electromagnetic and particle emissions

B-007-5-8.... All communication frequencies throughout the spectrum are affected in varying degrees by the:

1. ionosphere
2. aurora borealis
3. atmospheric conditions
4. sun

B-007-5-9.... Average duration of a solar cycle is:

1. 11 years
2. 3 years
3. 6 years
4. 1 year

B-007-5-10.... The ability of the ionosphere to reflect high frequency radio signals depends on:

1. the amount of solar radiation
2. the power of the transmitted signal
3. the receiver sensitivity
4. upper atmosphere weather conditions

B-007-5-11.... HF radio propagation cycles have a period of approximately 11:

1. years
2. months
3. days
4. centuries

DUCTING & SPORADIC E

INTRODUCTION

SURFACE WAVE - also known as ground wave. The electromagnetic wave propagates near the surface of the earth.

TROPOSPHERIC WAVE - also known as direct wave. These electromagnetic waves propagate within the troposphere which extends from the earth's surface to approximately 10 Km above the earth. Temperature inversions can cause tropospheric ducting of radio signals in the 50 to 450 MHz range. Communications for up to 800 Km is possible with tropospheric ducting.

IONOSPHERIC WAVE - also known as sky wave. An electromagnetic wave is affected by the following ionospheric layers:

> D - The height of this layer extends between 50 and 100 Km and exists during daylight hours. This layer tends to absorb the lower HF frequencies and is not suitable for refracting signals.

> F - The height of this layer extends between 150 and 400 Km. During night time hours this is usually a single layer but in the daytime it can split into two layers called F1 and F2. This layer has the greatest effect on HF propagation.

INTRODUCTION continued

> E - This layer can exist between the D and F layers in the daytime and usually dissipates at night. It has limited effect on wave propagation. Occasionally dense ionization patches form in the E layer. These patches are referred to as SPORADIC E and can propagate 10, 6 and 2 meter band signals. The 6 meter band is where this type of propagation is most frequently observed.

AURORAL EFFECTS - HF and VHF signals can be reflected by northern lights. For best results, orient antennas north and use narrow modes such as CW. Signal distortion will be noted, even on SSB. Auroral activity occurs at E region heights.

SOLAR FLARES - Occasionally, solar flare eruptions greatly affect D layer ionization. When this happens, HF communications can be completely disrupted because of D region absorption. This normally only affects the side of the earth that faces the sun. Disturbed propagation conditions can last from a few minutes to days.

QUESTIONS

B-007-7-1.... Which ionospheric region most affects sky-wave propagation on the 6 metre band?

1. the F2 region
2. the F1 region
3. *the E region*
4. the D region

B-007-7-2.... What effect does tropospheric bending have on 2 metre radio waves?

1. it causes them to travel shorter distances
2. it garbles the signal
3. it reverses the sideband of the signal
4. *it lets you contact stations farther away*

B-007-7-3.... What causes tropospheric ducting of radio waves?

1. lightning between the transmitting and receiving stations
2. an aurora to the north
3. *a temperature inversion*
4. a very low pressure area

B-007-7-4.... That portion of the radiation kept close to the earth's surface due to bending in the atmosphere is called the:

1. inverted wave
2. ground wave
3. *tropospheric wave*
4. ionospheric wave

B-007-7-5.... What is a sporadic-E condition?

1. *patches of dense ionization at E region height*
2. partial tropospheric ducting at E region height
3. variations in E region height caused by sunspot variations
4. a brief decrease in VHF signals caused by sunspot variations

B-007-7-6.... On which amateur frequency band is the extended distance propagation effect of sporadic E most often observed?

1. 160 metres
2. 20 metres
3. *6 metres*
4. 2 metres

B-007-7-7.... In the northern hemisphere, in which direction should a directional antenna be pointed to take maximum advantage of auroral propagation?

1. east
2. *north*
3. west
4. south

B-007-7-8.... Where in the ionosphere does auroral activity occur?

1. at F region height
2. *at E region height*
3. in the equatorial band
4. at D region height

B-007-7-9.... Which emission mode is best for auroral propagation?

1. RTTY
2. FM
3. *CW*
4. SSB

B-007-7-10.... Excluding enhanced propagation modes, what is the approximate range of normal VHF tropospheric propagation?

1. 2400 Km (1500 miles)
2. *800 Km (500 miles)*
3. 3200 Km (2000 miles)
4. 1600 Km (1000 miles)

Finish question section on page 234.

SCATTER PROPAGATION

INTRODUCTION

Scatter propagation can be used when normal sky wave propagation places two stations within each other's skip zones. Scatter is generally weak since only part of the energy is scattered. It exhibits rapid flutter with a hollow sounding distortion or wavering sound. The distortion occurs when energy is scattered into the skip zone through several radio-wave paths. Some of the common types of scatter are:

TROPOSPHERIC SCATTER - Changes in the index of refraction of the lower atmosphere can cause HF & VHF signals to be scattered making communications in the 100 to 500 Km range possible. At much higher frequencies (above 1 GHz), scattering from rain, snow and clouds can also occur.

IONOSPHERIC SCATTER - D layer forward scatter peaks during mid-day hours when ionization is greatest. Maximum communication distance is in the 2000 Km range. Signals are weak. This mode of communication suits the 10 and 6 meter bands best.

METEOR SCATTER - Ionization from trails left by meteors in the E layer region are effective in reflecting 30 to 100 MHz signals. The 6 metre ham band is the best band for meteor scatter communications. Effective range is 800 to 2300 Km.

INTRODUCTION continued

AURORAL EFFECTS - Higher HF and VHF signals can be reflected by northern lights. Best results occur when stations point antennas north and narrow modes (CW/SSB) are used. Effective range is up to 2300 Km.

BACKSCATTER - This occurs when some of the transmitted signal is reflected back into the ionosphere from the earth towards the transmitting station.

Scatter propagation is most likely to be involved when weak and distorted signals near or above the maximum usable frequency for normal propagation can be heard over unusual paths.

QUESTIONS

B-007-8-1.... What kind of unusual HF propagation allows weak signals from the skip zone to be heard occasionally?

1. ground-wave
2. sky-wave with low radiation angle
3. ducting
4. *scatter-mode*

B-007-8-2.... If you receive a weak, distorted signal from a distance, and close to the maximum usable frequency, what type of propagation is probably occurring?

1. ground-wave
2. line-of-sight
3. *scatter*
4. ducting

B-007-8-3.... What is a characteristic of HF scatter signals?

1. reversed modulation
2. *rapid flutter or hollow sounding distortion*
3. reversed sidebands
4. high intelligibility

B-007-8-4.... What makes HF scatter signals often sound distorted?

1. *energy scattered into the skip zone through several radio-wave paths*
2. auroral activity and changes in the earth's magnetic field
3. propagation through ground waves that absorb much of the signal
4. the state of the E region at the point of refraction

B-007-8-9.... Meteor scatter is most effective on what band?

1. 40 metres
2. *6 metres*
3. 15 metres
4. 160 metres

B-007-8-5.... Why are HF scatter signals usually weak?

1. propagation through ground waves absorbs most of the signal energy
2. *only a small part of the signal energy is scattered into the skip zone*
3. the F region of the ionosphere absorbs most of the signal energy
4. auroral activity absorbs most of the signal energy

B-007-8-6.... What type of propagation may allow a weak signal to be heard at a distance too far for ground-wave propagation but too near for normal sky-wave propagation?

1. short path skip
2. sporadic E skip
3. *scatter*
4. ground wave

B-007-8-7.... On the HF bands, when is scatter propagation most likely involved?

1. when the sunspot cycle is at a minimum and D region absorption is high
2. at night
3. when the F1 and F2 regions are combined
4. *when weak and distorted signals near or above the maximum usable frequency for normal propagation can be heard over unusual paths*

B-007-8-8.... Which of the following is NOT a scatter mode?

1. meteor scatter
2. tropospheric scatter
3. ionospheric scatter
4. *absorption scatter*

B-007-8-10.... Which of the following is NOT a scatter mode?

1. side scatter
2. back scatter
3. *inverted scatter*
4. forward scatter.

Finish question section on page 234

ANTENNA TERMS

INTRODUCTION

Antenna gain is the ratio which compares the radiated signal strength of an antenna to that of another antenna.

Some examples: 6.0 dBi means 6.0 dB gain over an isotropic antenna.
6.0 dBd means 6.0 dB gain over a dipole antenna.

An isotropic antenna is a theoretical antenna in space which is used for reference purposes. This theoretical antenna has 0 dB gain.

A half wave dipole antenna has maximum radiation broadside and minimum radiation from the ends. The gain of a dipole is 2.1 dBi (referenced to an isotropic antenna).

Bandwidth is the frequency range over which an antenna performs well. The bandwidth of antenna can be increased by increasing the diameter of the radiating element.

Front to back ratio is express in dB and is the ratio of maximum forward power in the major lobe as compared to the maximum power radiated in the opposite direction.

INTRODUCTION continued

Parasitic elements are used in beam antennas. These elements obtain their radio energy by induction or radiation from a driven element.

If a shorter parasitic element, slightly shorter than a horizontal dipole antenna, is placed parallel to the dipole 0.1 wavelength from it and at the same height, a major lobe will develop in the horizontal plane, from the dipole toward the parasitic element. If that parasitic element had been slightly longer than a horizontal dipole, the result would be a major lobe directed from the parasitic element toward the dipole.

Antenna - conductors that collect or radiate radio frequency energy.

Beamwidth - width, in degrees, of the major lobe measured at the peak's half power points.

Driven Element - the antenna element which is connected to the transmission line.

Impedance - ohmic value of the antenna feed point.

QUESTIONS

B-006-9-1.... What is a parasitic beam antenna?

1. An antenna where the driven element obtains its radio energy by induction or radiation from director elements
2. an antenna where all elements are driven by direct connection to the transmission line
3. *an antenna where some elements obtain their radio energy by induction or radiation from a driven element*
4. an antenna where wave traps are used to magnetically couple the elements

B-006-9-2.... How can the bandwidth of a parasitic beam antenna be increased?
1. use traps on the elements
2. *use larger diameter elements*
3. use tapered-diameter elements
4. use closer element spacing

B-006-9-7.... What is meant by antenna gain?

1. the numerical ratio of the signal in the forward direction to the signal in the back direction
2. the numerical ratio of the amount of power radiated by an antenna compared to the transmitter output power
3. the power amplifier gain minus the transmission line losses
4. *the numerical ratio relating the radiated signal strength of an antenna to that of another antenna*

B-006-9-3.... If a parasitic element slightly shorter than a horizontal dipole antenna is placed parallel to the dipole 0.1 wavelength from it and at the same height, what effect will this have on the antenna's radiation pattern?

1. a major lobe will develop in the horizontal plane, parallel to the two elements
2. *a major lobe will develop in the horizontal plane, from the dipole toward the parasitic element*
3. a major lobe will develop in the vertical plane, away from the ground
4. the radiation pattern will not be affected

B-006-9-4.... If a parasitic element slightly longer than a horizontal dipole antenna is placed parallel to the dipole 0.1 wavelength from it and at the same height, what effect will this have on the antenna's radiation pattern?

1. a major lobe will develop in the horizontal plane, parallel to the two elements
2. a major lobe will develop in the vertical plane, away from the ground
3. *a major lobe will develop in the horizontal plane, from the parasitic element toward the dipole*
4. the radiation pattern will not be affected

B-006-9-5.... The property of an antenna, which defines the range of frequencies to which it will respond is called its:

1. *bandwidth*
2. front-to-back ratio
3. impedance
4. polarization

B-006-9-6.... Approximately how much gain does a half-wave dipole have over an isotropic radiator?

1. 1.5 dB
2. 3.0 dB
3. 6.0 dB
4. *2.1 dB*

B-006-9-8.... What is meant by antenna bandwidth?

1. antenna length divided by the number of elements
2. the angle between the half-power radiation points
3. the angle formed between two imaginary lines drawn through the ends of the elements
4. *the frequency range over which the antenna may be expected to perform well*

Finish question section on page 233.

WAVELENGTH

INTRODUCTION

Electromagnetic waves travel at the speed of light in space which is at a velocity of:

- 300 000 000 meters per second
- 300 000 kilometers per second

The wavelength of a frequency is calculated by dividing 300 by the frequency in MHz.

The resonant frequency of an antenna is increased by shortening the radiating element.
The resonant frequency of an antenna is decreased by lengthening the radiating element.
Insulators at the ends of suspended wire antennas limit the electrical length of the antenna.

Adding an inductor in series with a radiating element will lower the resonant frequency of the antenna.
Adding a capacitor in series with a radiating element will increase the resonant frequency of the antenna.

Parallel resonant circuits, constructed with coils and capacitors of appropriate values, can be used as traps in antenna systems to isolate segments of antenna elements. These make multi-band operation possible from single antennas.

SUPPLEMENT

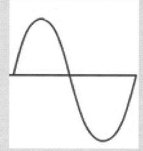

Wavelength is the distance traversed by one period of an electromagnetic wave. This is the distance between a point on the first wave and the same point on the following wave.

For example, the wavelength of a 2 MHz signal = 300 / 2 = 150 meters.

The diagram shows a sine wave. The waveform in the positive direction is identical to the waveform in the negative direction. The horizontal line is the time line.

Electromagnetic waves travel slower along transmission lines. The dielectric constant of the medium causes this. Transmission lines have a specification called the velocity factor. This has to be considered for certain antenna designs.

QUESTIONS

B-006-8-1.... If an antenna is made longer, what happens to its resonant frequency?

1. it decreases
2. it increases
3. it stays the same
4. it disappears

B-006-8-2.... If an antenna is made shorter, what happens to its resonant frequency?

1. it stays the same
2. it increases
3. it disappears
4. it decreases

B-006-8-3.... The wavelength for a frequency of 25 MHz is:

1. 15 metres (49.2 ft)
2. 4 metres (13.1 ft)
3. 12 metres (39.4 ft)
4. 32 metres (105 ft)

B-006-8-4.... The velocity of propagation of radio frequency energy in free space is:

1. 300 000 kilometers per second
2. 3 000 kilometers per second
3. 150 kilometers per second
4. 186 000 kilometers per second

B-006-8-5.... Adding a series inductance to an antenna would:

1. increase the resonant frequency
2. have little effect
3. decrease the resonant frequency
4. have no change on the resonant frequency

B-006-8-6.... The resonant frequency of an antenna may be increased by:

1. lowering the radiating element
2. increasing the height of the radiating element
3. shortening the radiating element
4. lengthening the radiating element

B-006-8-7.... The speed of a radio wave:

1. is infinite in space
2. is the same as the speed of light
3. is always less than half speed of light
4. varies directly with frequency

B-006-8-8.... At the end of suspended antenna wire, insulators are used. These act to:

1. limit the electrical length of the antenna
2. increase the effective antenna length
3. allow the antenna to be more easily held vertically
4. prevent any loss of radio waves by the antenna

B-006-8-9.... To lower the resonant frequency of an antenna, the operator should:

1. shorten it
2. lengthen it
3. ground one end
4. centre feed it with TV ribbon transmission line

B-006-8-10.... One solution to multiband operation with a shortened radiator is the "trap dipole" or trap vertical. These "traps" are actually:

1. large wire-wound resistors
2. a coil and capacitor in parallel
3. coils wrapped around a ferrite rod
4. hollow metal cans

B-006-8-11.... The wavelength corresponding to a frequency of 2 MHz is:

1. 360 m (1181 ft)
2. 150 m (492 ft)
3. 1500 m (4921 ft)
4. 30 m (98 ft)

ANTENNA POLARIZATION

INTRODUCTION

Electromagnetic waves radiated from antennas have an electric field and a magnetic field.

The polarization of an electromagnetic wave is determined by the alignment of the electric field. Vertical antennas radiate vertically polarized signals. Dipoles and Yagi antennas positioned horizontally radiate horizontally polarized signals.

Reception is best when the polarity of transmitted signals are received with similarly polarized antennas. The polarization of HF signals changes unpredictably after the signal passes through the ionosphere. The polarization for HF signals is therefore less of a concern.

An isotropic antenna is a theoretical antenna in space which is used for reference purposes. The theoretical radiation from this antenna is spherical.

SUPPLEMENT

The antennas on this tower are vertically polarized. The exception is the lowest antenna which is a 6 meter band horizontally polarized dipole.

QUESTIONS

B-006-7-1.... What does horizonal wave polarization mean?

1. the electric and magnetic lines of force of a radio wave are perpendicular to the earth's surface
2. the electric lines of force of a radio wave are perpendicular to the earth's surface
3. *the electric lines of force of a radio wave are parallel to the earth's surface*
4. the magnetic lines of force of a radio wave are parallel to the earth's surface

B-006-7-2.... What does vertical wave polarization mean?

1. the magnetic lines of force of a radio wave are perpendicular to the earth's surface
2. *the electric lines of force of a radio wave are perpendicular to the earth's surface*
3. the electric and magnetic lines of force of a radio wave are parallel to the earth's surface
4. the electric lines of force of a radio wave are parallel to the earth's surface

B-006-7-5.... Polarization of an antenna is determined by:

1. the height of the antenna
2. *the orientation of the electric field relative to the earth's surface*
3. the type of antenna
4. the magnetic field

B-006-7-6.... An isotropic antenna is:

1. *a hypothetical point source*
2. an infinitely long piece of wire
3. a dummy load
4. a half wave reference dipole

B-006-7-7.... What is the antenna radiation pattern for an isotropic radiator?

1. a parabola
2. a cardioid
3. a unidirectional cardioid
4. *a sphere*

B-006-7-3.... What electromagnetic wave polarization does a Yagi antenna have when its elements are parallel to the earth's surface?

1. helical
2. *horizontal*
3. vertical
4. circular

B-006-7-4.... What electromagnetic wave polarization does a half-wavelength antenna have when it is perpendicular to the earth's surface?

1. circular
2. horizontal
3. parabolical
4. *vertical*

B-006-7-8.... VHF signals from a mobile station using a vertical whip antenna will normally be best received using a:

1. random length of wire
2. horizontal ground-plane antenna
3. *vertical ground-plane antenna*
4. horizontal dipole antenna

B-006-7-9.... A dipole antenna will emit a vertically polarized wave if it is:

1. fed with the correct type of RF
2. too near to the ground
3. parallel with the ground
4. *mounted vertically*

B-006-7-10.... If an electromagnetic wave leaves an antenna vertically polarized, it will arrive at the receiving antenna, by ground wave:

1. polarized at right angles to original
2. *vertically polarized*
3. horizontally polarized
4. polarized in any plane

Finish question section on page 232

VERTICAL ANTENNA

INTRODUCTION

Single vertical antennas transmit and receive signals equally well in all horizontal directions. Quarter wavelength verticals are referred to as Marconi antennas.

The length of a quarter wavelength vertical antenna in feet, is calculated by dividing 234 by the frequency in MHz. For example, the calculations for a quarter wave vertical to operate on 21.125 MHz is:

$$234/21.125 = 11 \text{ feet}$$

The 5/8 wavelength vertical antenna is favoured for 2 meter mobile installations as it has gain in the horizontal plane with a low angle of radiation. A mobile antenna placed on the roof of a car gives almost equal coverage in all horizontal directions.

A vertical antenna with 4 ground plane radials sloping downwards has a feed point impedance of approximately 50 ohms. A vertical antenna with 4 ground plane radials in the horizontal plane has a feed point impedance of approximately 30 ohms. Feed point impedance increases when radials are sloped.

On the lower HF bands, it is more difficult to use full size 1/4 wavelength vertical antennas. A loading coil may be used to increase the electrical length of short antennas. This tunes out capacitive reactance.

SUPPLEMENT

Almost all mobile antennas are of the vertical variety. The picture shows an HF antenna mounted near the rear of the truck's box. The loading coil near the top makes the antenna resonate in the 20 meter band. With this particular model, if you remove the loading coil, the remaining mast would resonate in the 6 meter band. Loading coils are available for most HF bands.

QUESTIONS

B-006-10-1.... How do you calculate the length in metres (feet) of a quarter-wavelength vertical antenna?

1. divide 468 (1532) by the antenna's operating frequency in MHz
2. divide 300 (982) by the antenna's operating frequency in MHz
3. *divide 71.5 (234) by the antenna's operating frequency in MHz*
4. divide 150 (491) by the antenna's operating frequency in MHz

B-006-10-2.... If you made a quarter-wavelength vertical antenna for 21.125 MHz, how long would it be?

1. 3.6 meters (11.8 ft)
2. *3.36 meters (11.0 ft)*
3. 7.2 meters (23.6 ft)
4. 6.76 meters (22.2 ft)

B-006-10-3.... If you made a half-wavelength vertical antenna for 223 MHz, how long would it be?

1. *64 cm (25.2 in)*
2. 128 cm (50.4 in)
3. 105 cm (41.3 in)
4. 134.6 cm (53 in)

B-006-10-4.... Why is a 5/8 wavelength vertical antenna better than a 1/4 wavelength vertical antenna for VHF or UHF mobile operations?

1. a 5/8-wavelength antenna has less corona loss
2. *a 5/8-wavelength antenna has more gain*
3. a 5/8-wavelength antenna is easier to install on a car
4. a 5/8-wavelength antenna can handle more power

B-006-10-5.... If a magnetic-base whip antenna is placed on the roof of a car, in what direction does it send out radio energy?

1. most of it is aimed high into the sky
2. most of it goes equally in two opposite directions
3. *it goes out equally well in all horizontal directions*
4. most of it goes in one direction

B-006-10-6.... What is an advantage of downward sloping radials on a ground plane antenna?

1. it increases the radiation angle
2. it brings the feed point impedance closer to 300 ohms
3. *it brings the feed point impedance closer to 50 ohms*
4. it lowers the radiation angle

B-006-10-7.... What happens to the feed point impedance of a ground-plane antenna when its radials are changed from horizontal to downward sloping?

1. *it increases*
2. it decreases
3. it stays the same
4. it approaches zero

B-006-10-8.... Which of the following transmission lines will give the best match to the base of a quarter wave ground-plane antenna?

1. 300 ohms balanced transmission line
2. 75 ohms balanced transmission line
3. 300 ohms coaxial cable
4. *50 ohms coaxial cable*

B-006-10-9.... The main characteristic of a vertical antenna is that it will:

1. *receive signals equally well from all compass points around it*
2. be very sensitive to signals coming from horizontal antennas
3. require few insulators
4. be easy to feed with TV ribbon transmission line

B-006-10-10.... Why is a loading coil often used with an HF mobile vertical antenna?

1. *to tune out capacitive reactance*
2. to lower the losses
3. to lower the Q
4. to filter out electrical noise

Finish question section on page 233

WIRE ANTENNA

INTRODUCTION

The dipole or doublet antenna is one half wavelength long and fed in the middle where the impedance is approximately 73 ohms. A dipole that folds back on itself is a folded dipole and has an impedance of approximately 300 ohms. The folded dipole has greater bandwidth.

The formula for determining the length of a half wave dipole is 468 divided by frequency in MHz.

Dipole antennas have a radiation pattern which is broadside to the antenna and can be described as a figure 8 like pattern.

The trap dipole antenna can be used on more than one band. Traps are parallel resonant circuits which isolates the appropriate segments of the antenna. The advantage is multi-band operation using one feedline. Harmonic radiation is a disadvantage.

A random wire antenna is sometimes used with an antenna tuner and is able to operate on many HF amateur bands. The disadvantage is that frequently RF feedback in the station becomes a problem. A good ground system for the station is required with these antennas.

SUPPLEMENT

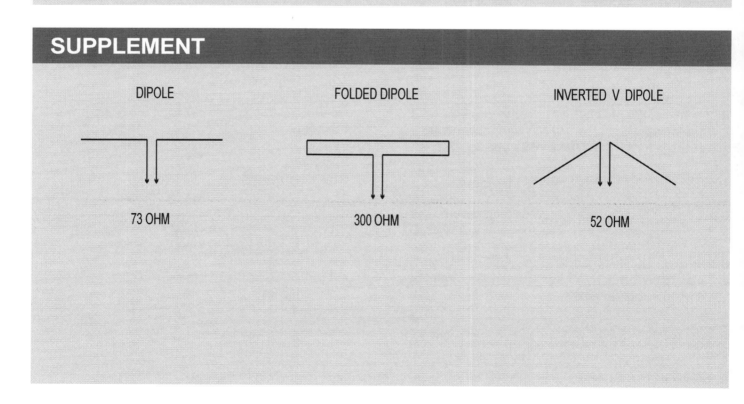

DIPOLE	FOLDED DIPOLE	INVERTED V DIPOLE
73 OHM	300 OHM	52 OHM

B-006-12-1.... If you made a half wavelength dipole antenna for 28.150 MHz, how long would it be?

1. 10.5 metres (34.37 ft)
2. 28.55 metres (93.45 ft)
3. *5.08 metres (16.62 ft)*
4. 10.16 metres (33.26 ft)

B-006-12-2.... What is one disadvantage of a random wire antenna?

1. it usually produces vertically polarized radiation
2. it must be longer than 1 wavelength
3. *you may experience RF feedback in your station*
4. you must use an inverted T matching network for multi-band operation

B-006-12-3.... What is the low angle radiation pattern of an ideal half wavelength dipole HF antenna in free space installed parallel to the earth?

1. *it is a figure-eight, perpendicular to the antenna*
2. it is a circle (equal radiation in all directions)
3. it is two smaller lobes on one side of the antenna, and one larger lobe on the other side
4. it is a figure eight, off both ends of the antenna

B-006-12-4.... The impedances in ohms at the feed point of the dipole and folded dipole in free space are, respectively:

1. 73 and 150
2. 52 and 200
3. 52 and 100
4. *73 and 300*

B-006-12-5.... A horizontal dipole transmitting antenna, installed at an ideal height, so that the ends are pointing North/South, radiates:

1. mostly to the South and North
2. mostly to the South
3. equally in all directions
4. *mostly to the East and West*

B-006-12-6.... How does the bandwidth of a folded dipole antenna compare with that of a simple dipole antenna?

1. it is essentially the same
2. it is less than 50%
3. it is 0.707 times the bandwidth
4. *it is greater*

B-006-12-7.... What is a disadvantage of using an antenna equipped with traps?

1. it is too sharply directional at lower frequencies
2. *it may radiate harmonics more readily*
3. it must be neutralized
4. it can only be used for one band

B-006-12-8.... What is an advantage of using a trap antenna?

1. *it may be used for multi-band operation*
2. it has high directivity at the higher frequencies
3. it has high gain
4. it minimizes harmonic radiation

B-006-12-9.... If you were to cut a half wave dipole for 3.75 MHz, what would be its approximate lenth?

1. *38 meters (125 ft)*
2. 32 meters (105 ft)
3. 45 meters (145 ft)
4. 75 meters (245 ft)

YAGI-UDA ANTENNA

INTRODUCTION

The Yagi-Uda or Yagi directional antenna is common in the amateur radio service. A typical Yagi has three elements mounted on an aluminum boom.

The center element is the driven element which is normally insulated from the boom and also insulated at the center to form a 1/2 wave-length dipole. The driven element is connected to the transmission line through impedance matching devices.

The reflector element is longer than the driven element. The director element is shorter than the driven element. These elements need not be insulated from the boom provided the mounting point is at the element center point. The gain is in the direction of the director element.

Boom length is a large factor in antenna performance. Forward gain is in the 6 dB range (compared to a dipole). Front to side rejection can be very high. Front to back rejection is in the 20 dB range. These type of antennas perform best when they are high above ground (e.g. 1 wavelength). There are many computer software packages available that predict the performance of Yagi designs.

SUPPLEMENT

The driven element needs to be connected to the feedline through a matching device.

There are several configurations to accomplish this. Delta, T, Omega and Gamma matching is described in many articles available on the internet..

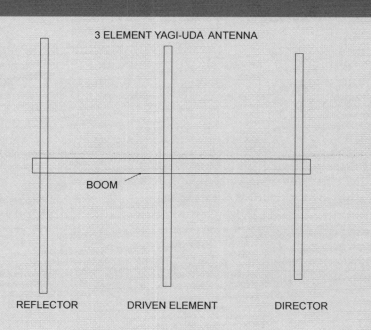

3 ELEMENT YAGI-UDA ANTENNA

BOOM

REFLECTOR   DRIVEN ELEMENT   DIRECTOR

QUESTIONS

B-003-9-1.... In a Yagi 3 element directional antenna, the _____ is primarily for mechanical support purposes.

1. reflector
2. driven element
3. director
4. *boom*

B-003-9-2.... In a Yagi 3 element directional antenna, the _____ is the longest radiating element.

1. director
2. driven element
3. *reflector*
4. boom

B-003-9-3.... In a Yagi 3 element directional antenna, the _____ is the shortest radiating element.

1. boom
2. reflector
3. *director*
4. driven element

B-003-9-4.... In a Yagi 3 element directional antenna, the _____ is not the longest nor the shortest radiating element.

1. boom
2. director
3. *driven element*
4. reflector

YAGI ANTENNA

INTRODUCTION

The Yagi antenna has two or more elements mounted on a boom. The transmitter power output is fed to the driven element which, by itself, is a dipole antenna. Other elements are parasitically excited from the driven element. Director elements are made consecutively shorter and reflector elements consecutively longer. The approximate length of a half wave driven element is computed by dividing the frequency in MHz into 468. Director elements could be 5% shorter and reflector elements 5% longer.

Increasing the number of elements on a Yagi antenna increases gain. Element spacing also affects gain. Element spacing of 0.2 wavelength is considered optimally spaced and offers high gain, less critical tuning and low SWR. Yagi design software is a great tool for optimizing directional antennas.

Front-to-back ratio refers to the ratio of power radiated in the forward direction to the power radiated in the opposite direction. This ratio is expressed in dB. The front-to-back and also front-to-side characteristics of a Yagi antenna helps to greatly minimize interference to and from stations operating in directions from the back and side.

Stacking two similar antennas can yield 3 dB system gain. For example, two 10 dB gain yagis stacked one over the other with optimal spacing can result in an antenna system gain of 13 dB.

SUPPLEMENT

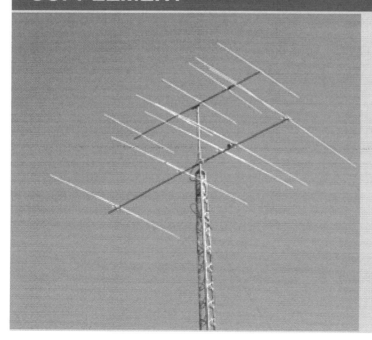

Driven elements for yagis are half wave dipoles. Use the formula 468/f (MHz) to calculate length. Examples:

    For 14.0 MHz - length = 468/14 or 33.4 ft.
    For 21.1 MHz - length = 468/21.1 or 22.2 ft.
    For 28.1 MHz - length = 468/28.1 or 16.7 ft.

The formula used by yagi designers may vary so use the closest answer in the question bank.

The photo shows two yagi antennas installed on a 64 foot tower with rotator. The lower antenna is for 10 meters. The higher antenna is a 6 meter yagi.

QUESTIONS

B-006-11-1.... How many directly driven elements do most Yagi antennas have?

1. none
2. two
3. three
4. one

B-006-11-2.... Approximately how long is the driven element of a Yagi antenna for 14.0 MHz?

1. 5.21 metres (17 feet))
2. 10.67 metres (35 feet)
3. 20.12 metres (66 feet))
4. 10.21 metres (33.5 feet)

B-006-11-3.... Approximately how long is the director element of a Yagi antenna for 21.1 MHz?

1. 5.18 metres (17 feet)
2. 6.4 metres (21 feet)
3. 3.2 metres (10.5 feet)
4. 12.8 metres (42 feet)

B-006-11-4.... Approximately how long is the reflector element of a Yagi antenna for 28.1 MHz?

1. 4.88 metres (16 feet)
2. 5.33 metres (17.5 feet)
3. 10.67 metres (35 feet)
4. 2.66 metres (8.75 feet)

B-006-11-5.... What is one effect of increasing the boom length and adding directors to a Yagi antenna?

1. SWR increases
2. weight decreases
3. wind load decreases
4. gain increases

B-006-11-6.... What are some advantages of a Yagi with wide element spacing?

1. high gain, less critical tuning and wider bandwidth
2. high gain, lower loss and a low SWR
3. high front-to-back ratio and lower input resistance
4. shorter boom length, lower weight and wind resistance

B-006-11-7.... Why is a Yagi antenna often used for radiocommunications on the 20 metre band?

1. it provides excellent omnidirectional coverage in the horizontal plane
2. it is smaller, less expensive and easier to erect than a dipole or vertical antenna
3. it provides the highest possible angle of radiation for the HF bands
4. it helps reduce interference from other stations off to the side or behind

B-006-11-8.... What does "antenna front-to-back ratio" mean in reference to a Yagi antenna?

1. the relative position of the driven element with respect to the reflectors and directors
2. the power radiated in the major radiation lobe compared to the power radiated in exactly the opposite direction
3. the power radiated in the major radiation lobe compared to the power radiated 90 degrees away from that direction
4. the number of directors versus the number of reflectors

B-006-11-9.... What is a good way to get maximum performance from a Yagi antenna?

1. optimize the lengths and spacing of the elements
2. use RG-58 transmission line
3. use a reactance bridge to measure the antenna performance from each direction around the antenna
4. avoid using towers higher than 9 metres (30 feet) above the ground

Finish question section on page 233.

QUAD & LOOP ANTENNAS

INTRODUCTION

The cubical quad antenna consists of two or more closed loops. One is the driven loop, the others are parasitically excited. The driven loop is one wavelength. When fed at the center of a horizontal side, the polarization is horizontal. When fed at the center of a vertical side, the polarization is vertical.

The formula for determining the total length of the the driven element is 1005 divided by frequency in MHz.

Reflective loops are made approximately 5% longer than the directive loops.

The gain of a 2 element cubical quad or delta loop compares favorably with a three element Yagi.

The delta loop antenna is similar to the quad antenna but with triangular sides.

SUPPLEMENT

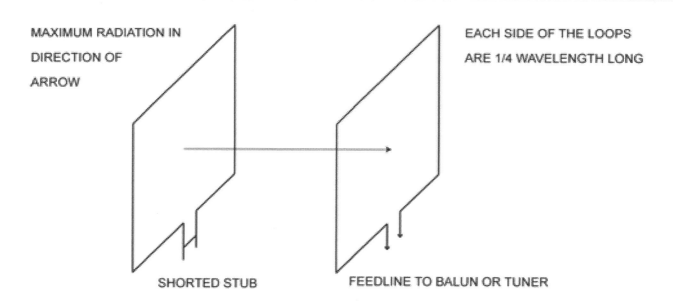

MAXIMUM RADIATION IN DIRECTION OF ARROW

EACH SIDE OF THE LOOPS ARE 1/4 WAVELENGTH LONG

SHORTED STUB

FEEDLINE TO BALUN OR TUNER

QUESTIONS

B-006-13-1.... What is a cubical quad antenna?

1. a center-fed wire 1/2 electrical wavelength long
2. a vertical conductor 1/4 electrical wavelength high, fed at the bottom
3. *two or more parallel four-sided wire loops, each approximately one electrical wavelength long*
4. four straight, parallel elements in line with each other, each approximately 1/2 electrical wavelength long

B-006-13-2.... What is a delta loop antenna?

1. *an antenna whose elements are each a three sided loop whose total length is approximately one electrical wavelength*
2. a large copper ring or wire loop, used in direction finding
3. an antenna system made of three vertical antennas, arranged in a triangular shape
4. an antenna made from several triangular coils of wire on an insulating form

B-006-13-3.... Approximately how long is each side of a cubical-quad antenna driven element for 21.4 MHz?

1. *3.54 metres (11.7 feet)*
2. 0.36 metres (1.17 feet)
3. 14.33 metres (47 feet)
4. 143 metres (469 feet)

B-006-13-4.... Approximately how long is each side of a cubical-quad antenna driven element for 14.3 MHz?

1. 21.43 metres (70.3 feet)
2. *5.36 metres (17.6 feet)*
3. 53.34 metres (175 feet)
4. 7.13 metres (23.4 feet)

B-006-13-5.... Approximately how long is each leg of a symmetrical delta loop antenna driven element for 28.7 MHz?

1. 2.67 metres (8.75 feet)
2. 7.13 metres (23.4 feet)
3. 10.67 metres (35 feet)
4. *3.5 metres (11.5 feet)*

B-006-13-6.... Which statement about two-element delta loops and quad antennas is true?

1. they perform very well only at HF
2. *they compare favorably with a three-element Yagi*
3. they are effective only when constructed using insulated wire
4. they perform poorly above HF

B-006-13-7.... Compared to a dipole antenna, what are the directional radiation characteristics of a cubical quad antenna?

1. *the quad has more directivity in both horizontal and vertical planes*
2. the quad has more directivity in the horizontal plane but less directivity in the vertical plane
3. the quad has less directivity in the horizontal plane but more directivity in the vertical plane
4. the quad has less directivity in both horizontal and vertical planes

B-006-13-8.... Moving the feed point of a multi-element quad antenna from a side parallel to the ground to a side perpendicular to the ground will have what effect?

1. it will change the antenna polarization from vertical to horizontal
2. it will significantly decrease the antenna feed point impedance
3. *it will change the antenna polarization from horizontal to vertical*
4. it will significantly increase the antenna feed point impedance

Finish question section on page 233-234.

TRANSMISSION LINES

INTRODUCTION

Transmission lines connect antennas to receivers and transmitters. They are often referred to as feed lines.

Maximum transfer of energy occurs when the impedance of the transmitter/receiver, the transmission line and the antenna are equal.

The characteristic impedance of a transmission line is determined by the physical dimension and relative positions of the conductors. In the case of coaxial transmission lines the ratio of the diameter of the inner conductor to the diameter of the outer shield determines the characteristic impedance. Transmission line length and the frequency used, have no effect on impedance.

If a transmission line is terminated with a resistor of the same value as the characteristic impedance, the transmission line will appear to be infinitely long.

If the impedance of a load at the end of a transmission line is significantly different than the characteristic impedance of the transmission line, the resulting load impedance will be influenced by transmission line length.

SUPPLEMENT

COAXIAL CABLE

Coaxial transmission lines may be buried. Twin lead type transmission lines need to be kept clear of conductive surfaces and therefore should not be buried.

This sample has a solid center conductor. A solid or foamed dielectric separates the center conductor from the foil shield and braid. Many coaxial cables only use a braid. The outside covering is the jacket.

50 Ohm coaxial cables such as RG-58, RG-8, RG-213 and LMR-400 are commonly used in the amateur radio service. The variety of available coaxial cables is huge. Use transmission lines with the lowest loss characteristics for best operation of your amateur radio equipment.

QUESTIONS

B-006-1-1.... What connects your transceiver to your antenna?

1. the power cord
2. a ground wire
3. *a transmission line*
4. a dummy load

B-006-1-2.... The characteristic impedance of a transmission line is determined by the:

1. length of the line
2. *physical dimensions and relative positions of the conductors*
3. frequency at which the line is operated
4. load placed on the line

B-006-1-3.... The characteristic impedance of a 20 metre piece of transmission line is 52 ohms. If 10 metres were cut off, the impedance would be:

1. *52 ohms*
2. 26 ohms
3. 39 ohms
4. 13 ohms

B-006-1-4.... The characteristic impedance of a coaxial line:

1. *can be the same for different diameter line*
2. changes significantly with the frequency of the energy it carries
3. is correct for only one size of line
4. is greater for larger diameter line

B-006-1-6.... The characteristic impedance of a transmission line is:

1. the impedance of a section of the line one wavelength long
2. the dynamic impedance of the line at the operating frequency
3. the ratio of the power supplied to the line to the power delivered to the load
4. *equal to the pure resistance which, if connected to the end of the line, will absorb all the power arriving along it*

B-006-1-5.... What commonly available antenna transmission line can be buried directly in the ground for some distance without adverse effects?

1. 300 ohm twin-lead
2. 600 ohm open-wire
3. 75 ohm twin-lead
4. *coaxial cable*

B-006-1-7.... A transmission line differs from an ordinary circuit or network in communications or signaling devices in one very important way. That important aspect is:

1. capacitive reactance
2. inductive reactance
3. *propagation delay*
4. resistance

B-006-1-8.... The characteristic impedance of a parallel wire transmission line does not depend on the:

1. *velocity of energy on the line*
2. radius of the conductors
3. centre to centre distance between conductors
4. dielectric

B-006-1-9.... If the impedance terminating a transmission line differs significantly from the characteristic impedance of the line, what will be observed at the input of the line?

1. *some value of impedance influenced by line length*
2. a negative impedance
3. an impedance nearly equal to the characteristic impedance
4. an infinite impedance

Finish question section on page 232

BALANCED & UNBALANCED TRANSMISSION LINES

INTRODUCTION

Two parallel conductors can be used as a balanced transmission line. One such transmission line is the twin insulated 300 ohm lead that used to be in common use for television reception. Another is the 450 ohm ladder line which has a similar appearance but the conductors are a bit further apart. Open wire line separated by air and non conductive spreaders was frequently designed to obtain 600 ohm impedance. All of these types of transmission lines have relatively low loss but need to be kept clear of conductive surfaces.

A coaxial cable is composed of a center wire inside an insulating material which is then covered by an outer metal sleeve or conductive braid. This is an unbalanced transmission line.

Coaxial cable is generally fairly flexible and some types are rated to be buried. The characteristic of an unbalanced transmission line is that one of the conductors (the sleeve or braid in this case) is grounded or is at ground potential. Most amateur radio installations use 52 ohm coaxial cable. Typically 75 ohm coaxial cable is used in the television industry. For VHF and higher frequencies, use of rigid hardline or heliax is popular. These transmission cables generally have lower loss than standard coaxial cable and are designed for permanent installations where cable flexibility is not required.

INTRODUCTION continued

A balun is a special type of transformer used to connect balanced and unbalanced transmission lines and also to match impedances.

Another name used for the balun is an "impedance transformer".

One very common balun is the 300 ohm to 75 ohm transformer used to connect CATV to older television sets.

QUESTIONS

B-006-2-1.... What is a coaxial cable?

1. two wires side-by-side in a plastic ribbon
2. two wires side-by-side held apart by insulating rods
3. two wires twisted around each other in a spiral
4. *a center wire inside an insulating material which is covered by a metal sleeve or shield*

B-006-2-2.... What is parallel-conductor transmission line?

1. two wires twisted around each other in a spiral
2. a center wire inside an insulating material which is covered by a metal sleeve or shield
3. a metal pipe which is as wide or slightly wider than a wavelength of the signal it carries
4. *two wires side-by-side held apart by insulating material*

B-006-2-8.... A flexible coaxial line contains:

1. four or more conductors running parallel
2. only one conductor
3. *braided shield conductor and insulation around a central conductor*
4. two parallel conductors separated by spacers

B-006-2-4.... What does the term "balun" mean?

1. balanced unloader
2. *balanced to unbalanced*
3. balanced unmodulator
4. balanced antenna network

B-006-2-5.... Where would you install a balun to feed a dipole antenna with 50 ohm coaxial cable?

1. *between the coaxial cable and the antenna*
2. between the transmitter and the coaxial cable
3. between the antenna and the ground
4. between the coaxial cable and the ground

B-006-2-9.... A balanced transmission line:

1. *is made of two parallel wires*
2. has one conductor inside the other
3. carries RF current on one wire only
4. is made of one conductor only

B-006-2-6.... What is an unbalanced line?

1. transmission line with neither conductor connected to ground
2. transmission line with both conductors connected to ground
3. transmission line with both conductors connected to each other
4. *transmission line with one conductor connected to ground*

B-006-2-7.... What device can be installed to feed a balanced antenna with an unbalanced transmission line?

1. a triaxial transformer
2. *a balun*
3. a wavetrap
4. a loading coil

B-006-2-3.... What kind of antenna transmission line is made of two conductors held apart by insulated rods?

1. *open-wire line*
2. coaxial cable
3. twin lead in a plastic ribbon
4. twisted pair

B-006-2-10.... A 75 ohm transmission line could be matched to the 300 ohm feedpoint of an antenna:

1. with an extra 250 ohm resistor
2. *by using a 4 to 1 impedance transformer*
3. by using a 4 to 1 trigatron
4. by inserting a diode in one leg of the antenna

B-006-2-11.... What kind of antenna transmission line can be constructed using two conductors which are maintained a uniform distance apart using insulated spreaders?

1. coaxial cable
2. 75 ohm twin-lead
3. *600 ohm open wire line*
4. 300 ohm twin-lead

CABLES & CONNECTORS

INTRODUCTION

Transmission lines & connectors commonly used in amateur radio stations:

- RG-8 & RG-213 50 ohm coaxial cable is mainly used on HF & VHF bands. It is weather proof, handles legal power, impedance matches most amateur antennas, can be used near other conductive materials and can be buried. PL-259 connectors are mostly used for HF. Lower loss, type N connectors are preferred for VHF and UHF. PL-259 connectors can be used with a variety of adaptors. SMA connectors have become very common for hand-held to antenna connections,

- RG-58 50 ohm coaxial cable is mainly used for HF. Long lengths are not suitable for VHF due to cable loss. It is weather proof, handles a few hundred watts of power, can be used near other conductors and can be buried. Frequently used for making patch cords with BNC (the type used on most handheld transceivers) connectors. PL-259 connectors can be used with an adaptor.

- Parallel conductor feed lines have lower loss than the coaxial cables mentioned above. For good performance, these need to be kept clear of conductive surfaces and should not be buried. TV 300 ohm twin-lead feedline is used by some amateurs.

SUPPLEMENT

The outside patch cord has BNC connectors. One end of this cable is fitted with a BNC-T.

The inside cable is fitted on the left side with an N type connector and on the right side it has a UHF connector.

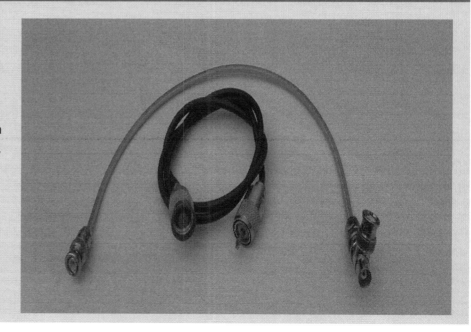

QUESTIONS

B-006-3-1.... Why does coaxial cable make a good antenna transmission line?

1. it is weatherproof, and its impedance is higher than that of most amateur antennas
2. *it is weatherproof, and its impedance matches most amateur antennas*
3. it can be used near metal objects, and its impedance is higher than that of most amateur antennas
4. you can make it at home, and its impedance matches most amateur antennas

B-006-3-2.... What is the best antenna feed line to use, if it must be put near grounded metal objects?

1. ladder-line
2. twisted pair
3. *coaxial cable*
4. twin lead

B-006-3-3.... What are some reasons not to use parallel conductor transmission line?

1. you must use an impedance-matching device with your transceiver, and it does not work very well with a high SWR
2. it does not work well when tied down to metal objects, and it cannot operate under high power
3. *it does not work well when tied down to metal objects, and you should use a balun and may have to use an impedance-matching device with your transceiver*
4. it is difficult to make at home, and it does not work very well with a high SWR

B-006-3-4.... What common connector type usually joins RG-213 coaxial cable to an HF transceiver?

1. *a PL-259 connector*
2. an F type cable connector
3. a banana plug connector
4. a binding post connector

B-006-3-5.... What common connector usually joins a hand-held transceiver to its antenna?

1. *an SMA connector*
2. a PL-259 connector
3. an F type cable connector
4. a binding post connector

B-006-3-6.... Which of these common connectors has the lowest loss at UHF?

1. an F type cable connector
2. a BNC connector
3. a PL-259 connector
4. *a type N connector*

B-006-3-7.... If you install a 6 metre Yagi on a tower 60 metres (200 feet) from your transmitter, which of the following transmission lines provides the least loss?

1. RG-174
2. RG-59
3. *RG-213*
4. RG-58

B-006-3-8.... Why should you regularly clean and tighten all antenna connectors?

1. *to help keep their contact resistance at a minimum*
2. to keep them looking nice
3. to keep them from getting stuck in place
4. to increase their capacitance

B-006-3-9.... What commonly available antenna transmission line can be buried directly in the ground for some distance without adverse effects?

1. 75 ohm twin-lead
2. 600 ohm open-wire line
3. *coaxial cable*
4. 300 ohm twin-lead

Finish question section on page 232.

TRANSMISSION LINES (FEED LINES)

INTRODUCTION

Transmission cables exhibit loss that increases with frequency and is expressed in decibels.

A transmission line that exhibits 3 dB loss will only deliver 50 watts to an antenna where the transmitted power is 100 watts. Received signals are affected similarly.

The type of transmission line used, affects the power radiated from the antenna, and also the ability to receive weaker signals. For HF, the open-wire parallel conductor transmission line exhibits the least loss but is not suitable if it needs to be routed next to conductive materials.

For coaxial type cables, it is prudent to check and compare manufacturers specifications.

- shorten cable - decrease loss
- lengthen cable - increase loss
- lower frequency - less loss
- higher frequency - higher loss

SUPPLEMENT

Choose coaxial cables for your antenna system that have the lowest loss specifications.

Before installing previously used coaxial cable, it is a good idea to strip the ends to determine whether or not the cable has good braid coverage. The braid should be bright and shiny. Discoloration would indicate that moisture has at one time penetrated the cable. New connectors are also recommended.

If an accurate wattmeter and a dummy load are available, measure the power with the meter connected between the transmitter and the start of the coaxial cable, which is then connected to the dummy load. Record the RF power. Then place the meter just before the dummy load at the end of the coaxial cable. Using the same transmitter settings, record the RF power. The difference between the two recorded measurements equates to the actual power loss.

QUESTIONS

B-006-4-1.... Why should you use only good quality coaxial cable and connectors for a UHF antenna system?

1. to keep television interference high
2. to keep the power going to your antenna system from getting too high
3. to keep the standing wave ratio of your antenna system high
4. *to keep RF loss low*

B-006-4-2.... What are some reasons to use parallel-conductor transmission line?

1. *it will operate with a high SWR, and has less loss than coaxial cable*
2. it has low impedance, and will operate with a high SWR
3. it will operate with a high SWR, and it works well when tied down to metal objects
4. it has a low impedance, and has less loss than coaxial cable

B-006-4-4.... As the length of a transmission line is changed, what happens to signal loss?

1. signal loss decreases as length increases
2. *signal loss increases as length increases*
3. signal loss is the least when the length is the same as the signal's wavelength
4. signal loss is the same for any length of transmission line

B-006-4-6.... Losses occurring on a transmission line between transmitter and antenna results in:

1. an SWR reading of 1:1
2. *less RF power being radiated*
3. reflections occurring in the line
4. the wire radiating RF energy

B-006-4-8.... In what values are RF transmission line losses expressed?

1. ohms per MHz
2. dB per MHz
3. ohms per metre
4. *dB per unit length*

B-006-4-3.... If your transmitter and antenna are 15 metres (50 ft) apart, but are connected by 60 metres (200 ft) of RG-58 coaxial cable, what should be done to reduce transmission line loss?

1. shorten the excess cable so the transmission line is an odd number of wavelengths long
2. *shorten the excess cable*
3. roll the excess cable into a coil which is as small as possible
4. shorten the excess cable so the transmission line is an even number of wavelengths long

B-006-4-9.... If the length of coaxial transmission line is increased from 20 metres (66 ft) to 40 metres (132 ft), how would this affect the line loss?

1. *it would be increased by 100%*
2. it would be reduced by 10%
3. it would be increased by 10%
4. it would be reduced to 50%

B-006-4-5.... As the frequency of a signal is changed, what happens to signal loss in a transmission line?

1. signal loss increases with decreasing frequency
2. *signal loss increases with increasing frequency*
3. signal loss is the least when the signal's wavelength is the same as the transmission line's length
4. signal loss is the same for any frequency

B-006-4-7.... The lowest loss transmission line on HF is:

1. *open wire line*
2. 75 ohm twin-lead
3. coaxial cable
4. 300 ohm twin-lead

B-006-4-10.... If the frequency is increased, how would this affect the loss on a transmission line?

1. it is independent of frequency
2. *it would increase*
3. it depends on the line length
4. it would decrease

202

IMPEDANCE MATCHING

INTRODUCTION

Maximum transfer of energy occurs when the impedance of the transmitter, transmission line and antenna are equal. This is a matched system and in this situation the length of transmission line has no effect on matching.

Antenna tuners can be used for matching a mismatched antenna system and also make it possible to operate on bands the antenna was not designed for.

Baluns are also useful for matching antennas to a transmission line. For example a 6:1 balun could be used to match a 300 ohm antenna to 50 ohm coaxial cable.

SUPPLEMENT

This is a picture of a typical balun that mounts on the boom of a yagi antenna. The wires connect to the driven element. Input is from a 50 ohm coaxial cable.

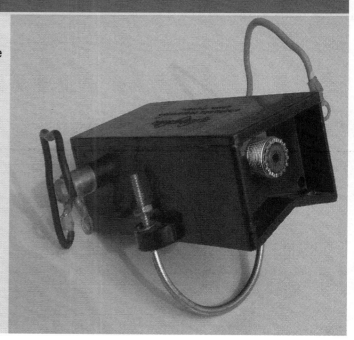

QUESTIONS

B-006-6-1.... What device might allow use of an antenna on a band it was not designed for?

1. an antenna tuner
2. an SWR meter
3. a low pass filter
4. a high pass filter

B-006-6-2.... What does an antenna tuner do?

1. it matches a transceiver to a mismatched antenna system
2. it helps a receiver automatically tune in stations that are far away
3. it switches an antenna system to a transmitter when sending, and to a receiver when listening
4. it switches a transceiver between different kinds of antennas connected to one transmission line

B-006-6-3.... What would you use to connect a coaxial cable of 50 ohms impedance to an antenna of 17 ohms impedance?

1. an SWR meter
2. an impedance-matching device
3. a low pass filter
4. a terminating resistor

B-006-6-4.... When will a power source deliver maximum output to the load?

1. when air wound transformers are used instead of iron-core transformers
2. when the power-supply fuse rating equals the primary winding current
3. when the impedance of the load is equal to the impedance of the source
4. when the load resistance is infinite

B-006-6-5.... What happens when the impedance of an electrical load is equal to the internal impedance of the power source?

1. the electrical load is shorted
2. the source delivers maximum power to the load
3. no current can flow through the circuit
4. the source delivers minimum power to the load

B-006-6-6.... Why is impedance matching important?

1. so the load will draw minimum power from the source
2. to ensure that there is less resistance than reactance in the circuit
3. to ensure that the resistance and reactance in the circuit are equal
4. so the source can deliver maximum power to the load

B-006-6-7.... To obtain efficient power transmission from a transmitter to an antenna requires:

1. high load impedance
2. low load resistance
3. matching of impedances
4. inductive impedance

B-006-6-8.... To obtain efficient transfer of power from a transmitter to an antenna, it is important that there is a:

1. high load impedance
2. matching of impedance
3. proper method of balance
4. low load resistance

B-006-6-9.... If an antenna is correctly matched to a transmitter, the length of transmission line:

1. must be a full wavelength long
2. must be an odd number of quarter-waves
3. must be an even number of half-waves
4. will have no effect on the matching

B-006-6-10.... The reason that an RF transmission line should be matched at the transmitter end is to:

1. ensure that the radiated signal has the intended polarization
2. transfer the maximum amount of power to the antenna
3. prevent frequency drift
4. overcome fading of the transmitted signal

Finish question section on page 232.

VSWR

INTRODUCTION

VSWR, or the short form SWR, refers to voltage standing wave ratio.

If no energy is reflected back on a transmission line from the load, the transmission line is said to be flat or matched. In this case the SWR is said to be 1:1 and the maximum transfer of energy occurs. An SWR reading of less than 1.5:1 is considered to be a fairly good impedance match. In this case, it denotes a maximum standing wave amplitude that is 1.5 times greater than the minimum standing wave value.

If SWR is present, reflected energy will travel back and forth along the transmission line between the transmitter and antenna and is dissipated as heat because of the ohmic resistance of the transmission line.

SWR is not critical, however most modern solid state transceivers require the SWR ratio to be 2:1 or less for proper operation. Should you see the SWR reading fluctuate greatly during a transmission, it may be indicative of antenna or connector problems.

Open wire, 600 ohm feed lines perform well in high SWR situations.

SUPPLEMENT

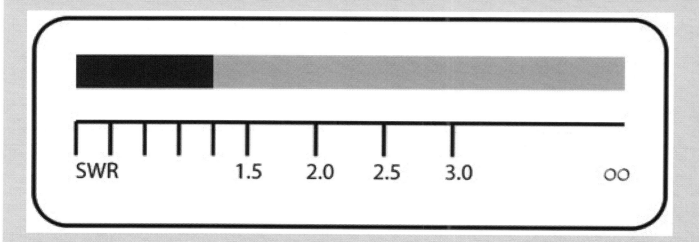

Representation of a SWR meter. In this case, the meter reading would be interpreted to be 1.4:1
The lowest reading is 1.0 and the highest possible reading is assumed to reach infinity.

QUESTIONS

B-006-5-1.... What does an SWR reading of 1:1 mean?

1. the best impedance match has been attained
2. an antenna for another frequency band is probably connected
3. no power is going to the antenna
4. the SWR meter is broken

B-006-5-2.... What does an SWR reading of less than 1.5:1 mean?

1. a fairly good impedance match
2. an impedance match which is too low
3. a serious impedance mismatch, something may be wrong with the antenna system
4. an antenna gain of 1.5

B-006-5-3.... What kind of SWR reading may mean poor electrical contact between parts of an antenna system?

1. a negative reading
2. no reading at all
3. a jumpy reading
4. a very low reading

B-006-5-4.... What does a very high SWR reading mean?

1. the transmitter is putting out more power than normal, showing that it is about to go bad
2. the antenna is the wrong length for the operating frequency, or the transmission line may be open or short circuited
3. there is a large amount of solar radiation, which means very poor radio conditions
4. the signals coming from the antenna are unusually strong, which means very good radio conditions

B-006-5-7.... If the characteristic impedance of the transmission line does not match the antenna input impedance then:
1. heat is produced at the junction
2. the SWR reading falls to 1:1
3. the antenna will not radiate any signal
4. standing waves are produced in the transmission line

B-006-5-5.... What does standing-wave ratio mean?

1. the ratio of maximum to minimum voltages on a transmission line
2. the ratio of maximum to minimum inductances on a transmission line
3. the ratio of maximum to minimum resistances on a transmission line
4. the ratio of maximum to minimum impedances on a transmission line

B-006-5-6.... If your antenna transmission line gets hot when you are transmitting, what might this mean?

1. you should transmit using less power
2. the conductors in the transmission line are not insulated very well
3. the transmission line is too long
4. the SWR may be too high, or the transmission line loss may be high

B-006-5-8.... The result of the presence of standing waves on a transmission line is:

1. perfect impedance match between transmitter and transmission line
2. maximum transfer of energy to the antenna from the transmitter
3. lack of radiation from the transmission line
4. reduced transfer of RF energy to the antenna

B-006-5-9.... An SWR meter measures the degree of match between transmission line and antenna by:
1. comparing forward and reflected voltage
2. measuring radiated RF energy
3. measuring the conductor temperature
4. inserting a diode in the ftransmission line

Finish question section on page 232.

HAZARDS & SAFETY

INTRODUCTION

Electricity can be dangerous. As little as 20 milliamperes of current through a person can result in death. The heart is the body organ that can be fatally affected by a very small amount of current. Under the right conditions, it is possible for this to occur with voltages of low as 30 volts.

Coming upon someone who has received a severe electric shock:

- turn off the source of the current
- quickly check immediate surroundings for hazards
- safely remove the victim from contact with the current source. If you are not sure that the source of current is off, use adequate non-conductive material to move the victim from the current source. Do not endanger yourself.
- call for help
- administer first aid

INTRODUCTION continued

Equipment cabinets with high voltages should have switches that automatically turn off the power supply if the cabinet is opened.

Trouble-shooting amateur equipment may be dangerous, especially if it is done with the power supply operating.

Should unauthorized access to an amateur station be possible, a good preventative measure is to install a key-operated on/off switch which controls the electrical supply for the station.

Operators of mobile stations should remove their microphones if others will be operating these vehicles.

QUESTIONS

B-003-18-1.... How could you best keep unauthorized persons from using your amateur station at home?

1. use a key-operated on/off switch in the main power line
2. use a carrier-operated relay in the main power line
3. put a "Danger - High Voltage" sign in the station
4. put fuses in the main power line

B-003-18-2.... How could you best keep unauthorized persons from using a mobile amateur station in your car?

1. tune the radio to an unused frequency when you are done using it
2. turn the radio off when you are not using it
3. disconnect the microphone when you are not using it
4. put a "Do not touch" sign on the radio

B-003-18-3.... Why would you use a key-operated on/off switch in the main power line of your station?

1. for safety, in case the main fuses fail
2. to keep the power company from turning off your electricity during an emergency
3. for safety, to turn off the station in the event of an emergency
4. to keep unauthorized persons from using your station

B-003-18-4.... Why would there be a switch in a high-voltage power supply to turn off the power if its cabinet is opened?

1. to keep anyone opening the cabinet from getting shocked by dangerous high voltages
2. to keep dangerous RF radiation from leaking out through an open cabinet
3. to keep dangerous RF radiation from coming in through an open cabinet
4. to turn the power supply off when it is not being used

Finish question section on page 228-229

B-003-18-5.... How little electrical current flowing through the human body can be fatal?

1. approximately 10 amperes
2. more than 20 amperes
3. current flow through the human body is never fatal
4. as little as 20 milliamperes

B-003-18-6.... Which body organ can be fatally affected by a very small amount of electrical current?

1. the heart
2. the brain
3. the liver
4. the lungs

B-003-18-7.... What is the minimum voltage which is usually dangerous to humans?

1. 100 volts
2. 1000 volts
3. 2000 volts
4. 30 volts

B-003-18-8.... What should you do if you discover someone who is being burned by high voltage?

1. wait for a few minutes to see if the person can get away from the high voltage on their own, then try to help
2. immediately drag the person away from the high voltage
3. turn off the power, call for emergency help and provide first- aid if needed
4. run from the area so you won't be burned too

B-003-18-9.... What is the safest method to remove an unconscious person from contact with a high voltage source?

1. turn off the high voltage switch before removing the person from contact with the source
2. wrap the person in a blanket and pull him to a safe area
3. call an electrician
4. remove the person by pulling an arm or a leg

ANTENNA STRUCTURES

INTRODUCTION

The Minister of Innovation, Science and Economic Development (formerly Minister of Industry) has authority over antenna installations including antenna masts and towers. Refer to Client Procedures Circular CPC-2-0-03 titled "Radiocommunication and Broadcasting Antenna Systems" for planning and building significant antenna systems.

Amateur radio operators are expected to address community concerns in a responsible manner. Prior to installing antenna structures for which community concerns could be raised, radio amateurs may be required to consult with their land-use authority. The taller height applies If there are multiple exclusions.

If the land-use authority does not have a process for public consultation for antenna systems, the radio amateur must fulfill the public consultation requirements set out in CPC-2-0-03 unless the land-use authority excludes their type of proposal from consultation or if it conforms to an exclusion in CPC-2-0-03.

If the land-use authority has developed a public consultation process, public consultation may not be required if the land-use authority excludes the proposed type of antenna structure or if it conforms to an exclusion listed in CPC-2-0-03. Where required, how a public consultation should take place is determined by the municipality or local land-use authority.

SUPPLEMENT

When applicable, proponents with reasonable and relevant concerns will have to express this in writing within the 30 day public comment period. Where there is an impasse over the proposed antenna system, the final decision will be made by the Department of Innovation, Science and Economic Development (formerly Industry Canada).

The Department does not need to be advised prior to erecting amateur antenna structures but does expect radio amateurs to consult with land-use authorities and follow the requirements of CPC-2-0-03.

Proposals for antenna systems must be reviewed by Transport Canada and Nav Canada for an assessment of hazard to air navigation, impact to navigation systems and/or lighting requirements. This is done by:
- submitting an Aeronautical Obstruction Clearance form to Transport Canada (#26-0427)
- submitting a Land-use Proposal Submission form to Nav Canada (NAVCAN10-0441E)
- consulting with land-use authorities and follow the land-use authority process for structures 15 meters above ground level or higher.

QUESTIONS

B-001-23-1.... Which of these statements about the installation or modification of an antenna structure is NOT correct?

1. a radio amateur must follow Industry Canada's antenna siting procedures
2. *a radio amateur may erect any size antenna structure without consulting neighbors or the local land-use authority*
3. Industry Canada expects radio amateurs to address community concerns in a responsible manner
4. prior to an installation, for which community concerns could be raised, radio amateurs may be required to consult with their land-use authority

B-001-23-2.... Who has authority over antenna installations including antenna masts and towers?

1. the majority of neighbours residing within a distance of three times the proposed antenna structure height
2. the person planning to use the tower or their spouse
3. *the Minister of Industry*
4. the local municipal government

B-001-23-3.... If you are planning to install or modify an antenna system under what conditions may you not be required to contact land use authorities to determine public consultation requirements?

1. when transmitting will only be done at low power
2. *when an exclusion criterion defined by Industry Canada applies*
3. in a rural area
4. when the structure is part of an amateur radio antenna

B-001-23-6.... The Default Public Consultation Process for antenna systems requires proponents to address:

1. opposition to the project
2. *reasonable and relevant concerns provided in writing within the 30 day public comment period*
3. all questions, comments and concerns raised
4. comments reported in media reporting on the proposal

B-001-23-4.... The land use authority has not established a process for public consultation for antenna systems. The radio amateur planning to install or modify an antenna system:

1. can proceed with their project without public consultation
2. *must fulfil the public consultation requirements set out in Industry Canada's Default Public Consultation Process unless the land use authority excludes their type of proposal from consultation or it is excluded by Industry Canada's process*
3. must implement a public consultation process of their own design
4. must wait for the land use authority to develop a public consultation process

B-001-23-5.... Which is NOT an element of the Industry Canada Public Consultation Process for antenna systems?
1. providing written notice
2. *participating in public meetings on the project*
3. addressing relevant questions, comments and concerns
4. providing an opportunity for the public to respond regarding measures to address reasonable and relevant concerns

B-001-23-7.... Where a municipality has developed a public consultation process, which of the following options best describes all circumstances when public consultation may not be required?

1. *exclusions listed in either CPC-2-0-03 or the Local land use authority process*
2. exclusions listed in the Industry Canada Client Procedures Circular on Radiocommunications and Broadcasting Antenna Systems CPC-2-0-03
3. exclusions defined in the Local land use authority process
4. exclusions listed in both CPC-2-0-03 and the Local land use authority process

Finish question section on page 226-227

ANTENNA AND TOWERS

INTRODUCTION

To protect the station and building from lightning damage, antenna and rotor cables should be grounded when the station is not in use. Lightening arrestors on antenna transmission lines are usually installed outside and close to earth grounding. Disconnecting all equipment from antennas and AC power is the best protection from lightning damage.

Only qualified competent persons should work on antenna structures. Approved fall arrest equipment should be used.

Horizontal wire antennas should be installed high enough so that no one can touch any part of the antenna from the ground. Contact with an antenna or open wire feed lines during transmissions may cause RF burns. For the same reason, ground mounted antennas must be protected so no one can come in contact with the radiating element.

The transmitter should be turned off and the antenna transmission lines disconnected before commencing work on antennas.

NOTES

If you decide to install an amateur station with many antennas, one way to ensure grounding of all the feed lines is to have all cables terminate on bulkhead connectors installed on aluminum angle stock. Note how the grounding wires are connected with lugs that are available from electrical wholesalers.

QUESTIONS

B-003-20-1.... Why should you ground all antenna and rotator cables when your amateur station is not in use?

1. to lock the antenna system in one position
2. *to help protect the station equipment and building from lightning damage*
3. to avoid radio frequency interference
4. to make sure everything will stay in place

B-003-20-2.... You want to install a lightning arrestor on your antenna transmission line, where should it be inserted?

1. close to the antenna
2. behind the transceiver
3. anywhere on the line
4. *outside, as close to earth grounding as possible*

B-003-20-3.... How can amateur station equipment best be protected from lightning damage?

1. *disconnect all equipment from the power lines and antenna cables*
2. use heavy insulation on the wiring
3. never turn off the equipment
4. disconnect the ground system from all radios

B-003-20-6.... For safety, how high should you place a horizonal wire antenna?

1. above high-voltage electrical lines
2. just high enough so you can easily reach it for adjustments or repairs
3. *high enough so that no one can touch any part of it from the ground*
4. as close to the ground as possible

B-003-20-4.... What equipment should be worn or working on an antenna tower?

1. a reflective vest of approved color
2. *approved equipment in accordance with applicable standards concerning fall protection*
3. a flashing red, yellow or white light
4. a grounding chain

B-003-20-5.... Why should you wear approved fall arrest equipment if you are working on an antenna tower?

1. to safely bring any tools you might use up and down the tower
2. to keep the tower from becoming unbalanced while you are working
3. *to prevent you from accidentally falling*
4. to safely hold your tools so they don't fall and injure someone on the ground

B-003-20-7.... Why should you wear a hard hat if you are on the ground helping someone work on an antenna tower?

1. so you won't be hurt if the tower should accidentally fall
2. to keep RF energy away from your head during antenna testing
3. so someone passing by will know that work is being done on the tower and will stay away
4. *to protect your head from something dropped from the tower*

B-003-20-8.... Why should your outside antennas be high enough so that no one can touch them while you are transmitting?

1. touching the antenna might reflect the signal back to the transmitter and cause damage
2. touching the antenna might radiate harmonics
3. *touching the antenna might cause RF burns*
4. touching the antenna might cause television interference

B-003-20-9.... Why should you make sure that no one can touch an open wire transmission line while you are transmitting with it?

1. because contact might break the transmission line
2. *because high-voltage radio energy might burn the person*
3. because contact might cause spurious emissions
4. because contact might cause a short circuit and damage the transmitter

Finish question section on page 230

GROUNDING

INTRODUCTION

It is a good practice to ground all station equipment. The station ground system must conform to applicable electrical code requirements.

A separate grounding system using copper-clad steel ground rods are recommended for amateur stations. If this is not possible, grounding to the water system at the point where a metallic water pipe enters the home may be a good alternative. Do not connect directly to the natural gas pipe.

Keep connections to ground as short as possible. Long ground wires have significant reactance and can act like an antenna in which case it is possible to receive RF burns when touching the transmitter.

Many components and accessories of an amateur station are designed to be powered from an AC source with a 3 wire color coded power cord. The green wire will be connected to the chassis. If the electrical system is wired in accordance with current standards, the connection through the wall receptacle can be traced back to the electrical distribution panel and its ground. This ground connection prevents a high voltage (with respect to ground) from developing on the chassis.

SUPPLEMENT

Two ground lugs are bolted to the bottom leg of a Delhi 64 foot tower. One of the #6 copper wire leads is connected to a 10 ft long grounding rod. The other grounding wire is buried under the surface of the ground and connects to a common grounding connection point in the ham shack. Avoid sharp bends in the grounding conductor to keep the path to ground at the lowest possible impedance.

QUESTIONS

B-003-19-1.... For best protection from electrical shock, what should be grounded in an amateur station?

1. the antenna transmission line
2. *all station equipment*
3. the AC power line
4. the power supply primary

B-003-19-2.... If a separate ground system is not possible for your amateur station, an alternative indoor grounding point could be:

1. *a metallic cold water pipe*
2. a plastic cold water pipe
3. a window screen
4. a metallic natural gas pipe

B-003-19-3.... To protect you against electrical shock, the chassis of each piece of your station equipment should be connected to:

1. *a good ground connection*
2. a dummy load
3. insulated shock mounts
4. the antenna

B-003-19-8.... What is one good way to avoid stray RF energy in your amateur station?

1. make a couple of loops in the ground wire where it connects to your station
2. drive the ground rod at least 4m (14 feet) into the ground
3. *keep the station's ground wire as short as possible*
4. use a beryllium ground wire for best conductivity

B-003-19-5.... If you ground your station equipment to a ground rod driven into the earth, what is the shortest length the rod should be?

1. 1.2 metres (4 ft)
2. *the station ground system must conform to applicable electrical code requirements*
3. 3 metres (10 ft)
4. 2.5 meters (8 ft)

B-003-19-6.... Where should the green wire in a three-wire AC line cord be connected in a power supply?

1. to the white wire
2. to the "hot" side of the power switch
3. *to the chassis*
4. to the fuse

B-003-19-7.... If your third-floor amateur station has a ground wire running 10 meters (33 feet) down to a ground rod, why might you get an RF burn if you touch the front panel of your HF transceiver?

1. because of a bad antenna connection, allowing the RF energy to take an easier path out of the transceiver through you
2. because the transceiver's heat-sensing circuit is not working to start the cooling fan
3. *because the ground wire has significant reactance and acts more like an antenna than an RF ground connection*
4. because the ground rod is not making good contact with moist earth

B-003-19-4.... Which of these materials is best for a ground rod driven into the earth?

1. hard plastic
2. iron or steel
3. fiberglass
4. *copper-clad steel*

B-003-19-9.... Which statement about station grounding is true?

1. a ground loop is an effective way to ground station equipment
2. if the chassis of all station equipment is connected with a good conductor, there is no need to tie them to an earth ground
3. *RF hot spots can occur in a station located above the ground floor if the equipment is grounded by a long ground wire*
4. the chassis of each piece of station equipment should be tied together with high-impedance conductors

Finish question section on page 230

214

RF FIELD LIMITS

INTRODUCTION

Health Canada publishes Safety Code 6 (2015), "Limits of Human Exposure to Radiofrequency Electromagnetic Energy in the Frequency Range from 3 kHz to 300 GHz."

Limits of exposure to RF, are lowest in the 30 to 300 MHz frequency range. It has been determined that the human body absorbs more RF energy in this range than any other radio frequency range.

Permissible exposure levels of RF fields increases as frequency is increased from 300 MHz to 1.5 GHz.

Permissible exposure levels of RF fields decreases as frequency is decreased from 10 MHz to 1 MHz.

The maximum safe power output to the antenna of hand-held VHF or UHF radio equipment is not specified.

SUPPLEMENT

Some practical considerations are:

- Maximize the antenna distance away from people. Higher antennas are usually better than lower antennas.

- Use good grounding for your equipment.

- Use good quality coaxial cables and other feedlines.

- In vehicles, VHF powers in excess of 30 watts should be avoided.

- Avoid indoor antennas if at all possible.

- Point handheld antennas away from the head, especially away from eyes.

QUESTIONS

B-001-24-1.... What organization has published safety guidelines for the maximum limits of RF energy near the human body?

1. Canadian Standards Association
2. Environment Canada
3. Transport Canada
4. *Health Canada*

B-001-24-3.... According to Safety Code 6, what frequencies cause us the greatest risk from RF energy?

1. 300 to 3000 MHz
2. *30 to 300 MHz*
3. above 1500 MHz
4. 3 to 30 MHz

B-001-24-4.... Why is the limit of exposure to RF the lowest in the frequency range of 30 MHz to 300 MHz, according to Safety Code 6?

1. there are more transmitters operating in this range
2. there are fewer transmitters operating in this range
3. most transmissions in this range are for a longer time
4. *the human body absorbs RF energy the most in this range*

B-001-24-5.... According to Safety Code 6, what is the maximum safe power output to the antenna of a hand-held VHF or UHF radio?

1. 10 watts
2. *not specified*
3. 25 watts
4. 125 milliwatts

B-001-24-9.... Which statement is correct?

1. Safety Code 6 regulates the operation of receivers only
2. the operation of portable transmitting equipment is of no concern in Safety Code 6
3. portable transmitters, operating below 1 GHz, with an output power equal to, or less than 7 watts, are exempt from the requirements of Safety Code 6
4. *Safety Code 6 sets limits for RF exposure from all radio transmitters regardless of power output*

B-001-24-2.... What is the purpose of the Safety Code 6?

1. *it gives RF exposure limits for the human body*
2. it lists all RF frequency allocations for interference protection
3. it sets transmitter power limits for interference protection
4. it sets antenna height limits for aircraft protection

B-001-24-6.... Which of the following statements is NOT correct?

1. maximum exposure levels of RF fields to the general population, in the frequency range 10 to 300 MHz, is 28 V/RMS per metre (E-field)
2. permissible exposure levels of RF fields increases as frequency is increased from 300 MHz to 1.5 Ghz
3. permissible exposure levels of RF fields increases as frequency is decreased from 10 MHz to 1 MHz
4. *permissible exposure levels of RF fields decreases as frequency is decreased below 10 MHz*

B-001-24-7.... The permissible exposure level of RF fields:

1. *increases, as frequency is increased from 300 MHz to 1.5 GHz*
2. decreases, as frequency is decreased below 10 MHz
3. increases, as frequency is increased from 10 MHz to 300 MHz
4. decreases, as frequency is increased above 300 MHz

B-001-24-8.... Which statements is NOT correct?

1. Antenna gain, distance, transmitter power and frequency are all factors which influence the electric field strength and a person's exposure to radio energy
2. Safety Code 6 uses different units for the magnetic field strength and the electric field strength when stating limits
3. Safety Code 6 specifies lower exposure limits for the general public in uncontrolled areas than it does for people in controlled areas
4. *hand-held transmitters are excluded from Safety Code 6 requirements*

Finish question section on page 227

RF EXPOSURE

INTRODUCTION

Health Canada publishes limits of exposure to radiofrequency fields in a publication titled Safety Code 6 (2015).

Body tissue temperature can be affected when in very close proximity to strong radio frequency energy. This effect is more pronounced for UHF and higher frequencies. In the human body, eyes are the most sensitive.

It is prudent to keep hand held radio antennas pointing as far away from the body as possible. Outdoor antennas should be installed as high as possible for maximum clearance to living areas. When using indoor antennas, locate them as far as possible from living spaces that may be occupied while you are operating.
Before working on UHF and higher frequency equipment, disable the transmitter before removing covers installed for shielding.

Using the minimum power required for effective communications between stations is the recommended way to operate amateur stations.

SUPPLEMENT

Safety code 6 is available on the internet. Some of the tables refer to power density. Measuring power density at a specific locations is complex and requires specialized equipment.

Health Canada's website indicates that the current version of Safety Code 6 reflects the scientific literature published up to August 2014 and replaces the previous version published in 2009.

An expert panel of the Royal Society of Canada (RSC) was contracted in 2013 to ensure that the results of emerging research related to the safety of radiofrequency energy were reflected in the latest review of Safety Code 6.

QUESTIONS

B-003-21-1.... What should you do for safety when operating at at UHF and microwave frequencies?

1. keep antenna away from your eyes when RF is applied
2. make sure that an RF leakage filter is installed at the antenna feed point
3. make sure the standing wave ratio is low before you conduct a test
4. never use a horizontally polarized antenna

B-003-21-2.... What should you do for safety if you put up a UHF transmitting antenna?

1. make sure the antenna is near the ground to keep its RF energy pointing in the correct direction
2. make sure the antenna will be in a place where no one can get near it when you are transmitting
3. make sure you connect an RF leakage filter at the antenna feed point
4. make sure that RF field screens are in place

B-003-21-3.... What should you do for safety, before removing the shielding on a UHF power amplifier?

1. make sure that RF leakage filters are connected
2. make sure the antenna transmission line is properly grounded
3. make sure the amplifier cannot accidentally be turned on
4. make sure all RF screens are in place at the antenna transmission line

B-003-21-9.... If you operate your amateur station with indoor antennas, what precautions should you take when you install them?

1. position the antennas parallel to electrical power wires to take advantage of parasitic effects
2. position the antennas along the edge of a wall where it meets the floor or ceiling to reduce parasitic radiation
3. locate the antenna as far away as possible from living spaces that will be occupied while you are operating
4. locate the antennas close to your operating position to minimize transmission line length

B-003-21-4.... Why should you make sure the antenna of a hand-held transceiver is not close to your head when transmitting?

1. to use your body to reflect the signal in one direction
2. to reduce your exposure to the radio-frequency energy
3. to keep static charges from building up
4. to help the antenna radiate energy equally in all directions

B-003-21-5.... How should you position the antenna of a hand-held transceiver while you are transmitting?

1. pointed towards the station you are contacting
2. pointed away from the station you are contacting
3. pointed down to bounce the signal off the ground
4. away from your head and away from others

B-003-21-6.... How can exposure to a large amount of RF energy affect body tissue?

1. it causes hair to fall out
2. it lowers blood pressure
3. it paralyzes the tissue
4. it heats the tissue

B-003-21-7.... Which body organ is the most likely to be damaged from the heating effects of RF radiation?

1. heart
2. eyes
3. liver
4. hands

B-003-21-8.... Depending on the wavelength of the signal, the energy density of the RF field, and other factors, in what way can RF energy affect body tissue?
1. it has no effect on the body
2. it causes ionizing radiation poisoning
3. it causes blood flow to stop
4. it heats the tissue

Finish question section on page 228.

FRONT-END OVERLOAD & CROSS-MODULATION

INTRODUCTION

Front-end-overload is also referred to as fundamental overload. This is probably the most common type of interference. Design deficiencies are the main reasons some equipment is susceptible to the presence of strong radio signals. Strong fundamental signals can enter equipment through interconnecting cables, power lines and antenna feed lines.

The interfering effect is directly related to the strength of the fundamental signal entering the equipment. By doubling the separation distance of devices from the source of the radio frequency signal, the fundamental signal will be 1/4 the strength. Increasing distance separation can provide significant improvement.

The characteristic of front-end-overload interference is that the interference is about the same, no matter what frequency is used for the transmitter. If only audio stages of broadcast receivers are affected, the interference will appear wherever the receiver is tuned.

In a receiver, if the modulation of an unwanted signal is heard in addition to the desired signal, the effect is referred to as cross-modulation.

INTRODUCTION continued

Filtering for front-end-overload and cross-modulation problems has to be done at the affected receiver.

The first thing to try if a television receiver is affected by front-end-overload or cross-modulation, is to install a high-pass filter in the antenna transmission line as close to the TV tuner as practical. These filters are relatively small and inexpensive.

Occasionally multiple stations are assembled in the same location for groups of amateurs to participate in a field day or a contest. When two stations try to operate on the same band at the same time, most receivers would suffer from strong front-end overload and cross modulation if no additional external filtering and/or significant antenna spacing is employed.

Intermodulation interference is different than crossmodulation interference in that there are multiple frequencies involved, including second order and higher order intermodulation distortions. Receiver intermodulation interference is more common than transmitter intermodulation. One example: 2A+B=C means that two times frequency A, plus frequency B, results in interference on frequency C.

QUESTIONS

B-008-1-1.... What is meant by receiver overload?

1. interference caused by turning the volume up too high
2. too much current from the power supply
3. *interference caused by strong signals from a nearby transmitter*
4. too much voltage from the power supply

B-008-1-2.... What is one way to tell if radio frequency interference to a receiver is caused by front-end overload?

1. if grounding the receiver makes the problem worse
2. if connecting a low-pass filter to the receiver greatly cuts down the interference
3. *if the interference is about the same no matter what frequency is used for the transmitter*
4. if connecting a low-pass filter to the transmitter greatly cuts down the interference

B-008-1-3.... If a neighbour reports television interference whenever you transmit, no matter what band you use, what is probably the cause of the interference?

1. incorrect antenna length
2. receiver VR tube discharge
3. *receiver overload*
4. too little transmitter harmonic suppression

B-008-1-4.... What type of filter should be connected to a TV receiver as the first step in trying to prevent RF overload from an amateur HF station transmission?

1. *high-pass*
2. low-pass
3. band-pass
4. no filter

B-008-1-5.... During a club ARRL Field Day outing, reception on the 20 m SSB station is compromised every time the 20 m CW station is on the air. What might cause such interference?

1. both stations are fed from the same generator
2. *receiver desensitization*
3. improper station grounding
4. harmonic radiation

B-008-1-6.... intermodulation in a broadcast receiver by a nearby transmitter would be noticed in the receiver as:

1. interference only when a broadcast signal is tuned
2. *the undesired signal in the background of the desired signal*
3. distortion on transmitted voice peaks
4. interference continuously across the dial

B-008-1-7.... You have connected your hand-held VHF transceiver to an outside gain antenna. You now hear a mixture of signals together with different modulation on your desired frequency. What is the nature of this interference?

1. harmonic interference from other stations
2. audio stage overload interference
3. audio stage intermodulation interference
4. *receiver intermodulation interference*

B-008-1-8.... Two or more strong out-of-band signals mix in your receiver to produce interference on a desired frequency. What is this called?

1. receiver quieting
2. *intermodulation interference*
3. capture effect
4. front-end desensitization

Finish question section on page 235

AUDIO RECTIFICATION

INTRODUCTION

Audio rectification can occur when electronic circuitry, usually an amplifier, detects strong nearby radio frequency signals. This type of interference in a radio receiver would be present across the entire dial.

If the transmitter is using amplitude modulated phone, the detected speech will sound fairly clear. If the transmission is single-sideband phone, it will sound like distorted speech. If the transmission is Morse code, it will sound like on-and-off clicking or humming.

Some ways to reduce or eliminate audio rectification in audio devices include:

- shortening the leads to speakers and other devices, as much as possible

- installing bypass capacitors at input/output devices of home entertainment systems

- installing coils on ferrite cores and/or wrapping speaker leads around ferrite core material

- installing a modular plug-in telephone RFI filter close to the telephone device

INTRODUCTION continued

Properly grounding all transmitting and station equipment is a good practice to adopt and may alleviate audio rectification issues.

Increasing the distance between the transmitting antenna and the affected device will reduce the effect of audio rectification interference. Increasing antenna height is also an option for increasing the distance separation.

Using the higher allowable transmitting powers increases the likelihood of audio rectification occurring. Reducing transmitting power to the minimum power required for communications may be a valid consideration to resolve audio rectification interference.

Similar audio devices from other manufacturers may prove to not be affected by audio rectification.

QUESTIONS

B-008-2-1.... What devices would you install to reduce or eliminate audio frequency interference to home entertainment systems?

1. bypass resistors
2. metal-oxide varistors
3. *coils on ferrite cores*
4. bypass inductors

B-008-2-2.... What should be done if a properly operating amateur station is the cause of interference to a nearby telephone?

1. ground and shield the local telephone distribution amplifier
2. stop transmitting whenever the telephone is in use
3. *install a modular plug-in telephone RFI filter close to the telephone device*
4. make internal adjustments to the telephone equipment

B-008-2-3.... What sound is heard from a public address system if audio rectification of a nearby single-sideband phone transmission occurs?

1. clearly audible speech from the transmitter's signals
2. on-and-off humming or clicking
3. *distorted speech from the transmitter's signals*
4. a steady hum whenever the transmitter's carrier is on the air

B-008-2-4.... What sound is heard from a public address system if audio rectification of a nearby CW transmission occurs?

1. audible, possibly distorted speech
2. muffled, severely distorted speech
3. a steady whistling
4. *on-and-off humming or clicking*

B-008-2-5.... How can you minimize the possibility of audio rectification of your transmitter's signals?

1. install bypass capacitors on all power supply rectifiers
2. use CW only
3. *ensure that all station equipment is properly grounded*
4. use a solid-state transmitter

B-008-2-6.... An amateur transmitter is being heard across the entire dial of a broadcast receiver. The receiver is most probably suffering from:

1. harmonic interference from the transmitter
2. *audio rectification in the receiver*
3. poor image rejection
4. splatter from the transmitter

B-008-2-7.... Your SSB HF transmissions are heard muffled on a sound system in the living room regardless of its volume setting. What causes this?

1. *audio rectification of strong signals*
2. harmonics generated at the transmitter
3. improper filtering in the transmitter
4. lack of receiver sensitivity and selectivity

B-008-2-8.... What device can be used to minimize the effect of RF pickup by audio wires connected to stereo speakers, intercom amplifiers, telephones, etc.?

1. magnet
2. attenuator
3. diode
4. *ferrite core*

B-008-2-9.... Stereo speaker leads often act as antennas to pick up RF signals. What is one method you can use to minimize this effect?

1. *shorten the leads*
2. lengthen the leads
3. connect the speaker through an audio attenuator
4. connect a diode across the speaker

B-008-2-10.... One method of preventing RF from entering a stereo set through the speaker leads is to wrap each of the speaker leads:

1. around a copper bar
2. around an iron bar
3. *through a ferrite core*
4. around a wooden dowel

Finish question section on page 235

RESOLUTION OF COMPLAINTS

INTRODUCTION

Innovation, Science and Economic Development Canada's electromagnetic compatibility advisory bulletin EMCAB-2 titled "Criteria for Resolution of Immunity Complaints Involving Fundamental Emissions of Radiocommunications Transmitters" will be used by the Department to resolve interference complaints.

The Minister may make determinations regarding immunity-related interference complaints involving both radio apparatus and radio sensitive equipment and to issue orders to resolve them. Although a transmitting station may be operating normally and in full compliance of all regulations, operators are still responsible for taking all practical steps to minimize potential interference problems.

In the event of a neighbour's broadcast receiving or stereo equipment is malfunctioning when an amateur's transmitter is operating, it will be deemed by the Department that the affected equipment's lack of immunity is the cause, if the field strength on the premises of the affected equipment is below the specified immunity criteria.

In the event of interference to a neighbour's television receiver when an amateur's transmitter is operating, it will be deemed by the Department that the amateur's transmission is the cause of the problem, if the field strength on the neighbour's premises is above the specified immunity criteria.

SUPPLEMENT

The following levels specified in EMCAB-2, in Volts per meter, will be the technical criteria used to resolve disputes:

- 1.83 V/m - Broadcasting Receivers
- 1.83 V/m - Associated Equipment (radio sensitive equipment used with radio apparatus)
- 3.16 V/m - Radio-Sensitive Equipment (any device, machinery or equipment, other than radio apparatus, the use or functioning of which is or can be adversely affected by radiocommunication emissions.)

The other useful document is CPC-3-14-01 "Determinations of Harmful Interference with Respect to Radio-Sensitive Equipment".

QUESTIONS

B-001-25-1.... In the event of the malfunctioning of a neighbour's broadcast FM receiver and stereo system, it will be deemed that the affected equipment's lack of immunity is the cause if the field strength:

1. at the transmitting location is below the radio amateur's maximum allowable transmitter power
2. at the transmitting location is above 100 watts
3. *on the premises of the affected equipment is below Industry Canada's specified immunity criteria*
4. near the affected equipment is above Industry Canada's specified immunity criteria

B-001-25-2.... In the event of interference to a neighbour's television receiver, according to EMCAB-2 it will be deemed that a radio amateur's transmission is the cause of the problem if the field strength:

1. near the TV is below Industry Canada's specified immunity criteria
2. *on the neighbour's premises is above Industry Canada's specified immunity criteria*
3. at the transmitting location is below the radio amateur's maximum allowable transmitter power
4. at the transmitting location is above the radio amateur's maximum allowable transmitter power

B-001-25-3.... Which of the following is defined in EMCAB-2 as "any device, machinery or equipment, other than radio apparatus, the use or functioning of which is, or can be, adversely affected by radiocommunication emissions"?

1. cable television converters
2. audio and video recorders
3. *radio-sensitive equipment*
4. broadcast receivers

B-001-25-4.... According to EMCAB-2 which of the following types of equipment is NOT included in the list of field strength criteria for resolution of immunity complaints?

1. *broadcast transmitters*
2. broadcast receivers
3. associated equipment
4. radio-sensitive equipment

HAMSTUDY Basic 2017/2018

ADDITIONAL QUESTIONS

RESTRICTIONS

B-001-7-10.... A radio amateur may be engaged in communication which includes the transmission of:

1. programming that originates from a broadcasting undertaking
2. Q signals
3. radiocommunication in support of industrial, business, or professional activities
4. commercially recorded material

EMERGENCY COMMUNICATIONS

B-001-11-9.... Messages from recognized public service agencies may be handled by amateur radio stations:

1. using Morse code only
2. when Industry Canada has issued a special authorization
3. only on the 7 and 14 MHz band
4. during peace time and civil emergencies and exercises

B-001-11-10.... It is permissible to interfere with the working of another station if:

1. the other station is not operating according to the Radiocommunication Regulations
2. you both wish to contact the same station
3. the other station is interfering with your transmission
4. your station is directly involved with a distress situation

IDENTIFICATION

B-001-13-10.... The call sign of an amateur station must be sent:

1. every minute
2. every 15 minutes
3. at the beginning and end of each exchange of communications, and at least every 30 minutes, while in communications
4. once after initial contact

B-001-13-11.... The call sign of a Canadian amateur radio station would normally start with the letters:

1. VA, VE, VO or VY
2. GA, GE, MO or VQ
3. A, K, N or W
4. EA, EI, RO or UY

THIRD PARTY COMMUNICATIONS

B-001-14-007....International third party amateur radio communication in case of emergencies or disaster relief is expressly permitted unless:

1. internet service is working well in the foreign country involved
2. specifically prohibited by the foreign administration concerned
3. satellite communication can be originated in the disaster area
4. the foreign administration is in a declared state of war

B-001-14-9.... One of the following is not considered to be communications on behalf of a third party, even though the message may be originated by, or addressed to, a non-amateur:

1. messages that originate from the United States Military Auxiliary Radio System (MARS)
2. all messages originated by Canadian amateur stations
3. messages addressed to points within Canada from the United States
4. messages that are handled within local networks during a simulated emergency exercise

B-001-14-10.... Which of the following is NOT correct? While operating in Canada a radio amateur licensed by the Government of the United States must:

1. add to his call sign the Canadian call sign prefix for the geographic location of the station
2. qualify his identification when operating phone by adding to the call sign the word "mobile" or "portable" or when operating Morse code by adding a slash "/"
3. obtain a Canadian amateur certificate before operating in Canada
4. identify with the call sign assigned by the FCC

ADDITIONAL QUESTIONS

B-001-14-11.... Which of the following statements is NOT correct? A Canadian radio amateur may, on amateur frequencies:

1. *pass third party traffic with all duly licensed amateur stations in any country which is a member of the ITU*
2. pass messages originating from, or destined to the United States Military Auxiliary Radio System (MARS)
3. pass messages originating from, or destined to the Canadian Forces Affiliated Radio System (CFARS)
4. communicate with a similar station of a country which has not notified ITU that it objects to such communications

QUALIFICATIONS & HF BANDS

B-001-15-10.... In Canada, the 10 metre amateur band corresponds in frequency to:

1. *28.000 to 29.700 MHz*
2. 24.890 to 24.990 MHz
3. 21.000 to 21.450 MHz
4. 50.000 to 54.000 MHz

B-001-15-11.... In Canada, radio amateurs may use which of the following for radio control of models:

1. 50 to 54 MHz only.
2. all amateur frequency bands
3. *all amateur frequency bands above 30 MHz*
4. 50 to 54, 144 to 148 and 222 to 225 MHz only

BANDWIDTH

B-001-16-10.... Which of the following answers is not correct? Based on the bandwidth required, the following modes may be transmitted on these frequencies:

1. *fast-scan television (ATV) on 14.23 MHz*
2. slow-scan television (SSTV) on 14.23 MHz
3. frequency modulation (FM) on 29.6 MHz
4. single-sideband (SSB) on 3.76 MHz

POWER RESTRICTIONS

B-001-17-10....Which of the following is the most powerful equipment the holder of a Basic with Honours certificate can legally operate at full power?

1. *160 watts carrier power VHF amplifier*
2. 100 watts carrier power HF transmitter
3. 200 watts carrier power HF transceiver
4. 600 watts PEP HF linear amplifier

ANTENNA STRUCTURES

B-001-23-8.... Where the proponent and a stakeholder other than the general public reach an impasse over a proposed antenna system, the final decision will:

1. *be made by Industry Canada*
2. be postponed until those in dispute reach an agreement
3. be made by the municipality in which the antenna is to be built
4. be made by a majority vote of those residing within a radius of three times the antenna structure height

B-001-23-9.... In general, what is the tallest amateur radio antenna system excluded from the requirement to consult with the land-use authority and the public where there is a land-use authority defined public consultation process?

1. *the taller of the height exclusion in the land-use authority public consultation process and Industry Canada's antenna siting procedures*
2. 10m
3. 15m
4. 21m

ADDITIONAL QUESTIONS

B-001-23-10.... Where a land-use authority or municipality has established a public consultation process for antenna systems, who determines how public consultation should take place?

1. the provincial government
2. *the municipality or local land use authority*
3. Industry Canada
4. the person planning to erect an antenna structure

RF FIELD LIMITS

B-001-24-10.... Which of these statements about Safety Code 6 is false?

1. Safety Code 6 sets limits for induced currents, electrical field strength and magnetic field strength from electromagnetic radiation
2. Safety Code 6 sets limits for allowable rates at which RF energy is absorbed in the body (Specific Absorption Rate)
3. *Safety Code 6 sets limits in terms of power levels fed into antennas*
4. Safety Code 6 sets limits for contact currents that could be drawn from ungrounded or poorly grounded objects

REPEATER OPERATING PROCEDURES

B-002-1-11.... FM repeater operation on the 2 metre band uses one frequency for transmission and one for reception. The difference in frequency between the transmit and receive frequency is normally:

1. 800 kHz
2. *600 kHz*
3. 1 000 kHz
4. 400 kHz

COURTEOUS OPERATING

B-002-4-9.... When selecting a single-sideband phone transmitting frequency, what minimum frequency separation from a contact in progress should you allow (between suppressed carriers) to minimize interference?

1. *approximately 3 kHz*
2. 150 to 500 Hz
3. approximately 6 kHz
4. approximately 10 kHz

B-002-4-10.... What is a band plan?

1. a plan of operating schedules within an amateur band published by Industry Canada
2. *a guideline for using different operating modes within an amateur band*
3. a plan devised by a club to best use a frequency band during a contest
4. a guideline for deviating from amateur frequency band allocations

B-002-4-11.... Before transmitting, the first thing you should do is:

1. ask if the frequency is occupied
2. make an announcement on the frequency indicating that you intend to make a call
3. decrease your receiver's volume
4. *listen carefully so as not to interrupt communications already in progress*

OPERATING CW

B-002-5-11.... Good Morse telegraphy operators:

1. always give stations a good readability report
2. *listen to the frequency to make sure that it is not in use before transmitting*
3. save time by leaving out spaces between words
4. tune the transmitter using the operating antenna

ADDITIONAL QUESTIONS

EMERGENCY PROCEDURES

B-002-8-10.... In order of priority, a distress message comes before:
1. no other messages
2. a government priority message
3. *an emergency message*
4. a safety message

B-002-8-11.... If you hear distress traffic and are unable to render direct assistance you should:
1. *contact authorities and then maintain watch until you are certain that assistance will be forthcoming*
2. enter the details in the log book and take no further action
3. take no action
4. tell all other stations to cease transmitting

OPERATOR AIDS

B-002-9-9.... Station logs and confirmation (QSL) cards are always kept in UTC (Universal Time Coordinated). Where is that time based?
1. *Greenwich, England*
2. Geneva, Switzerland
3. Ottawa, Canada
4. Newington, Connecticut

B-002-9-10.... When referring to contacts in the station log, what do the letters UTC mean?
1. *Universal Time Coordinated (formerly Greenwich Mean Time - GMT)*
2. Universal Time Constant
3. Unlisted Telephone Call
4. Unlimited Time Capsule

B-002-9-11.... To set your station clock accurately to UTC, you could receive the most accurate time off the air from _____?
1. a non-directional beacon station
2. your local television station
3. *CHU, WWV or WWVH*
3. your local radio station

TRANSMITTER FUNDAMENTALS

B-003-11-11.... The difference between DC input power and RF output power of a transmitter RF amplifier?
1. *appears as heat dissipation*
2. is lost in the transmission line
3. is due to oscillating
4. radiates from the antenna

SINGLE SIDEBAND FUNDAMENTALS

B-003-12-3.... What is the term for the average power supplied to an antenna transmission line during one RF cycle, at the crest of the modulation envelope?
1. *peak envelope power*
2. peak output power
3. average radio-frequency power
4. peak transmitter power

B-003-12-4.... What is the usual bandwidth of a single-sideband amateur signal?
1. 1 kHz
2. 2 kHz
3. between 3 and 6 kHz
4. *between 2 and 3 kHz*

B-003-012-8.... How should the microphone gain control be adjusted on a single-sideband phone transmitter?
1. for full deflection of the ALC meter on modulation peaks
2. for 100% frequency deviation on modulation peaks
3. for a dip in plate current
4. *for slight movement of the ALC meter on modulation peaks*

B-003-12-11.... The automatic level control (ALC) in a SSB transmitter:
1. reduces transmitter audio feedback
2. increases the occupied bandwidth
3. reduces the system noise
4. *controls the peak audio input so that the power amplifier is not overdriven*

ADDITIONAL QUESTIONS

B-003-12-11.... The automatic level control (ALC) in a SSB transmitter:

1. reduces transmitter audio feedback
2. increases the occupied bandwidth
3. reduces the system noise
4. *controls the peak audio input so that the power amplifier is not overdriven*

FM FUNDAMENTALS

B-003-13-6.... What is the usual bandwidth of a frequency-modulated amateur signal for +/- 5 kHz deviation?

1. greater than 20 kHz
2. *between 10 and 20 kHz*
3. less than 5 kHz
4. between 5 and 10 kHz

B-003-13-9.... Why isn't frequency modulated (FM) phone used below 28.0 MHz?

1. harmonics could not be attenuated to practical levels
2. the frequency stability would not be adequate
3. *the bandwidth would exceed limits in the Regulations*
4. the transmitter efficiency for this mode is low

B-003-13-11.... FM receivers perform in an unusual manner when two or more stations are present. The strongest signal, even though it is only two or three times stronger than the other signals, will be the only transmission demodulated. This is called:

1. *capture effect*
2. attach effect
3. interference effect
4. surrender effect

BATTERIES -

B-003-16-11.... A lithium-ion battery should never be:
1. left disconnected
2. left overnight at room temperature
3. recharged
4. *short circuited*

STATION ACCESSORIES

B-003-14-4.... Why might a dummy antenna get warm when in use?

1. because it absorbs static electricity
2. because it stores radio waves
3. because it stores electric current
4. *because it changes RF energy into heat*

BATTERIES

B-003-16-8.... Battery capacity is commonly stated as a value of current delivered over a specified period of time. What is the effect of exceeding that specified current?

1. the internal resistance of the cell is short-circuited
2. the battery will accept the subsequent charge in shorter time
3. the voltage delivered will be higher
4. *a battery charge will not last as long*

POWER SUPPLIES

B-003-17-11.... You have a very loud low-frequency hum appearing on your transmission. In what part of the transmitter would you first look for the trouble?

1. *the power supply*
2. the variable-frequency oscillator
3. the driver circuit
4. the power amplifier circuit

HAZARDS AND SAFETY

B-003-18-10.... Before checking a fault in a mains operated power supply unit, it would be safest to first:

1. *turn off the power and remove power plug*
2. short out leads of filter capacitor
3. check action of capacitor bleeder resistance
4. remove and check fuse from power supply

ADDITIONAL QUESTIONS

B-003-18-11.... Fault finding in a power supply of an amateur transmitter while the supply is operating is not a recommended technique because of the risk of:

1. *electric shock*
2. damaging the transmitter
3. overmodulation
4. blowing the fuse

GROUNDING

B-003-19-10.... On mains operated power supplies, the ground wire should be connected to the metal chassis of the power supply. This ensures, in case there is a fault in the power supply, that the chassis:

1. does not become conductive to prevent electric shock
2. becomes conductive to prevent electric shock
3. develops a high voltage compared to the ground
4. *does not develop a high voltage with respect to the ground*

B-003-19-11.... The purpose of using a three wire power cord and plug on amateur radio equipment is to:

1. prevent the plug from being reversed in the wall outlet
2. *prevent the chassis from becoming live*
3. prevent internal short circuits
4. make it inconvenient to use

ANTENNA AND TOWERS

B-003-20-10.... What safety precautions should you take before beginning repairs on an antenna?

1. *be sure to turn off the transmitter and disconnect the transmission line*
2. be sure you and the antenna structure are grounded
3. inform your neighbors so they are aware of your intentions
4. turn off the main power switch in your house

B-003-20-11.... What precaution should you take when installing a ground-mounted antenna?

1. it should be painted so people or animals do not accidentally run into it
2. it should not be installed in a wet area
3. *it should be installed so no one can come in contact with it*
4. it should not be installed higher than you can reach

RF EXPOSURE

B-003-21-10.... Why should directional high-gain antennas be mounted higher than nearby structures?

1. *so they will not direct RF energy toward people in nearby structures*
2. so they will be dried by the wind after a heavy rain storm
3. so they will not damage nearby structures with RF energy
4. so they will receive more sky waves and few ground waves

B-003-21-11.... For best RF safety, where should the ends and center of a dipole antenna be located?

1. *as high as possible to prevent people from coming in contact with the antenna*
2. near or over moist ground so RF energy will be radiated away from the ground
3. as close to the transmitter as possible so RF energy will be concentrated near the transmitter
4. close to the ground so simple adjustments can be easily made without climbing a ladder

FIELD EFFECT TRANSISTORS

B-004-4-11.... Which two elements in a field effect transistor exhibit fairly similar characteristics?

1. source and gate
2. gate and drain
3. source and base
4. *source and drain*

ADDITIONAL QUESTIONS

RESISTANCE & CONDUCTANCE

B-005-2-11.... The most common material used to make a resistor is:

1. carbon
2. gold
3. mica
4. lead

OHM'S LAW

B-005-4-11.... If a 3 volt battery supplies 300 milliamperes to a circuit, the circuit resistance is:

1. 10 ohms
2. 9 ohms
3. 5 ohms
4. 3 ohms

SERIES & PARALLEL CIRCUITS

B-005-5-10.... Two resistors are in parallel. Resistor A carries twice the current of resistor B, which means that:

1. the voltage across B is twice that across A
2. the voltage across A is twice that across B
3. A has half the resistance of B
4. B has half the resistance of A

B-005-5-11.... The total current in a parallel circuit is equal to the:

1. source voltage divided by the value of one of the resistive elements
2. sum of the currents through all the parallel branches
3. source voltage divided by the sum of the resistive elements
4. current in any one of the parallel branches

POWER

B-005-6-11.... Resistor wattage ratings are:

1. calculated according to physical size and tolerance rating
2. expressed in Joules
3. determined by heat dissipation qualities
4. variable in steps of one hundred

ALTERNATING CURRENT

B-005-7-11.... A signal is composed of a fundamental frequency of 2 kHz and another of 4 kHz. This 4 kHz signal is referred to as:

1. the DC component of the main signal
2. a dielectric signal of the main signal
3. a harmonic of the 2 kHz signal
4. a fundamental of the 2 kHz signal

DECIBEL

B-005-8-11.... A local amateur reports your 100W 2M simplex VHF transmission as 30 dB over S9. To reduce your signal to S9, you could reduce your power to _____ watts.

1. 1 W
2. 10 W
3. 33.3 W
4. 100 mW

REACTANCE

B-005-10-11.... In general, the reactance of inductors increases with:

1. increasing AC frequency
2. decreasing AC frequency
3. decreasing applied voltage
4. increasing applied voltage

ADDITIONAL QUESTIONS

TRANSMISSION LINES

B-006-1-10.... What factors determine the characteristic impedance of a parallel conductor antenna transmission line?

1. *the distance between the centres of the conductors and the radius of the conductors*
2. the distance between the centres of the conductors and the length of the line
3. the radius of the conductors and the frequency of the signal
4. the frequency of the signal and the length of the line

B-006-1-11.... What factors determine the characteristic impedance of a coaxial antenna transmission line?

1. *the ratio of the diameter of the inner conductor to the diameter of the outer shield*
2. the diameter of the shield and the length of the line
3. the diameter of the shield and the frequency of the signal
4. the frequency of the signal and the length of the line

CABLES & CONNECTORS

B-006-3-10.... When antenna transmission lines must be placed near grounded metal objects, which of the following transmission lines should be used?

1. 300 ohm twin-lead
2. 600 ohm open wire line
3. 75 ohm twin-lead
4. *coaxial cable*

B-006-3-11.... TV twin-lead transmission line can be used for a transmission line in an amateur station. The impedance of this line is approximately:

1. 600 ohms
2. 50 ohms
3. *300 ohms*
4. 70 ohms

VSWR

B-006-5-10.... A resonant antenna having a feed point impedance of 200 ohms is connected to a transmission line which has an impedance of 50 ohms. What will the standing wave ratio of this system be?

1. 6:1
2. 3:1
3. *4:1*
4. 5:1

B-006-5-11.... The type of transmission line best suited to operating at a high standing wave ratio is:

1. 75 ohm twin-lead
2. coaxial line
3. *600 ohm open wire line*
4. 300 ohm twin-lead

IMPEDANCE MATCHING

B-006-6-11.... If the centre impedance of a folded dipole is approximately 300 ohms, and you are using RG8U (50 ohms) coaxial lines, what is the ratio required to have the line and the antenna matched?

1. 2:1
2. 4:1
3. 10:1
4. *6:1*

ANTENNA POLARIZATION

B-006-7-11.... Compared with a horizontal antenna, a vertical antenna will receive a vertically polarized radio wave:

1. at weaker strength
2. without any comparative difference
3. if the antenna changes the polarization
4. *at greater strength*

ADDITIONAL QUESTIONS

ANTENNA TERMS

B-006-9-9.... In free space, what is the radiation characteristic of a half-wave dipole?

1. *minimum radiation from the ends, maximum broadside*
2. maximum radiation from the ends, minimum broadside
3. omnidirectional
4. maximum radiation at 45 degrees to the plane of the antenna

B-006-9-10.... The gain of an antenna, especially on VHF and above, is quoted in dBi. The "i" in this expression stands for:

1. *isotropic*
2. ideal
3. ionosphere
4. interpolated

B-006-9-11.... The front-to-back ratio of a beam antenna is:

1. the forward power of the major lobe to the power in the backward direction both being measured at the 3 dB points
2. *the ratio of the maximum forward power in the major lobe to the maximum backward power radiation*
3. undefined
4. the ratio of the forward power at the 3 dB points to the power radiated in the backward direction

VERTICAL ANTENNA

B-006-10-11.... What is the main reason why so many VHF base and mobile antennas are 5/8 of a wavelength?

1. the angle of radiation is high giving excellent local coverage
2. *the angle of radiation is low*
3. it is easy to match the antenna to the transmitter
4. it's a convenient length on VHF

YAGI ANTENNA

B-006-11-10.... The spacing between the elements on a three element Yagi antenna, representing the best overall choice, is _____ of a wavelength?

1. 0.10
2. 0.50
3. 0.75
4. *0.20*

B-006-11-11.... If the forward gain of a six element Yagi is about 10 dBi, what would the gain of two of these antennas be if they were "stacked"?

1. 7 dBi
2. *13 dBi*
3. 20 dBi
4. 10 dBi

QUAD & LOOP ANTENNAS

B-006-13-9.... What does the term "antenna front-to-back ratio" mean in reference to a delta loop antenna?

1. the relative position of the driven element with respect to the reflectors and directors
2. *the power radiated in the major radiation lobe compared to the power radiated in exactly the opposite direction*
3. the power radiated in the major radiation lobe compared to the power radiated 90 degrees away from that direction
4. the number of directors versus the number of reflectors

B-006-13-10.... The cubical quad or "quad" antenna consists of two or more square loops of wire. The driven element has an approximate overall length of:

1. three-quarters of a wavelength
2. *one wavelength*
3. two wavelengths
4. one-half wavelength

ADDITIONAL QUESTIONS

B-006-13-11.... The delta loop antenna consists of two or more triangular structures mounted on a boom. The overall length of the driven element is approximately:

1. one-quarter of a wavelength
2. *one wavelength*
3. two wavelengths
4. one-half of a wavelength

SKIP

B-007-3-11.... If the height of the reflecting layer of the ionosphere increases, the skip distance of a high frequency (HF) transmission:

1. stays the same
2. varies regularly
3. *becomes greater*
4. decreases

FADING

B-007-4-10.... Polarization change often takes place on radio waves that are propagated over long distances. Which of these does NOT cause polarization change?

1. *parabolic interaction*
2. reflections
3. passage through magnetic fields (Faraday rotation)
4. refractions

B-007-4-11.... Reflection of a SSB transmission from the ionosphere causes:

1. *little or no phase shift distortion*
2. phase shift distortion
3. signal cancellation at the receiver
4. a high-pitch squeal at the receiver

CRITICAL & MAXIMUM USABLE FREQUENCY

B-007-6-10....The optimum working frequency provides the best long range HF communication. Compared with the maximum usable frequency (MUF), it is usually:

1. double the MUF
2. half the MUF
3. *slightly lower*
4. slightly higher

DUCTING & SPORADIC-E

B-007-7-11.... What effect is responsible for propagating a VHF signal over 800 Km (500 miles)?

1. faraday rotation
2. *tropospheric ducting*
3. D region absorption
4. moonbounce (EME earth-moon-earth)

SCATTER PROPAGATION

B-007-8-11.... In which frequency range is meteor scatter most effective for extended-range communication?

1. *30 - 100 MHz*
2. 10 - 30 MHz
3. 3 - 10 MHz
4. 100 - 300 MHz

ADDITIONAL QUESTIONS

FRONT-END OVERLOAD & CROSS-MODULATION

B-008-1-9.... Two mobile stations are travelling along the same road in close proximity to each other and having trouble communicating through a local repeater. Why may it be necessary to use simplex operation to communicate between these cars?

1. simplex operation does not require the use of CTCSS tones
2. there is less time delay using simplex operation compared to using a repeater
3. there are many more simplex frequencies than repeater frequencies available
4. *the strong signal of one mobile transmitter may desensitize the receiver of the other mobile receiver*

B-008-1-10.... A television receiver suffers interference on channel 5 (76 - 82 MHz) only when you transmit on 14 MHz. From your home you see the tower of a commercial FM station known to broadcast on 92.5 MHz. Which of these solutions would you try first?

1. insert a high pass filter at the antenna connector of the HF transmitter
2. insert a low pass filter at the antenna connector of the HF transmitter
3. *insert a high pass filter at the antenna connector of the television*
4. insert a low pass filter at the antenna connector of the television

B-008-1-11.... How can intermodulation be reduced?

1. *by installing a suitable filter at the receiver*
2. by using a better antenna
3. by increasing the receiver RF gain while decreasing the AF gain
4. by adjusting the passband tuning

AUDIO RECTIFICATION

B-008-2-11.... Stereo amplifiers often have long leads which pick up transmitted signals because they act as:

1. transmitting antennas
2. RF attenuators
3. frequency discriminators
4. *receiving antennas*

HARMONICS & SPLATTER

B-008-4-11.... Harmonics may be produced in the RF power amplifier of a transmitter if:

1. *excessive drive signal is applied to it*
2. the output tank circuit is tuned to the fundamental frequency
3. the oscillator frequency is unstable
4. modulation is applied to a high level stage

CONGRATULATIONS

Now that you have become familiar with the material in this manual, it is time make contact with an accredited examiner in your area..

A current list of accredited examiners can be found by a web search for "Amateur Radio Operator Accredited Examiner".

If you have any comments or suggestions about this study guide, please pass them on to: frankvdz@telus.net

Many thanks to Diana, VE7XYL for all the help with the first, second and now the third edition of this study guide.

73 - VE7AV
Frank VanderZande

Manufactured by Amazon.ca
Bolton, ON

12914913R00133